THE SECRET HISTORY
OF THE
HELL-FIRE
CLUBS

"Geoffrey Ashe, one of Britain's most outstanding historians, paints a vivid picture of Francis Dashwood's Hell-Fire Club and other similar secret societies in this page-turning review of one of England's most audacious periods of history."

ANDREW COLLINS,
BESTSELLING AUTHOR OF *GÖBEKLI TEPE*

"A sweeping history of libertinism seen through the lens of the English 'clubs' of the eighteenth century. Precise and cogent, it also freely wanders the halls of infamy, painting portraits of some of the subject's most notorious figures. The motto 'do what thou will' defines a stance through this history, one that pulls at the Gordian knots of pain and pleasure, freedom and destiny."

JESSE BRANSFORD, ASSOCIATE PROFESSOR OF
VISUAL ARTS AND CHAIR OF THE DEPARTMENT OF ART AND
ART PROFESSIONS AT NYU

THE SECRET HISTORY
OF THE
HELL-FIRE
CLUBS

From RABELAIS *and*
JOHN DEE *to* ANTON LAVEY
and TIMOTHY LEARY

GEOFFREY ASHE

Bear & Company
Rochester, Vermont

Bear & Company
One Park Street
Rochester, Vermont 05767
www.bearandCompanyBooks.com

Text stock is SFI certified

Bear & Company is a division of Inner Traditions International

First edition published in 1974 by W. H. Allen under the title *Do What You Will: A History of Anti-morality*
Second edition published in 2000 by Sutton Publishing under the title *The Hell-Fire Clubs: A History of Anti-morality*
Third edition published in 2005 by Sutton Publishing under the title *The Hell-Fire Clubs: Sex, Rakes and Libertines*
Fourth edition published in 2019 by Bear & Company under the title *The Secret History of the Hell-Fire Clubs: From Rabelais and John Dee to Anton LaVey and Timothy Leary*

Cataloging-in-Publication Data for this title is available from the Library of Congress

ISBN 978-1-59143-348-4 (print)
ISBN 978-1-59143-349-1 (ebook)

Printed and bound in the United States by Lake Book Manufacturing, Inc. The text stock is SFI certified. The Sustainable Forestry Initiative® program promotes sustainable forest management.

10 9 8 7 6 5 4 3 2 1

Text design and layout by Priscilla Baker
This book was typeset in Garamond Premier Pro with Caredrock, Gandhi Serif, Snell Roundhand, Gill Sans, and Bergamot used as display typefaces

To send correspondence to the author of this book, mail a first-class letter to the author c/o Inner Traditions • Bear & Company, One Park Street, Rochester, VT 05767, and we will forward the communication.

CONTENTS

ACKNOWLEDGMENTS   VII

PREFACE TO THE 2019 EDITION   IX

Prologue "HELL IS THE PLACE FOR ME"   XV

PART ONE
Speculation

1   THE ABBEY OF ALL DELIGHTS   2

2   OCCULT WIFE-SWAPPING   21

PART TWO
Realization

3   WHIGS AND RAKES   32

4   A DUKEDOM IN HELL   47

5   WHATEVER IS, IS RIGHT   68

6   BUBB AND FRED   94

7   CASTLE BUILDING   113

8   MEDMENHAM   130

9   THE FAVORITE AND THE MAVERICK   146

10   THE HELL-FIRE MINISTRY   162

11   AFTERMATH   185

PART THREE
Nightmare

12   THE GOTHIC PLUNGE   208

13   THE DIVINE MARQUIS   216

14   END OR BEGINNING?   248

A NOTE ON SEX   269

BIBLIOGRAPHY   270

INDEX   274

ACKNOWLEDGMENTS

I am deeply indebted to Sir Francis Dashwood (the present baronet, not his namesake, who founded the "Monks of Medmenham") for much hospitality and interest, and for permission to use various documents.

I must also acknowledge my debt to the following authors, translators, and publishers for use made of extracts from the works mentioned.

The Daily Telegraph, London. From a leading article entitled "The Son of Man," January 27, 1971.

Gargantua and Pantagruel, Francois Rabelais, translation by J. M. Cohen. Penguin Books, London, 1955.

Jezebel, a poem by Aleister Crowley, by permission of Mr. John Symonds.

Juliette, the Marquis de Sade, translation by Austryn Wainhouse. Grove Press Inc., New York, 1968.

Justine, the Marquis de Sade, translation by Alan Hull Walton. Neville Spearman, London, 1964; Corgi Books, London, 1965.

PREFACE TO THE 2019 EDITION

This book had its origin in a casual remark by a publisher, who told me that there was no good account of the Hell-Fire clubs of the eighteenth century. While the topic was remote from anything I had written till then, he was generous enough to suggest that I might be able to fill the gap.

I knew nothing about these organizations, except for the well-known one associated with a Thames-side retreat at Medmenham. And virtually all I knew about that was from *Three Men in a Boat*. Jerome K. Jerome had this to say about it:

> The famous Medmenham monks, or "Hell-Fire Club," as they were commonly called, and of whom the notorious Wilkes was a member, were a fraternity whose motto was "Do as you please," and that invitation still stands over the ruined doorway of the abbey.

Jerome called the Club "a congregation of irreverent jesters" but said nothing further about it, being more interested in the real Cistercian abbey that formerly occupied the site.

That motto over the doorway, more accurately, "Do what you will," was in French, and as I looked into the subject I realized that it was not original. It had a distinguished ancestry. "Do what you will" appeared in Rabelais's *Gargantua*, as the rule—the only rule—of his imagined Utopian "abbey" of Thélème. This was an intriguing linkage. Did the motto appear anywhere else, I wondered, whether in its Rabelaisian form or in some equivalent? Was there such a thing as a spelled-out anti-moral tradition? If so, who expressed it and where did it lead? Such questions were topical at that time, because of what many regarded as a wave of moral anarchy unleashed by the "hippie" activities of the sixties; activities that took not only cheerful and creative forms but perverted and dreadful ones, such as the murderous Family of Charles Manson in California. Reflecting on all this, I thought it raised a real issue.

It is tempting to suppose that uninhibited "doing what you will," without restraints from religion or conventional ethics, is a way to freedom; that libertinism, to use an old-fashioned word, means Liberty. But is that actually so? What has happened when people have tried it, in reality or fiction?

That question may sound rather abstract and academic. When considering it, I realized that the only way to answer it was by examining actual historical instances. What has happened when people have really tried to live and act this way, in open reality or in well-conceived fiction? The answers turned up a medley of out-of-the-way history around which this book took shape.

Here is a sample. After Rabelais himself, my first encounter with his motto was at the Elizabethan court. John Dee, the royal astrologer, fixed the date of the coronation. He was a polymath, employed on diplomatic and secret-service missions. During debates about England's policy in the New World, he coined the term "British Empire." Late in life, Dee became interested in an early form of spiritualism, working with a medium called Kelley, who transmitted messages in a secret language. One favored spirit was a young girl named Madimi. At first her messages were innocuous. She transmitted a Rabelaisian command: "Behold you are become free. Do that which pleases you. Do even as you list." Madimi followed this up with a specific order to Dee and Kelley to exchange wives. Mrs. Dee resented this order, but the foursome took shape. It is not clear whether Dee expanded Madimi's order into a general rule.

With the Rabelaisian precept in mind, I was interested to discover that eighteenth-century London had a Hell-Fire Club before Medmenham. There were about forty members, and women were admitted as well as men, an exception among London's many clubs. The members met for blasphemy sessions, including dinners with dishes given appropriate names, such as "Devil's Loins." In 1721 the Club was suppressed by royal decree.

It may seem strange, at this distance in time, that George I should be so concerned about anything so trivial. But while blasphemers were trivial, the president of the Club was not. He was the amazing and troublemaking Duke of Wharton, who rushed about Europe wasting his fortune, meddling in English politics, trying to help Spain recover Gibraltar, and aligning himself with Jacobite diehards. Wharton could not be ignored because he used his money to publish an opposition paper called *The True Briton* and clamored for "Liberty!" as he understood it. Long after Wharton's death, he was still a legend of lawlessness. The villain in Richardson's novel *Clarissa Harlowe* is based on him.

When I confronted the actual organization based at Medmenham, my first discovery was that it was not actually called the Hell-Fire Club. That was a nickname suggested by the one in London and one or two later ones in England and Ireland. Properly speaking, it was the Order of the Friars of St. Francis of Wycombe. The founder and head, Sir Francis Dashwood, apparently assembled a rich and exclusively male membership at regular intervals during the 1750s in the disused Medmenham Abbey with the Rabelaisian maxim over the door and led them in quasi-religious ritual making fun of religion, after which they adjourned for lavish banquets and orgies with imported women. Sir Francis supplied a private library for their use, which was doubtless well stocked with pornography.

Such then was Medmenham from which this book proceeded. To revert to the serious question: it certainly promoted libertinism, but did it, in any intelligible sense, promote liberty? Curiously, and indirectly, it did.

England was governed by dominant Whigs and disgruntled Tories. The regime was very stable and depended largely on wealth, patronage, and corruption. The only political dissent came from devotees of a book called *The Idea of a Patriot King,* in which the author maintained that an ideal monarch would stand above the parties, appointing ministers of his choice and breaking the oligarchy. Sir Francis Dashwood was one of these dissenters, and for a time he and his fellow dissenters actually influenced government, but Dashwood, to put it mildly, was not leadership material.

However, by an odd quirk of fate, one of the Hell-Fire brethren was. Jerome K. Jerome singled him out correctly as "the notorious Wilkes." Because of him, a popular cry of "Liberty!" was heard in the streets of London.

John Wilkes was MP for Aylesbury and a latecomer to Medmenham. He is described as ugly, unprincipled, brilliant, and sexually very active. Like Wharton, he brought out a paper of his own, the *North Briton.* When members of the Dashwood set came for a while into government, Wilkes assumed he would be offered a job. One of his ideas was that he should govern Canada. However, he was passed over. He took his revenge by publishing scandalous revelations about Medmenham.

He went on to declare in his paper that the proposed reform of the monarchy would be a step toward tyranny. That was too much. The government tried to lock him up in the Tower, but he managed to stay at large. Crowds of sympathizers followed him with cheers. He went on to become a popular hero, and for many years afterward the slogan of popular reform was "Wilkes and Liberty!"

Wilkes, at any rate, did combine liberty and libertinism. With his example, we can go on to explore the question more fully. Who else has done it?

When this book was completed in 1974, its centerpiece was the eighteenth-century Hell-Fire confraternity. However, to put them in perspective, the text looks as far back as Rabelais and as far ahead as the sixties ferment. Its original title, *Do What You Will: A History of Anti-morality,* reflects this wider scope.

A few words and phrases in the 1974 edition are no longer acceptable, such as *man* and *mankind* for humanity in general. They are still here in the text, but my use of them had no sexist intent; they were normal then. With one or two dated expressions such as "Women's Lib," it has seemed to me that such things should usually be left as they are, with the understanding that the book is a product of its time, and that these awkwardnesses (as they have now, unforeseeably, become) have no bearing on it as a historical study. The prologue is more especially a product of its time, but I have left even this as written, with a note intended to put it in perspective. The last few pages are necessarily somewhat remodeled. Here too I added a note.

Reconsidering the book, I am not sure how far it has any claim to be a contribution to history, or to the understanding of the human condition. I am quite sure, however, that it was fun to write, and that I am glad to have made the acquaintance of some of the people who figure in it . . . some, but not all. Most emphatically, not all.

GEOFFREY ASHE
GLASTONBURY, SEPTEMBER 20, 2018

PROLOGUE

"HELL IS THE PLACE FOR ME"*

"Paradise? What have I to do there?" said Aucassin . . . "None go to Paradise but I'll tell you who. Your old priests and your old cripples, and the halt and maimed, who are down on their knees day and night, before altars and in old crypts; those also that wear mangy old cloaks, or go in rags and tatters, shivering and shoeless and showing their sores, and who die in hunger and want and cold and misery. Such are they who go to Paradise; and what have I to do with them? Hell is the place for me. For to Hell go the fine churchmen, and the fine knights, killed in the tourney or in some grand war, the brave soldiers and the gallant gentlemen. With them will I go. There go also the fair gracious ladies who have lovers two or three besides their lord. There go the gold and the silver, the sables and ermines. There go the harpers and the minstrels and the kings of the earth. With them will I go, so I have Nicolette my most sweet friend with me."

Those are the words of the teenage lover in *Aucassin and Nicolette,* a graceful little French romance eight centuries old. Nicolette's guardian

---

*This is the original prologue as written in the early seventies, a kind of manifesto for the book as a whole. I would now word it rather differently in several respects, and of course, the part that was topical has long ceased to be so. I leave it unchanged, however, as an early-seventies statement that may have its interest as such and can still lead comprehensibly into the main story. —G.A., 2005

XVI   PROLOGUE

has locked her away. He can't allow Aucassin to marry her, he explains. As for just sleeping with her . . . well, according to the church, it would ruin the boy's chances of Paradise. When Aucassin retorts that he can do without Paradise and would rather go to Hell (in good company) so long as he can take her with him, generations of readers have felt like applauding.

Today we might not put the choice in quite the same terms. Yet the choice is real. Most people merely lack the courage to be fundamental enough. What Aucassin implies is this: "Forget all rules. Snap your fingers at all Establishments. Do your own thing. Be yourself." Now where, in fact, is the catch? Why shouldn't the clue to life be just as blindingly simple as that? Is it so absurd to suggest that the secret of freedom and fulfillment is to be free and fulfilled; and even to do what Society pronounces damnation upon, if the mood takes you?

Until recently such subversive questions have seldom been asked and, when asked, have seldom been pressed. Official ideals, codified virtues, have held a near monopoly of the media. And of course the right may indeed be on the angels' side. Yet whether they speak the language of the Bible, or Marx, or scientific humanism, it does seem as if those who challenge their point of view have a case to answer. A breeze of doubt is blowing. Arthur Koestler, for instance, has criticized the human species for being—in a sense—too good. He means that Man has far too much readiness for devotion to principles and causes; far too much readiness to persecute and crusade his way to salvation—to his own version of the Paradise that Aucassin, with naive wisdom, doesn't care about.

Organized goodness has had a long inning and, it must be confessed, often a painful one. In the Middle Ages, religious orders presided over the torture of heretics, while chivalric orders presided over the slaughter of infidels. At least the monks and knights seldom claimed to be fighting for liberty. But when liberty became the fashion, it produced tyrants of its own, such as the Jacobins, led by that austere moralist Robespierre. "Oh, Liberty!" exclaimed Madame Roland as she approached the guillotine. "What crimes are committed in your name!" Of course Liberty's moralists have also behaved better than that. We may think of the idealism of the pioneer Zionists, or the saintly nonviolence of Mahatma Gandhi. Yet we may still wonder whether the person who elects not to be so virtuous, who indeed does his own thing and goes to Hell by his own route, is perhaps a truer apostle of freedom than many professed zealots for it. Certainly he is less dangerous.

But what happens when people try it, consciously and deliberately? Can there be, has there ever been, an actual mystique of "badness," or at least ethical irresponsibility, like the mystique of goodness? An open-minded attempt to enrich and liberate human life through anti-morality?

Plenty of pro-moralists would retort: "It's all around you . . . and just look at it!" and some would go on to pour themselves out against permissiveness, pornography, and whatever else offends their own outraged virtue. Such clichés can be discounted. Still, the retort has something solid in it. This issue is not merely historical or academic. It is contemporary. The current anguish of Western society forces us to confront it and come to terms with it either by a firm "No" and moral commitment, or by an unprejudiced grapple with disturbing facts.

In the 1970s it does appear that anti-morality is not just a negation, that it can be a way of life, and sometimes indeed a horrifying way. For instance, the last word has yet to be said on the conviction of Charles Manson, in California, for what was inadequately known as the Sharon Tate murder. But there is no doubt that the case revealed how a paranoid, undersized, oversexed young man with a prison record could form a lawless community and call it his Family; could convince admirers that his squalid and boring pseudocommune was a base for the liberation of the oppressed; could surround himself with a religious aura; could attract all the women he wanted to his personal Cause; and could spellbind them and others into a vicious program of crime and assassination.

XVIII   PROLOGUE

The London *Daily Telegraph* commented editorially (January 27, 1971) with much literary allusion, a touch of verbal cleverness, and one deeply significant choice of words.

THE SON OF MAN

"And what rough beast, its hour come round at last, slouches towards Bethlehem to be born?" To this question, posed by Yeats in his terrifying poem "The Second Coming," Charles Manson may provide another part of the answer. Of course Yeats was not thinking of this particular murderer in California. But surely he was thinking of what Manson represents—the post-Christian chaos which we now see swirling and rising about us, a chaos in which good and evil are confounded. For Yeats knew that Christianity would be succeeded not by cold reason, tolerance, and abstract benevolence, or not only by these things; . . . that into the minds left vacant by God will pour not philosophy, or not always philosophy, but demons. In the Manson "family" we may clearly see the features, hideously distorted, of a pseudoreligion.

We live, the young of us in particular, in an age of wild, almost insane, romanticism. Rousseau himself would be amazed to know what is said, thought, and felt today. He thought that man was naturally good. The causes of evil he found in law, society, custom, restraint. This sentimental view was memorably rebuked by Coleridge. . . .

Yet some of the young have contrived to out-Rousseau Rousseau. For, where he modestly proclaimed that man without chains would be good, they proclaim that whatever unchained man does is good, even if it is manifestly evil. . . . Do what thou wilt, they cry, shall be the only law; and drugs are invoked to free the will of the last vestiges of the old tyranny of reason, morality, and charity. These or the like must be the beliefs of all those, far more numerous than the "family," who appear to respect or admire Manson as a man who has fearlessly and ruthlessly "done his thing." . . . We stand in awe and ask . . . whether the wickedness of Hitler and his disciples did not represent the future as much as the past.

Through all the righteousness comes a genuine question. The author of the article assumes that he knows the answer to it. Others are not so sure. It is best stated in slightly old-fashioned language. Is there any connection between liberty and libertinism? Do you, or can you, promote human freedom and fulfillment in general through the personal freedom that sheds morality? It may be a long way from Aucassin's slap at an ecclesiastical "Thou Shalt Not" to Manson's defiance of even liberal values. Yet unless we can draw a line between these two, or find some method of restating the issue, we must accept that the one implies the other. Both have the motto "Hell is the place for me."

A few months after the Manson verdict, a prosecution was brought in England against the underground magazine *Oz*. This magazine had carried an article offering a cautious plea in extenuation of Manson. It was prosecuted, however, for something else—a "schoolkids' issue," which, it was charged, might corrupt the schoolkids. *Oz* was pronounced obscene. When it resumed publication, the editors declared that the main result had been to draw sexual and political revolutionaries together. Within certain limits, at any rate, the Libertines and the Libertarians had found that they were allies.

But are they? Really?

Look again at that excerpt from the *Telegraph*. The writer sums up an attitude in a slogan: "Do what thou wilt, they cry, shall be the only law." That slogan happens to be a quotation (or to be precise, a slight misquotation) and a clue. To put Manson and *Oz* in true perspective, we have only to follow up the clue: to discover who proclaimed such a slogan first, who has echoed it since, who has tried to live by it, and with what results. These are not catchall questions of the kind that will bring in anybody who fits a thesis. They are exact, with exact answers. Over the past few centuries, guided by the key phrase in slightly varying forms, we can pick out our major anti-moralists. We can link them together, tracing the outlines and evolution of a credo, both in theory and in practice.

The quest is strange and unsettling. It discloses scenes of pleasure and laughter, and also some of the most extreme horrors ever conceived. It introduces us to cults of the Natural, the Unnatural, the Supernatural; to magic, black and otherwise; to proofs, in fact, that Charles Manson stands in a succession. It takes us into an underworld of banned books and revolutionary ideas too shocking for those whom historians label as revolutionaries. Also it gives intriguing glimpses of several public figures: a prime minister; a chancellor of the Exchequer; two founders of American independence; an eminent Victorian poet. In the words of an old phrase, daydreamers build castles in Spain. Taking a hint from Aucassin we might describe anti-moralists as building castles in Hell. Such castles, however alluring or alarming, have often been as unreal as the Spanish kind. But not always.

PART ONE

Speculation

1

THE ABBEY OF
ALL DELIGHTS

THE RESTLESS RABELAIS

In 1535 a brilliant, wayward French priest, who had been both a Franciscan and a Benedictine, reached certain conclusions about the monastic life. He not only reached them but published them, an act that took courage. The ideal community, he said, would house men and women under the same roof; and they could live together splendidly in defiance of Heaven, with no other rule than "Do what you will."

This priest has given a word to the language. In fact he has given two words to quite a number of languages. If you say "Rabelaisian," it will start an idea in the minds of more people than have read him. If you say "Gargantuan," it will start another idea, and a fairer one. François Rabelais was much more than a purveyor of smut. The word, which is taken from the name of his book, with its hint of vast, exuberant size, is a truer hint of what Rabelais is about: growth, the shaking off of petty controls, giant laughter, and giant zest.

The cleric who launched the slogan of anti-morality was a restless figure, more understandable today than at any other point in the stretch of time between him and us. With all the gifts needed for success, he refused to succeed. With a career mapped out for him, he refused to follow it. John Cowper Powys, the novelist and mystic, hailed him in the 1940s as a prophet for the dawning Aquarian Age.

Rabelais was no drifter. His roots were deep in the soil of France. His birthplace, the country round it, the speech and folk wisdom of the people, the everyday concerns of his family—these stayed with him wherever he went, keeping his thoughts close to the solid world. But because he chose his own irregular way, the places, the family involvements, the folklore, came through his mental prisms transformed into a fantasia that challenged every respectable assumption and united the spokesmen of religion (who were at war on all other issues) in a common hatred of Rabelais.

He was a lawyer's son, born at Chinon, probably in 1494: his life ran parallel with the opening up of the New World. Not attracted by his father's profession, he entered the Church and was sent to the Franciscans at La Baumette near Angers. It was precisely the wrong choice, made, perhaps, because of family influence: a bright boy with an ardor to learn was dumped on the least learned of the Church's orders.

Routine and regulation closed in on him. A lifeless liturgy bored him. Neither good talk nor good reading was available to make up for the dullness of the cloister. In 1520 and 1521 we catch glimpses of him at another Franciscan house in Fonteney-le-Comte. He had been sending feelers outside, writing to Guillaume Budé, an apostle of the New Learning and founder of the study of Greek in France. Rabelais tackled Greek himself. His superiors confiscated his books. He complained, made an issue of it and got them back, but the rift was too wide to close.

After this clash, it seems, Rabelais managed to break away. He had been ordained a priest, and a priest he remained. But he found—for a while—a happier haven as secretary to a broad-minded bishop. By pulling wires in Rome the bishop got his difficult secretary the rare privilege of a transfer. Rabelais left the unlettered Franciscans and joined the book-loving Benedictines.

Even there he could not settle. To exchange one set of rules for another, to be tied still to a monastery as one's base, to go nowhere in particular and do nothing in particular . . . it was too tamely acquiescent for him, in a Europe where restlessness like his own was approaching epidemic level.

RESENTMENT AND ENRICHMENT

For hundreds of years the Catholic Church had formed the mind of Christendom and imposed its own concept of the universe. At an inconceivable summit was God in his Heaven, with the angels and saints. His power descended through a system of subheavens containing the stars, planets, sun, and moon, to the Earth around which they revolved. Inside Earth was Hell, the home of the devils and the damned. Thus values were concretized in space. "Up" was good, and "down" was bad, with a scale of gradations from top to bottom.

Society was hierarchical like the cosmos. At any rate, it was supposed to be. There was the state hierarchy derived from the old feudal scheme: anointed kings at the top, and below them a pyramidal structure of nobles, priests, merchants, craftsmen, peasants. Overlapping it, not without conflict, was the Church hierarchy. God had founded this, coming to Earth as Jesus Christ. His "vicar" or deputy, the pope, stood at its apex, with the cardinals, bishops, and lesser clerics below.

The great chain of Being passed down from Man into the animal and vegetable creations, which existed to serve him. Every creature had a prescribed place, from the brightest archangel down to the humblest plant, indeed the most malign demon. And every rational being was subject to rules.

Supreme were the commandments of God, given through scripture in a clerically approved version, and through the teaching of Christ to his apostles. Then came the Church with commandments of its own—about marriage, confession, fasting, moneylending, and many other things—with the power to penalize anybody who broke them too flagrantly. Those who entered religious orders (Franciscans and Benedictines like Rabelais for instance) took special vows of poverty, chastity, and obedience, and submitted to the rules of their order.

Entangled with the Church's network was the huge complex of customs, obligations, statutes, and treaties governing lay society, which the king's decrees and the king's justice might or might not regulate for his subjects' welfare.

After its fashion the pattern was logical, even beautiful. It had satisfied one of the greatest of philosophers, St. Thomas Aquinas, and one of the greatest of poets, Dante. But by Rabelais's time, the time of the Renaissance, it was crumbling and tottering. Its logic could not cope with the facts anymore. Its stiff machinery creaked. The religion that sustained it had lost credit. The Church's scholars, even the best of them, had spun webs of abstract reasoning so enormous and fragile that their language sounded unreal, out of touch. They no longer carried conviction in a world of tangible urgencies. Their opponents, aided by the invention of printing, did.

For by now they had opponents, and vocal ones. The New Learning was spreading through Europe. However often its pioneers—Erasmus, Thomas More, and others—reaffirmed their Christian belief, they seemed to stand for another Christianity, scornful of the Church as it was. The protests of the poor and the grievances of the enterprising were sapping authority. So was the social criticism coming from such men as More himself in his *Utopia*. Science was beginning to shake the official cosmos. In the Mediterranean and the Balkans, conquests by the infidel Turk had weakened Christendom's morale; and the voyages of discovery to the Indies and America had not so much restored the old confidence as unleashed forces that were novel, incalculable, perhaps more subversive than despair itself.

Meanwhile Catholic doctrine was being challenged—if in very different, mutually contradictory ways—by Luther, Calvin, Henry VIII. Its custodians struck back with persecution and censorship. King Henry took to persecution himself, executing More among others; and Protestants did likewise when they achieved power. Fear was growing. So, even among Catholics, was dislike for the religious orders, which piled up wealth behind a rampart of privilege and condemned thousands of men and women to what was apt to look like a useless servitude. Growing also was resentment against the pope, his political meddling, and his incessant demands for money.

Through this toppling postmedieval society, François Rabelais wandered. A Benedictine monk, even a secretarial one, was not supposed to wander. Rabelais did. He opted out, ceasing, for practical purposes, to belong to his order. He visited universities and met scholars on their own ground as an equal. But he could not lose himself in the rarefied academic atmosphere. What kept him on the move was a feeling of loyalty to human beings, to the new science that he believed could enrich their lives, and the learning that he believed could release them from superstition.

In 1530 he enrolled at Montpellier University for a medical course. It gave him professional expertise, and also a fascination with the body, its structure, and workings, that never left him. In 1532 he went to Lyon, where the explosive art of printing flourished. Here he picked up jobs reading proofs and brought out the first part of the best seller that was to make his name. (He continued adding to it for the rest of his life and never quite finished.) At some point he fathered an illegitimate son. Nothing is known about the mother, very little about the boy.

Through all his further traveling—to Rome, to Turin, to Metz—Rabelais remained a priest, never unfrocked, if never active. Two influential patrons, the brothers Jean du Bellay (Archbishop of Paris) and Guillaume du Bellay, employed him in medical and other capacities. It was probably through Guillaume's sponsorship that Rabelais was able to take over two parishes as an ordinary cure. These gave him an income—two incomes in fact—and he could unload the duties onto assistants. Outside literature his interests were wide, but not, in the priestly sense, pastoral. He spent much time trying to acclimatize exotic plants from Italy. He was among the first Frenchmen to raise melons, artichokes, and carnations.

Rabelais died in Paris on April 9, 1553. Perhaps, by then, he looked old; when he was buried they put down his age as seventy. Although his masterpiece was unfinished, he left a heap of notes and rough copies that some unknown and none-too-congenial editor worked up into a conclusion.

THE DELIGHTS AND GROTESQUERIES OF RABELAIS

The five-part work entitled *The Histories of Gargantua and Pantagruel*—which contains among other things (many other things) the first plain statement of the rule "Do what you will," with a detailed imaginary application of it—is a strange book. It is about giants. At least, it starts out that way. Like a later book using the same motif, *Gulliver's Travels,* it looks simpler than it is. It also looks cruder. Its sophistication is not the sophistication of cultured pornography, and to read *Gargantua* for that is to be disappointed. Rabelais's notorious dirt is bluntly anatomical, often excretory, and not often funny. Many readers have come to him looking for the one thing his name suggests to them, and then been put off him altogether on finding out what he is actually like.

Even his more intellectual improprieties have very little in common with, say, *Myra Breckinridge* or *Portnoy's Complaint.* The intellectual part of the joke is apt to be donnish. A great deal of Rabelais is summed up in his account of the giant Gargantua's first visit to the French capital.

The people so pestered him, in fact, that he was compelled to take a rest on the towers of Notre-Dame; and when from there he saw so many, pressing all around him, he said in a clear voice:

"I think these clodhoppers want me to pay for my kind reception and offer them a *solatium.* They are quite justified, and I am going to give them some wine, to buy my welcome. But only in sport, *par ris.*"

Then, with a smile, he undid his magnificent codpiece and, bringing out his john-thomas, pissed on them so fiercely that he drowned two hundred and sixty thousand, four hundred and eighteen persons, not counting the women and small children.

A number of them, however, were quick enough on their feet to escape this piss-flood; and when they reached the top of the hill above the University, sweating, coughing, spitting, and out of breath, they began to swear and curse, some in a fury and others in sport (*par ris*). "Carymary, Carymara! My holy tart, we've been drenched in sport! We've been drenched *par ris*."

Hence it was that the city was ever afterwards called Paris. Formerly it had been named *Leucetia,* as Strabo tells us in his fourth book; which in Greek signifies *white place.* This was on account of the white thighs of the ladies of that city.

To expurgate Rabelais by the standards prevailing before the 1960s (it has been tried) would mean cutting many passages. Yet hardly anything in the parts you would have to cut is in the least erotic. As a matter of fact *Gargantua* has few female characters. Though half the action results from somebody's attempts to decide whether he ought to marry, we never meet any prospective wife. Rabelais was not homosexual, but his imagination did work better in a male milieu. Toward women his tone is often suspicious, sometimes hostile. Various theories have been offered, such as rejection by his mother, or a hangover from the medieval antifeminism complained of by Chaucer's Wife of Bath. Whatever these factors may have amounted to, sex never excited him as much as some other activities, which, in his time, were virtually male preserves. The point is important. The sexual emancipation that Rabelais does herald is only part of a grander vision.

In his zest for the new liberty of the Renaissance, one thing that distinguished him from most of its leaders was a rediscovery of the body and of physical life in general, which the Middle Ages had undervalued. Rabelais believed in material joys and sensual delights, to be found in eating and drinking and all sorts of pursuits besides fornication. Working outward from those fundamentals, he believed also in material progress. He dreamed of human potentialities realized to the full. Scholars such as Erasmus thought of advances of the mind and spirit;

Rabelais thought also of physical achievement, science, invention, exploration. If morals were a shackle, then so much the worse for morals. When he unleashed his imagination in fiction, the huge deeds of his giants reduced human constraints to pettiness.

Rabelais differed from the main Renaissance vanguard in another respect. He was rooted in the popular folkways. The ribaldry of his writing is functional in more senses than one. It boils up from social levels beneath the notice of the wealthy and cultured, though familiar long since to medieval craftsmen and scribes, who would carve absurd figures in the stones of cathedrals and draw amusing animals in the illuminated margins of prayer books. Behind Rabelais is an anonymous hubbub of rustic festivals, picnics, games, vulgar stories, coarse comic songs, street cries, and swear words.

Constantly his mind reverts to an age-old grotesquerie of the body—a realm of cartoons, comic masks, made-up clowns, deformity, lavatory jokes; of stock double entendre and allusion (such as saying "nose" when you mean another organ). The carnivals where all this flourished were free-spoken occasions, often "feasts of misrule," with a cheerful topsy-turvydom that repulsed care and fear by laughter. They had their ancestry in such events as the Roman Saturnalia, the crazy liberating feast where for a moment all were equal, anything went, and the golden age of the old god Saturn was supposed to return. Medieval popular laughter had a defiant quality. It was a retort of unbroken spirits to the world system: to the terror of overlords, clerics, natural forces, Heaven itself. All this, Rabelais had absorbed.

But he could express it as no one else could. He was a lover of words and their uninhibited use. His writing echoes the French of ordinary people. When he does turn to Latin like a respectable author, it is often to an impudent underworld Latin of parody and ridicule, employed long before him in rude travesties of biblical texts, comic prayers to go with drinking and gambling, pseudowills for farm animals.

In exploiting the gross ebullience of human nature, Rabelais half-believed, half-knew, that he was doing something more profound. As a doctor, he had learned from the classical authority Galen to look for God's true purposes in his works, and especially in the body and its functions, barring none. He had seen also how the rustic festivals followed the immemorial cycle of seedtime and harvest, birth and mating and death, giving a voice and ritual power to what was otherwise voiceless. He found the hint for his mythos of Liberty, as no other Renaissance celebrity did, in ancient and earthy peasant lore. Here he could get, so to speak, *behind* orthodox morality and the orthodox rule books of the medieval cosmos.

A Breton folk saga supplied Rabelais with the giant motif itself. Tales of Gargantua had been handed down orally for centuries and diffused gradually over the Loire country that was the writer's homeland. Gargantua was originally a Celtic titan or demigod, a Breton relative of the giants of Cornwall, belonging to the same magical realm as the Merlin and King Arthur of Cornish legend. His name is derived from a word meaning "to swallow," and he was famous for stupendous eating and drinking. He left his mark on the landscape. Rocks and megaliths came to be known as Gargantua's Finger, as his Bed, his Shoes, his Quoits. The giant was good-natured but unpredictable. He roamed about the country carrying servants in his pocket.

In 1522, at Lyon, an unknown author put some of the fables into print, probably improving on them in the process. The result was a parody of courtly Arthurian romance. He started with Gargantua's father Grant-Gosier. This senior giant, he explained, was made by Merlin out of blood from Sir Lancelot's wounds and the bones of a male whale. The wizard also created a giantess out of Guinevere's nail parings and the bones of a female whale and added a gigantic mare to carry the couple. Together they produced Gargantua. After various youthful exploits, such as stealing the bells of Notre-Dame, Gargantua was enlisted by Merlin in King Arthur's service and wafted to Britain on a cloud. He slew Arthur's enemies by the hundred thousand, ate shiploads of food, drank barrels of cider at a gulp, and finally departed to the same fairyland as the king himself, where they both still are.

The skit has a curious authenticity. It goes behind the chivalric Round Table image to a cruder stratum of popular tradition and resembles some of the earliest Arthur stories, those that were told in Wales before the court poets tidied him up. Hence Rabelais found it congenial, and when he also found that the reading public was buying it, he began his own work in the form of a sequel.

He invented Gargantua's son Pantagruel. The name came from a play that some other unknown had written under the appropriate pseudonym of Merlin. The proto-Pantagruel was a sprite representing the salt seawater and causing thirst; his name means "all-thirst." Rabelais, turning him into a further member of the giant family, explains that he was born during a drought—a topical illusion to a real drought in 1532. But the name now carries a hint, which grows clearer as the story advances, of that thirst for experience, enjoyment, and knowledge that the Establishment of Rabelais's youth had frowned on.

When his tale of Pantagruel was well received, Rabelais prefaced it with a new account of Gargantua himself, the book that now stands first in the series. This is the one that proclaims the rule "Do what you will": how, we shall see in a moment. He published it in 1535. It was a bold action. Religious fury was running high, all writers were suspect, and the Pantagruel volume had already been denounced as obscene. Rabelais went into hiding for a while. Then his protector Jean du Bellay, now a cardinal, took him to Rome and out of danger. The remaining books, dealing chiefly with Pantagruel's further career, followed some years later.

As a more or less complete work in five books, *Gargantua* (to shorten its title) defies summary. It has no plot, and many different themes and targets. In the background is a symbolic idea of Past, Present, and Future. Rabelais presents three generations of giants. Grandgousier, as he calls Gargantua's father, belongs to an ancient world of rustic simplicity. Gargantua himself is a figure of civilized society up to now. Pantagruel looks ahead—sometimes—to a new wisdom that will liberate mankind. The giants themselves alter. At first they are colossal and make ordinary human beings look small and silly. As they come to embody fresh ideas, they shrink. Gargantua, having gone off to the Arthurian fairyland of Morgan le Fay, makes a brief return; and when he returns he can sit in an ordinary chair. Pantagruel, too, ceases to be gigantic. Both foreshadow human approaches to human problems. But before then, there is much upsetting to do.

Around his giants Rabelais builds an obstreperous topsy-turvydom, in the spirit of the old feats of misrule. He portrays parody wars that make real wars idiotic. He describes scholars' debates and lawyers' arguments that turn scholars and lawyers into clowns. One character visits the Underworld and finds every approved hero reduced to ignominy: Romulus making salt, Alexander darning socks. Other characters sail off on an Atlantic quest (a further borrowing from Celtic mythology) and discover islands where all the inhabitants are absurd in different ways. Yet we also get glimpses of what the author seriously desires: prophetic educational schemes; grandiose feasts and splendors; voyages of exploration; technological progress—including flight, not merely atmospheric but interplanetary.

At the end (if the end is Rabelais's own, as it probably is in substance) comes a visit to an oracle, and a strange touch of solemnity that finally turns the entire medieval order inside out. The priestess of the oracle commits the pilgrims to the protection of God and calls him "that sphere which has its centre everywhere and its circumference nowhere." The phrase is not Rabelais's. It occurs in the writings of medieval authors, including a saint, Bonaventure. But the Rabelaisian setting makes it defiant and radical. God is not "up there." The source of good is not "above," far away from ourselves. It is among us, within reach. The priestess goes on:

> So much as you can see in the heavens . . . so much as the earth reveals to you . . . is not to be compared with what is concealed in the earth.

Figuratively speaking, dig down. Don't gape at the sky, in spite of its reputation . . . as Samuel Beckett has put it since.

THE ANTI-MONASTERY

In all this medley, Rabelais seldom produces anything sympathetic. He seldom wants to. But he can, when he feels inclined, and once he does it on an impressive scale, in the episode of the Abbey of Thélème. Here conscious anti-morality, offered as a key to freedom and the enrichment of life, first appears in Christian Europe.

Why an abbey? Rabelais had sampled two religious orders and quit both. But the monastic pattern had left its imprint on him. Reading *Gargantua* we feel that he can't simply forget his old comrades in the cloister. He even has an amused affection for them. He does despite their besetting vices, laziness and hypocrisy. But he still cares enough to make a monk one of the heroes of his story; a monk who is neither lazy nor hypocritical.

Friar John, who becomes Abbot of Thélème, is introduced first at the monastery of Seuilly. During one of the grotesque mini-wars, raiders burst into the monastery vineyard. The monks' only idea of coping with this crisis is to chant Latin prayers. John alone, to his prior's indignation, actually urges them to do something. Armed with a large cross, he chases off the marauders himself. When Gargantua takes part in the war, Friar John aids him with the same energy and dash. After victory the giant, as a reward, offers to make him abbot of an existing community. But John won't have it.

> "How should I be able to govern others," he said, "when I don't know how to govern myself? . . . Give me leave to found an abbey after my own devices."

So Gargantua gives him an estate, Thélème, stretching along the Loire to within six miles of the forest of Port-Huault. Rabelais has a pun in mind. *Thelema* is Greek for "will." Friar John announces his plan, which is in keeping with the spirit of the whole story. He wants to found a religious order that shall be the opposite of all others. The Abbey of Thélème is to be an anti-monastery.

Gargantua approves the plan, financing it out of his gargantuan treasury, and the Abbey is built. Rabelais describes it carefully and lovingly, with masses of voluptuous detail. He may have taken a hint for his Thelemic Order from certain irreverent medieval parodies—pseudomonastic "rules" for fornicators and dropouts—but the main conception is purely his.

The Abbey stands on the south bank of the Loire. It is a hexagon, with round towers at the angles. Each tower is 60 yards across, and each connecting wall is 312 yards long, with six stories of rooms inside. Between the tower nearest the river and its neighbor on the west the six stories contain libraries, one above another, for books in Greek, Latin, Hebrew, French, Italian, and Spanish. Between two other towers are "fine wide galleries, all painted with ancient feats of arms, histories, and views of the world."

Inside the enclosure are courts and fountains, buildings with terraces on the roofs, spacious halls with pictures and sculptures; a theater, a tilting ground, a scented swimming bath. The living quarters have 9,332 apartments for the inmates, with green carpets, tapestries on the walls, embroidered bedclothes, long mirrors in golden frames. (Given the six-story plan throughout, this might just be feasible, though the apartments would be cell-like. But Rabelais probably hasn't worked it out. He likes to play with big, comically "exact" numbers.) Outside along the river are tennis courts, pleasure gardens, stables, a maze, an orchard, a park, a wood.

In this Renaissance luxury hotel Rabelais places his ideal community. Now the ex-monk's imagination really begins to soar. Thélème is to be made up of both sexes, admitted young. No woman is to be let in unless she is beautiful, well built, and sweet natured. Men must have corresponding good qualities. Because, in the Church, monks and nuns are expected never to leave, the Thelemites are allowed to leave when they choose, though we get the impression that they won't often want to. Because, in the Church, monks and nuns are vowed to poverty, chastity, and obedience, the Thelemites are allowed to make money and marry and generally suit themselves. Every encouragement is given them to develop their talents. They learn languages. They read and write. They compose music and play it. They compete in games. They deck themselves out with superb clothes and exotic perfumes, ringing the changes on every fashion.

Whereas the Church's religious orders carry regulated morality to a height, the Order of Thélème does the reverse.

> All their life was regulated not by laws, statutes, or rules, but according to their free will and pleasure. They rose from bed when they pleased, and drank, ate, worked and slept when the fancy seized them. Nobody woke them; nobody compelled them either to eat or to drink, or to do anything else whatever. . . . In their rules there was only one clause:
>
> DO WHAT YOU WILL

The French is *Fay ce que vouldras*. So here is the slogan, the clue we shall be following to the twentieth century. Rabelais means his readers to take it seriously. What does he intend by it?

To begin with, he has adapted it from an older saying, unimpeachably Christian. St. Augustine, in the fifth century CE, wrote: "Love, and do what you will." Only love enough, and you can't go wrong. But Augustine has no illusions about an emotional gush being a safe guide. You have to love rightly, wisely. In another place he says, "Virtue is the ordering of love." Rabelais drops the "ordering." In fact he drops the "love" part entirely, leaving only the "will."

Does he really suppose that a random assemblage of 9,332 high-caliber young men and women—or even a far smaller number—could live together in peace while at liberty to rape, steal, fight, and cheat, as they felt inclined? Well, no. Having stated the One Rule, he goes on:

People who are free, well-born, well-bred and easy in honest company have a natural spur and instinct which drives them to virtuous
deeds and deflects them from vice; and this they call honour. When
these same men are depressed and enslaved by vile constraint and
subjection, they use this noble quality, which once impelled them
freely towards virtue to throw off and break this yoke of slavery. For
we always strive after things forbidden and covet what is denied us.

Thélème is not anti-moral in the sense of promoting what society calls
evil. Diabolism is far off; the clue will lead us to that, but not yet.
Anything goes, but in practice not everything happens. In Rabelais's
opinion, evil attracts as forbidden fruit, and you can get rid of its attraction by lifting the veto. You can make people prefer the good if you give
them total liberty . . . *and if you handpick them first.*

A PROPENSITY FOR DECENT BEHAVIOR

Thélème brings us face to face with what we shall find to be a recurring fact. Anti-moralists tend to believe in privilege and selection.
They seldom extend their ideas to mankind at large. But while their
philosophy is not for all, it is not solitary either. Their minds run
on exclusive clubs, on coteries and enclosures. The phrase "Castles in
Hell" is apt, even when the Heaven-defying revolt is as idyllic and
Aucassin-like as it is at Thélème. Rabelais's monks and nuns are dis-
affiliated. They have opted out of the socially sanctioned religion and
ethic . . . but to form a society of their own in its own place. And their
hexagonal fortress beside the Loire has a number of descendants, some
imaginary, some real.

Thélème is adventurous, creative, artistic; but always within itself,
apart from people in general. It is an enclave, not a Utopia. Rabelais is
indulging a fancy that leads part of his mind in a direction where the
rest, the expansive "democratic" part, cannot follow. Even stylistically
his Thélème chapters break the flow and read unlike what is before and

after. The vulgar plebeian freedom of the rest of *Gargantua* is rarefied and refined.

True, there are reminders that we are still in the Rabelaisian world.

> In the middle of the first court was a magnificent fountain of fine alabaster, on the top of which were the three Graces with horns of abundance, spouting water from their breasts, mouths, ears, eyes, and other physical orifices.

Furthermore the abbot, Friar John, reappears later in the exploits of Pantagruel. But Thélème itself almost fades out of the story. It is aloof, an experiment, certainly not at odds with the tone of the carnival, but not quite in key with it either. This is the only place where Rabelais takes a chivalrous line and treats women with respect.

How does he picture his community running?

It is more than aloof. It is aristocratic, even feudal. Thélème is supported by an army of workers who aren't qualified to be members themselves. Inside are the house servants—chambermaids, barbers, perfumers, and many more. While outside . . .

> Around the Thélème wood was a great block of houses, a mile and a half long, very smart and well arranged, in which lived the goldsmiths, jewellers, embroiderers, tailors, wireworkers, velvet-weavers, tapestry makers, and upholsterers; and there each man worked at his trade, and all of them for the aforesaid monks and nuns.

As for the club's exclusiveness, Thélème has a long inscription over one of its gates, listing people who aren't wanted there and people who are. The first part of the list recalls Aucassin's description of those who go to Paradise.

> *Enter not here, vile hypocrites and bigots,*
> *Pious old apes, and puffed-up snivellers . . .*

Woebegone scoundrels, mock-godly sandal-wearers,
Beggars in blankets, flagellating canters . . .

This is only the beginning. The ban extends to lawyers, moneylenders, and the ill-natured; to the old, the ugly, and the diseased. Welcome types include generous and high-spirited men; "frank and fearless" women, "flowers of all beauty"; and those who proclaim "Christ's Holy Gospel," meaning apostles of the New Learning, whose religion, in Rabelais's time, was largely a campaign against the Church he was a priest in.

Having arrived at his well-screened body of inmates—young, good-looking, cultured, free from money worries, and (in view of their rejection of the old, ugly, and sick) rather heartless—Rabelais proposes "Do what you will" as a sufficient rule for them to live by, because a benevolent Nature will keep them in accord. The result is sometimes ominous. The Thelemites are so much in accord that they tend to act as a group rather than as individuals. When a number of them are together, they are willing to let the whim of any one decide the program for the whole party.

> They most laudably rivaled one another in all of them doing what they saw pleased one. If some man or woman said, "Let us drink," they all drank; if he or she said, "Let us play," they all played; if it was "Let us go and amuse ourselves in the fields," everyone went there.

"Do what you will" seems to work in Thélème because the inmates are so carefully chosen and conditioned that they can be trusted to "will" the same thing at the same time, or at any rate go along with it.

On close inspection Thélème does not lose its allure, but it does have an anticipatory whiff of a well-known story about a revolutionary orator.

"When the Revolution comes," he declared, "you'll have strawberries and cream for breakfast."

Somebody interjected: "I don't like strawberries and cream."

The speaker turned on him. "When the Revolution comes, you'll *eat* strawberries and cream."

In spite of the praise of Christ's Holy Gospel, Thélème is totally un-Christian. Rabelais admired Erasmus, the leader of Christian humanism, and adopted one comforting belief that Erasmus held: that Nature, if not interfered with, gives people a "propensity to decent behaviour." But in Thélème itself, when *Gargantua* was published, there was nothing to please Christians of any party. By implication it affronted Protestants even more than Catholics. A Renaissance pope could have adjusted himself to it. The earnest Luther and Calvin certainly couldn't.

The same is true of the whole of *The Histories of Gargantua and Pantagruel,* apart from some Protestant-tinged chapters near the end, which were probably added by the editor. Rabelais was assailed from both sides. Catholics called him a Protestant, Protestants called him an atheist, both called him an enemy of virtue and decency, in spite of which, or because of which, *Gargantua* was reprinted and bought and read. Rabelais's brand of satire influenced other French authors, especially those, thirty or forty years after his death, who led the protest against religious fanaticism of both kinds. His word-intoxicated style came through to English readers, exaggerated, in a bouncing translation started by an eccentric cavalier, Sir Thomas Urquhart, and completed less bouncingly by a bilingual Huguenot refugee, Peter Motteux. With the style came the ideas, or some of them.

So far as Rabelais has a message it is against regulated ethics always, though not in the conscious Thelemic sense outside Thélème itself. He makes fun of denials and restrictions of every kind and hardly ever spells out any definite ideals of his own. Everybody should accept Nature's guidance, say "yes" to life, and try all things, good-humoredly, uninhibitedly. There are no systems that work; no absolutes; no universal laws. The golden rule, as Shaw said centuries later, is that there are no golden rules. Enlightened common sense will give better results than morality as most people understand it.

Sometimes Rabelais seems to favor a childlike attitude and a sort of wise naïveté. Sometimes, in the popular medieval spirit, he seems to imply that the best way is to recognize that everything (including yourself) is pretty dreadful, yet "to defy all that is, and laugh." But he never sorts this out himself. Commentators do it for him. It is only in the Thélème scenes that he tries to show anti-morality in explicit action, with suggestions as to how it might work; and it is only there that he states the famous Rule that others, afterward, take up and try to put into practice.

2

OCCULT WIFE-SWAPPING

ESCAPE FROM AND DESCENT INTO SUPERSTITION

In the earlier Gargantua saga, there was one species of forbidden fruit that its adapter Rabelais never came to terms with: magic.

Of course, merely by taking over the giant motif he committed himself to a tale of fabulous marvels. Plenty of them appear in his story. Also, he knew and used odds and ends of magical lore. The expletives "Carymary, Carymara" in the Notre-Dame urination scene are said to be taken from a spell. Also Rabelais noticed the prominence of the wizard Merlin in his source materials, and Merlin is mentioned in his own book.

But the way in which this happens reveals his attitude. One of the best-known tales about Merlin concerned his "prophecies," a series of cryptic forecasts that he was supposed to have uttered when a British king was laying the foundation of a castle in Wales. Most of these were concocted in the twelfth century by the overimaginative historian Geoffrey of Monmouth. During the Middle Ages, however, various authors treated them as authentic and tried to interpret them. Though the prophecies did not figure in the "Gargantua" book that was written before Rabelais, he came across them in his reading, and he makes fun of them in the Thélème episode.

When the Abbey's foundations are being dug, Merlin is not present in person as on the similar Welsh occasion. The workmen, however, unearth a bronze plate with a long rigmarole in verse engraved on it. This darkly foretells a conflict, violence inflicted on "the globe," and eventual peace. Gargantua reads it and detects a religious message. Friar John isn't having this.

> "By St. Goderan!" exclaimed the monk. "That is not my explanation. The style is like Merlin the Prophet. You can read all the allegorical and serious meanings into it that you like, and dream on about it, you and all the world, as much as ever you will. . . ."

John refuses to do likewise. He construes the verses as a riddling account of a game of tennis, the "globe" being the much-battered ball. So much for prophecies.

To Rabelais the Renaissance meant an escape from superstition and an advance into enlightenment. The two trends went together, and for him superstition included magic. But not all his contemporaries agreed. The same Renaissance that inspired *Gargantua* also gave magic a new gloss. The quest for emancipation was pursued by some through suspect studies and practices. Rabelais would have been amazed—in fact he probably was—at some of his fellow travelers toward light; and he would have been amused as well, if he had lived to know the weird source from which his Thelemic Rule was to be reproclaimed.

Magic held a high place in sixteenth-century thought, not simply because of a hangover of superstition but because a good deal of what would now be distinguished from it as "science" and "philosophy" had not yet crystallized out. Chemistry, for instance, was still bound up with alchemy. Experimental research was fitted into a system of doctrines about the soul and its powers. The alchemist Paracelsus, whose life covered much the same span as Rabelais's, was a great scientist by any standard, a pioneer not only in chemistry but in medicine. He made the first useful studies of occupational diseases, of syphilis, of epilepsy. Yet he talked of astral bodies and the elixir of life and treated ailments (including those he understood best) with magnets.

In his *Occult Philosophy* Paracelsus wrote:

> Magic has the power to experience and fathom things which are inaccessible to human reason. For magic is a great secret wisdom, just as reason is a great public folly.

Magic, moreover, was not necessarily a black or devilish art. It could be black when wrongly applied. But the higher "natural" magic was white, an attempt to master the mysteries of the cosmos. Often it laid strong emphasis on the human side: on spiritual progress, wisdom, power. Galen's teaching, which Rabelais picked up—that God's purposes could be deciphered by studying human anatomy—was carried much further. Man was the "microcosm" and the key to all mysteries.

Cornelius Agrippa, another pioneer of scientific inquiry, pushed this theory to extremes. He claimed to perform feats of telepathy and said that this was only one instance of the boundless potentialities Man possessed, if he was bold enough to realize them:

> No one has such powers but he who has cohabited with the elements, vanquished nature, mounted higher than the heavens, elevating himself above the angels.

Agrippa was denounced by clerics. They said his magic was illicit and accused him of having a diabolical black poodle (Goethe transferred this beast to Faust) and a lodger who was strangled—or perhaps torn to bits—by a demon.

With Agrippa himself, magic was not anti-Christian, despite these critics. One of his telepathic partners was an abbot. A little after his time, a Jesuit, Benedict Pererius, called natural magic "the noblest part of physical science, medicine, and mathematics" and argued that Christians could lawfully practice such arts as dream interpretation. But the ground was growing shaky. Christians of speculative temper were ranging much further afield.

Many of them, Agrippa included, flirted with the mysticism of the Jews. Some did more than flirt. Their favorite study was the Kabbalah, a body of occult lore allegedly handed down from Abraham and other heroes of Hebrew tradition. The Bible has traces of it, but the surviving handbooks were written much later. The most important are the *Sepher Yetzirah* (Book of Formation) and the *Zohar.* They deal with the nature of God, the process of creation, sex in the spiritual realm, and other perilous topics, with much use of magical names, numbers, and formulae. In the sixteenth century Christian occultists discovered the system, with varied but generally unsettling results.

The Kabbalistic vogue reveals two of the reasons magic went the subversive way it did.

Among the Jews the Kabbalah itself was a form of protest. For century after century they had hung on under persecution, held together by the most minutely regulated morality on record: by the 613 commandments of the Law of Moses, plus thousands of bylaws added by rabbis. It was all endured as a divine discipline for survival, till the Messiah should come and set the Chosen People free. When he failed to arrive, the Kabbalah offered the ghetto-weary a path of release, for a privileged few at any rate. The secret wisdom that it taught made the Law less vital. Kabbalists rose above such things.

It was not a long step from this soft pedaling of the Law to a marking down of morals in general. The *Zohar* hinted that the Messiah himself, when he did come, would be outwardly evil. In the 1640s this heady book was to inspire an actual would-be Messiah, Sabbatai Zevi of Smyrna, who promised to do away with the Law. When, under Turkish pressure, he turned Moslem, his followers claimed that he had committed one of the worst sins a Jew could commit precisely to prove that morality was superseded.

Christian Kabbalists had no Jewish Law to rebel against. But some of the Kabbalah's potential ethical anarchism spilled over onto them. They also adopted a related feature, cliquishness. The true wisdom was held at first to belong to groups of initiates, superior to the masses, exempt from the normal rules. Among Jews this cliquishness became less acute with time. Among Christians it persisted. As the quotations from Paracelsus and Agrippa show, the magicians' besetting sin was apt to be arrogance. With the progress of Kabbalism we find them forming exclusive societies (Agrippa did himself) and claiming to possess secret traditions. Despite protestations of lofty aims, magic tended to be an affair of elite groups with elite ethics . . . or nonethics.

By a different road, a most un-Rabelaisian road, we come back within hailing distance of Thélème. Which is enough introduction for one of the most engaging of magicians, John Dee.

THE SCRYER, THE MAGE, AND MADIMI'S MESSAGE

Dee is a difficult man to label. The word *magician,* though correct, is inadequate. He was astrologer-royal to Elizabeth I. He was an early propagandist of overseas expansion, the first to employ the phrase "British Empire." He was an active and valued secret agent, foreshadowing not only James Bond but even the famous code number 007. Also he had conversations with angels.

Welsh, but born at Mortlake in 1527, he went to Cambridge at the age of fifteen and became one of the hardest-working undergraduates of his day. When Henry VIII founded Trinity College in 1546, Dee was among its earliest and youngest Fellows. Brought in as "effects" man for a college play, he built a huge mechanical beetle so frightening that he got a reputation for sorcery even before there were any grounds for it.

As a visiting lecturer on mathematics at Continental universities, he studied the works of Agrippa. Back in England his skill at casting horoscopes brought an invitation to cast Queen Mary's. He did so, but in 1555 he was arrested for plotting to kill her by black magic and remained under suspicion. Fortunately Mary's half sister Elizabeth came to the throne and favored him. He had already cast Elizabeth's horoscope as well as Mary's, and she now fixed her coronation date by his astrological reckonings. When a wax image of the queen was found in Lincoln's Inn Fields, with a pin through its heart, Dee was called in to nullify the hostile witchcraft.

Settling at Mortlake, he became a well-known and slightly dreaded figure, tall and thin, though healthy looking, with a big white beard. A flowing gown that he always wore made him look even more magelike. Once, when he was away, a local mob broke into his house and destroyed books and scientific instruments. But he had nothing malign about him. In the words of John Aubrey: "A mighty good man he was; he was a great peacemaker; if any of his neighbors fell out, he would never let them alone till he had made them friends." The queen herself visited him, and so did her chief minister William Cecil (Lord Burghley), and her beloved Leicester, and Sir Philip Sidney, and Sir Walter Raleigh.

Dee made a European tour, and then another and another. He went to Venice, to Hungary, to Germany, to Bohemia. From 1583 to 1589 he was out of England continuously. Count Adalbert Laski, a Polish envoy with astrological and alchemical interests, arranged an audience for him with the king of Poland. In Prague he met the Emperor Rudolph II, a crowned member of the magical-scientific fraternity, who afterward employed the astronomers Tycho Brahe and Kepler. Dee also received an alluring invitation from the tsar of Russia, which, however, he declined.

His long absences and foreign prestige did no harm to his reputation at home. Dee, it is essential to keep in mind, was a major figure, not an obscure crank. On some of his journeys he carried out secret-service commissions for the English government. He had commended himself to Cecil for the job by discovering a work on cryptography by Abbot Trithemius (the same abbot whom Agrippa practiced telepathy with) and inventing an improved method himself. Unlikely as it sounds, he sometimes used a code signature made up of two zeros in the angle of a large seven—007.

On the more open side of his activities, he urged English colonization across the Atlantic. He drew on his studies to prove English rights overseas. To Sir Francis Walsingham, head of the secret service, he said England had historical claims to Greenland, "Estotiland," and

"Frisland." The latter two countries did not exist. They were phantasms projected by mapmakers with blanks to fill. Dee, however, believed in both. In 1578 he told Richard Hakluyt, the historian of exploration, that Frisland had been conquered centuries earlier by King Arthur, so it was British territory: an idea that grew into a theory of an Arthurian colony in America itself, well ahead of Columbus and the Spaniards.

Meanwhile Dee was studying alchemy and the making of gold and writing on many subjects. But in spite of royal patronage, highly placed friends, transmutation, and authorship, he was never rich, and when he died he was poor.

His Arthurian flight of fancy links him, like Rabelais, with the mythology of his Celtic neighbors and ancestors. For him it was a by-product of research into the complex of mysteries surrounding Glastonbury, in Somerset, where the British king was supposed to have been buried. He wrote of the "enchanted" springs of the kingdom of Logres—Logres being an Arthurian name for England, and the springs, perhaps, being in Somerset. He acquired an obscure manuscript book, which he said had been dug up in the ruins of Glastonbury Abbey and contained the secret of turning base metal into gold. With it there was a red powder that was the Philosopher's Stone itself and could do the trick. He tested this—successfully, he maintained—on a warming pan. The alchemical text may have been a work ascribed to St. Dunstan, who was abbot of Glastonbury in the tenth century. The powder is inscrutable.

These things had been found and brought to him by a certain Edward Kelley. It was Kelley who led this good, credulous soul along a curious path.

Rather late in life Dee progressed from magical science or pseudo-science to an interest in the realm of spirits. He wondered whether his dreams were communications from unseen beings and also inquired into the dreams of his second wife, Jane Fromond, a lady-in-waiting from the court. Next (in May 1581) he took up crystal gazing as a technique by which the spirits might be induced to show themselves. The correct term for this branch of magic is "scrying," and the shiny object in which the scryer sees images—it need not be literally a crystal—is his "speculum" or "show-stone." The fully fledged scryer who sees and converses with entities in the crystal is a kind of medium. Dee found that he did not possess the gift himself and therefore needed an assistant who did.

His first choice was so blatantly bogus that Dee got rid of him. Edward Kelley entered his life as the scryer whom he tried next. Kelley was a shady apothecary and convicted forger nearly thirty years Dee's junior. He turned up at the Mortlake house on March 10, 1582, saying his name was Talbot, and quickly proceeded to see a vision in one of Dee's show-stones, while kneeling in front of the desk on which it was placed. This was the start of a lengthy association. Kelley confessed his real name and served Dee as a scrying medium in sessions that were set down on paper, covering hundreds of pages. How far this was a hoax it is difficult to tell. Certainly Kelley had some knowledge of occult lore and could have faked, but modern scrutiny of the records has left investigators with a feeling that he did not fake everything. Hallucination? Unintended hypnotic suggestion by Dee himself? Possibly.

Each session was prefaced with devout prayers and invocations. Kelley would gaze into the speculum and see beings that Dee considered to be angels—intelligent, passionless spirits with a knowledge of the past and future. Dee put questions to them and Kelley described what he saw and, in some way, heard. They had a special angelic language called Enochian. One angel that appeared often was Madimi, "a Spiritual Creature, like a pretty girl of seven or nine years of age." Dee set great store by her messages and named one of his daughters after her.

These angelic dialogues tended to be vague and erratic but were not pure nonsense. The whole proceeding was a pioneer exercise in spiritualism. In the course of it Kelley received, and passed on to his master, a restatement of the Rule of Thélème: "Behold you are become free: Do that which most pleaseth you. . . . Do even as you list."

Dee, still a convinced if most irregular Christian, hardly knew what to make of this. Given leisure to reflect, he might or might not have drawn radical conclusions from it. But the innocent-looking child-spirit Madimi insisted on a practical application. During the winter of 1586–1587 John and Jane Dee, with Edward Kelley and Mrs. Edward Kelley, were staying with Count Rosenberg of Bohemia at his castle in Trebona. Kelley had a fit of temperament and refused to scry, then suddenly had a look and contacted Madimi. She told him that the two experimenters should "share all things in common, including their wives."

It did not go down well. Jane "fell a-weeping and trembling for full quarter of an hour, then burst forth into a fury of anger." Her husband replied to Madimi that the message was "unmeet" and tried to ignore it. However, after a long and awkward hesitation, resistance crumbled and the magical quartet took shape. On May 3, 1587, all four signed a pact promising to obey the angels. The final outcome is unknown, but this was the last of Kelley's scrying. When Dee returned home in December 1589 he did not take his medium with him.

Kelley went to the Emperor Rudolph, talking now about alchemy instead of crystal gazing. Rudolph favored him for some years but lost patience when no gold materialized and put him in prison, where he was killed trying to escape. Dee lived on till 1608, leaving a Continental reputation that has never been fully reconstructed. His son by Jane, Arthur, pursued similar interests and likewise traveled abroad. While in Moscow Arthur made a Russian translation of some of his father's papers. It is said to have been studied three centuries later by Rasputin.

PART TWO
Realization

3

WHIGS AND RAKES

DISQUIET IN THE AGE OF REASON

Soon after the death of John Dee, much of Europe passed into a phase of ideological conflict and moral fervor. Germany was torn apart by the last great religious war. France under Louis XIV became aggressively Catholic. England was split between Cavaliers and Roundheads. Even the Restoration and easygoing Charles II could not prevent the struggle from continuing in other forms, because the issues were real. As long as they remained real, people with opposing outlooks could express them by supporting opposed parties. The conservative had his fields of action, the rebel had his. Both could be men of principle and conviction, on lines socially recognized; both frequently were.

The phase passed, and the atmosphere altered. Especially in England, events prepared the way for new attitudes and a new kind of questioning, a return of the Rabelaisian spirit with a difference . . . and, eventually, the building of an actual if reduced Thélème with his Rule over the door. As with Rabelais, the phenomenon appears in a context and the context is important. This time it is a context in which the main facts shed light, not simply on a single freak genius, but on a whole series of people.

The prolonged English crisis was resolved by the so-called Glorious Revolution of 1688. James II, a would-be absolute monarch, was forced into exile. William of Orange succeeded him; the Crown was confined within limits that the political magnates could approve; and the sacred watchwords of the regime were Liberty and Property. Parliament had won, a narrow-franchise Parliament representing the wealthy and landed, plus a largely docile Church. The battle was not quite over. Rumblings went on through the reign of William and Anne, and a Stuart comeback still appeared credible, especially in Scotland. But the Pretender—James III as his supporters called him— was overseas. The union of Scotland with England deprived him of a northern base and reconciled many Scots by opening up opportunities for them in the south. After the futile Jacobite rising of 1715, the Hanoverian George I, enthroned by Parliament, was accepted if not rejoiced at.

For the first time in many years England had a firmly entrenched "Establishment." It was dominated by the Whigs, who had led the Glorious Revolution. The early Whigs were men who inherited the Roundhead tradition in politics but shook off its puritanism— sometimes very thoroughly. England gravitated toward a state of affairs in which their successors comprised nearly everyone who mattered in politics. Whiggism was too broad and pervasive to count as a party at all in the modern sense. The Tories, who went on asserting the royal prerogative, and spoke for landed rather than moneyed interests, were still a party of sorts while Anne reigned and even held office for a spell. However, most of them more or less accepted the Whigs' 1688 settlement, and after Anne they dwindled into a mere scattered grumble, with a literary tinge and touches of Jacobite nostalgia. For most practical purposes Whiggism became the whole show, and nearly all people of power and influence were, in one sense or another, Whigs.

The spectacle of England from 1720 till the midcentury is the spectacle of a stable, balanced, oligarchic society, on the whole a successful society, with Liberty and Property well secured for a small class at the top, or most of them; *and no organized opposition, no real issues in public life, no clear basis for protest at all.* This is the crucial point to grasp in the seriocomic story that follows. It is the basic reason for the bizarre involvement of a section of English politics with the anarchic "Do what you will" and a cult of Hell-Fire.

The presiding genius of the prevailing order was Sir Robert Walpole, who, as prime minister, controlled government so expertly and for so long that he almost reduced official politics to the mere scramble for office. He and his coterie of Whig bosses hung on and on and prevented younger talents from rising. This was achieved partly by working closely with George I and George II (who succeeded him in 1727), partly by patronage and bribery on a lavish scale. Over two hundred MPs held government jobs that kept them in line. The Civil Service was staffed at its higher levels by influential friends of the Ministry. They delegated the actual work, pocketed the difference between their salaries and the pittances they paid to their deputies, and were satisfied with the system. Walpole himself had a vast private fortune, founded largely on using his inside information to get out of the South Sea Bubble just before its collapse—a disaster that he exploited further by presenting himself to the country as its savior from the resulting financial crisis.

On top of all this, paradoxically, Walpole dominated because he deserved to. A massive, philistine Norfolk squire with a common-sense outlook, he solved problems adroitly as they came and never got embroiled in dubious long-term programs. He worked hard, talked plainly, kept his temper, and was not vindictive. His presence was over-whelming. He enraged his enemies and gave them no weapons to use against him and no platform to take a stand on.

Against Walpole and his system, nicknamed the Robinocracy, noth-ing seemed possible. England was prosperous and at peace. Religious dissent had yet to find a voice. Jacobitism was a recognized stance but an ineffectual one. The only labor organizations were tiny craft unions without militancy. Cities could produce mobs, and riots occurred over local grievances, but the mobilization of class against class was a long way off. Population was small by modern standards, and the people were unawakened. The rich, however, were wide awake, and to some purpose. Profit seeking by a few—a close-knit, intermarried few—was spilling over into benefits for the nation. "Trade" was growing respectable. Walpole himself, the king's chief minister, married the daughter of a timber merchant.

Mercantile tastes and values increasingly shaped society. There was a growing tendency to be precise and explicit. The age saw a steady advance of time consciousness. In 1700 few Londoners carried watches; by the 1720s, those who could afford one habitually had one. Employers laid more and more stress on punctuality and on the hitherto unheard maxim that time is money. The bourgeois demand for up-to-date information created newspapers. In 1700 none was published at all outside London. Over the next half century a hundred local papers appeared, most of them serving the same middle- to upper-class readership and speaking the same language.

It was growth without radical change, growth with stability, on a foundation that 1688 was supposed to have made secure forever. The feeling that England had "arrived," so to speak, and that further progress could only mean carrying on along the same line, was reflected in a literature that took its tone from the last years of Queen Anne. Prose was dominated by Joseph Addison and the style he deployed in his little magazine the *Spectator*—cool, elegant, safe. The *Spectator* professed to give a running commentary on English life without being nastily controversial. It avoided politics (though Addison was a Whig when Toryism still counted), it never satirized the clergy, it never made fun of marriage, it never indulged in scandal or defamation. Stirring things up was now simply *not done*—a point of view that was novel, but rapidly took hold. In poetry too, thanks to Alexander Pope, the heroic couplet became the norm, and for several decades few poets used any other meter in longer works. All true culture was classical and rule bound.

While the English had this sense of "arrival" in a far higher degree than other nations, it was part of a trend that their own best minds had done much to initiate. The Age of Reason was flourishing. Newton, it was agreed, had discovered the reign of law in the universe, and Locke had done the same for the mind. If France (for example) had less ground for constitutional smugness, the monarchy of Louis XV at least rested on a solid consensus, and his thinking subjects could share a rational optimism. The cosmos had been cut down to size; it had been deprived of terror and mystery; Man could do very nicely by enlightened self-knowledge and study of his surroundings.

In other words, whereas Rabelais could rebel in the name of science and the free-ranging mind, this was far harder for a man of the earlier eighteenth century, and in England it was almost impossible. Science had been annexed by the Establishment, and the mind had been tamed. Nor was religion in itself a theme for serious revolt. Christianity was still professed, but stripped of its once tremendous claims. The eighteenth century was the time when even "enthusiasm" became a dirty word, and a parson's memorial might record in his praise that he preached for forty years without a trace of enthusiasm. Religion was not the cause of the complacency or, as a rule, of anything in particular. In 1728 an acute French traveler wrote: "In England there is no religion and the subject, if mentioned in society, evokes nothing but laughter." In 1736 Bishop Butler—one of the few Anglican clerics of high mental attainments—declared that most educated men had ceased to regard Christianity as even an object of inquiry, "its fictitious nature being so obvious." The Church nevertheless was part of the system; it helped to keep the populace quiet; and therefore a degree of religious practice was a gentleman's duty, and it was bad form to be outspokenly anti-Christian. (A similar view existed in Catholic countries, though without the same wholeheartedness in hypocrisy.)

But the real ideology of the Age of Reason was a pseudoscientific belief in Nature. God had set the whole beautiful machine going, and it now ran itself and was very good. From Newton's contemporary, Leibniz, literate Europe acquired a simple faith that this is the best of possible worlds; that everything in it is for the best; that whatever is, is right. This was a doctrine that blessed the status quo and fitted in with the well-being of the upper classes, especially in England. It was taken up there by Henry St. John, Viscount Bolingbroke, one of the more intellectual politicians. Bolingbroke's ideas were taken up in their turn, developed and versified by Pope in his *Essay on Man*.

> *All Nature is but art, unknown to thee;*
> *All chance, direction which thou canst not see;*
> *All discord, harmony not understood;*
> *All partial evil, universal good;*
> *And, spite of pride, in erring reason's spite,*
> *One truth is clear, Whatever is, is right.*

The *Essay on Man* expressed a mood that, for the moment, defied everything that might seem to shake it. Bolingbroke himself, as a practicing politician, was so deeply disaffected at one stage that he joined the Jacobites, and later he was the brain behind such opposition to the Robinocracy as did emerge. Yet as a philosopher he held that Nature was good and all was well. The same confidence could survive countless proofs that Hanoverian England was far from paradisal. Behind the prosperity were violence, poverty, crime, injustice. The new rich themselves, the merchant capitalists whose rise had created this happy kingdom, were constantly trying to push it into war for commercial gain. The law was savage, more savage than in the past: the number of capital crimes rose to 253—technically you could be hanged for shooting a rabbit or stealing property worth five shillings. London was a city of grim contrasts, with a West End that was magnificent and an East End that was unspeakable—a wilderness of stinking lodging houses, thieves' hideouts, gin shops, and squalor.

Anybody with eyes open was apt to have occasional feelings that behind the facade all was not well, that in spite of Pope something was wrong, that some piece of the puzzle was missing . . . yet, there it was again: no basis for protest existed. Thanks to Robinocracy, politics were empty. Religion was empty. The modish philosophy of benign Nature failed to acknowledge evil.

A symptom of disquiet that did emerge was a fondness for

romanticizing the lawbreaker. Highwaymen—at a safe distance—
enjoyed favor. *The Beggar's Opera* was a hit in 1728, and Dick Turpin,
hanged for murder at York in 1739, became an instant legend. At least
one of the underlying motives went deep. Vague rebelliousness could
fasten on a crook and build him up into a hero, because defiance was the
last way of rebellion still open. Under that regime of smiling, smother-
ing invulnerability the only method of revolt was to shock. Not perhaps
to be criminal outright, but at least to be eccentric; to be outrageous; to
be, perhaps, ostentatiously bad.

This was a state of things where liberty and libertinism clearly
might go together. Yet how, short of actual crime?

Given the waning of religion, and the prevailing tepid optimism,
it was hard to be even wicked with the old sense of damnation. Sin
scarcely seemed to matter enough. Atheism, though seldom avowed
publicly, provoked only yawns in private. Sexual mores in upper-
class western Europe took their tone largely from France, particularly
Versailles, where the Regent during Louis XV's minority gave his bless-
ing to everything including incest and sodomy, and the example later
set by Louis himself was not so different. If the flouting of moral rules
was easy, it was also devalued. The rare adventurer could still make
scandal in itself a declaration of independence. Such was Casanova a
little later. But in most cases, while shocking conduct could satisfy the
urge to rebel as nothing else could, it had to take a special form to be
really exciting. It had to be *group* activity, a way of life (part-time at any
rate) for a consciously and defiantly libertine set.

GANGS IN THE STREETS

Late in the reign of Anne, when the hardening shape of the new
Establishment was already visible, London's urban restlessness produced
a crop of street gangs—window breakers, "scowerers," and others. The
most famous, with a prophetic opting-out gesture, took the name of an
American Indian tribe. In 1710 four Iroquois chiefs visited England,

among them the "Emperor of the Mohocks" or Mohawks. Presently parties of young homegrown "Mohocks" began to trouble the streets after dark. During March and April of 1712 many journalists and letter writers were taking notice of them. Swift called them a "race of rakes," and Steele described them at length in the *Spectator*.

According to Steele they formed "a nocturnal fraternity with the title of the Mohock Club," headed by an emperor of their own, who had a Turkish crescent "engraved" (tattooed?) on his forehead. Having met in a tavern and consumed plenty of drinks, they would surge out into the streets with knives and razors, assaulting late pedestrians. Some went in for eye gouging. Some, called the Dancing Masters, forced men to jump about by lunging at their legs with swords. Some, the Tumblers, "set women upon their heads, and committed certain indecencies, or rather barbarities, on the limbs they exposed." A more elaborate method of harassing females was to nail them up in tubs and roll them down Snow Hill. When a strong party of Mohocks got together they would overturn coaches on to rubbish dumps or challenge the Watch—the only police—and count it a special triumph if the watchmen retreated. Their program seemed to be war on people in general, with the brothel keepers as their sole allies.

John Gay, author of *The Beggar's Opera*, mentions the gangs in his poem "Trivia." Speaking of the streets of London at night, he says:

> *Now is the time that rakes their revels keep;*
> *Kindlers of riot, enemies of sleep. . . .*
> *Who has not heard the Scowerer's midnight fame?*
> *Who has not trembled at the Mohock's name?*
> *Was there a watchman took his hourly rounds,*
> *Safe from their blows, or new-invented wounds?*
> *I pass their desperate deeds, and mischiefs done*
> *Where from Snow Hill black steepy torrents run;*
> *How matrons hoop'd within the hogshead's womb*
> *Were tumbled furious thence, the rolling tomb*

O'er the stones thunders, bounds from side to side:
So Regulus to save his country died.

These under-thirty delinquents were not criminals in the normal sense. Many were technically gentlemen, and they took no money from their victims. On April 8, 1712, the *Spectator* published an alleged letter and manifesto from the emperor himself. The statement made out, in a tongue-in-cheek manner, that the Mohocks' aim was to clean up London and Westminster by scaring persons "of loose and dissolute lives," and that their forays were confined—or were meant to be confined—to times and places where honest citizens shouldn't be wandering around anyway.

Whatever the value of the *Spectator* item, Authority scented more in this outbreak than skinhead rowdyism. A last Tory government was uneasily in office. Someone brought out a ballad, "Plot upon Plot," making fun of the Tories' continual suspicions of Whig scheming. The speaker is supposed to be a true-blue Tory denouncing the Whigs. After accusing them of such acts of terrorism as taking the screws out of the roof timbers of St. Paul's, he goes on:

You sent your Mohocks next abroad
With razors arm'd and knives,
Who on night-walkers made inroad,
And scared our maids and wives;
They scowered the Watch and windows broke,
But 'twas their true intent
(As our wise Ministry did smoke*)
T' o'erturn the Government.

Obviously the author of the ballad doesn't think so, but he indicates that some Tories did. In a way they were right. There was more in

---

*Discover (i.e., smoke out).

Mohock violence than fun and games. The Mohocks themselves faded out (their emperor married a rich widow and lost interest), but a few years later a shrewd French observer, B. L. de Muralt, noted a "roughness and fierceness" still current among the English and judged that it was linked with an assertion of liberty.

LADIES AND GENTLEMEN

Three key words in the Mohock documentation foreshadow what was soon to come. Swift and Gay call them "rakes"; Steele uses the term "club"; and the emperor's manifesto, whether genuine or bogus, names "the Devil Tavern" as their headquarters.

As England settled toward its Hanoverian deadlock, the Rake emerged as an ever more significant figure. Though never quite losing touch with his early association of street gang unruliness, he tended to become less crudely turbulent, to acquire character. More and more he was a gentleman of talent as well as nominal breeding, who drank, gamed, and wenched with impudent flamboyance and carried on in the same style long after the effervescence of youth had passed.

Several influences converged to mold him. One was the Grand Tour. Sons of wealthy families were sent to travel through France and Italy, with tutors, servants, and plentiful funds. They were intended to absorb culture, and they often did; but they absorbed other things with it—subversive promptings and tastes that their fathers rarely welcomed. In France, for instance, the Grand Tourist was apt to meet such notables as the Duc de Richelieu, who combined atheism, licentiousness, charm, diplomatic distinction, and prowess in war so brilliantly as to refute all preaching against the effects of debauch and irreligion. Then, going on to Italy, he could get seduced by popery or entangled in black magic. He tended to return home under a cloud of suspicion, and soon justify it, because the ever-duller Establishment denied him scope, and there was no proper opposition to go into.

A poem published in 1746, "The Fine Modern Gentleman" by

Soame Jenyns, shows what a tradition of outrage to the worthy majority had by then been built up.

> *Just broke from school, pert, impudent, and raw,*
> *Expert in Latin, more expert in Taw,**
> *His honour posts o'er Italy and France,*
> *Measures St. Peter's dome, and learns to dance.*
> *Thence having quick thro' various countries flown,*
> *Glean'd all their follies, and expos'd his own,*
> *He back returns, a thing so strange all o'er,*
> *As never ages past produc'd before;*
> *A monster of such complicated worth,*
> *As no one single clime could e'er bring forth.*
> *Half atheist, papist, gamester, bubble rook,*†
> *Half fiddler, coachman, dancer, groom, and cook.*

Of course most of them settled down, but some didn't.

The rakish mode of life was favored by the status of women. This, as it impinged on males in English higher society, comprised most of what Women's Lib dislikes. Though bought and sold in marriage, women were not consigned frankly to the nursery and kitchen, and in increasing numbers they entered the men's world, but they entered it on the men's terms. During Anne's reign a great rendezvous of top Whigs was the Kit-Cat Club. It always remained a male preserve, but it admitted girls of good breeding for a special ritual—a sort of Miss England contest in which the winner became a "toast" of the Club and had her name inscribed with a diamond on one of its toasting glasses. The wealth of the gentry offered expanding opportunities, which women with business talents were ready to exploit. However, since most trades and professions were closed to them, their enterprise often took the shape of keeping brothels and gaming houses.

---

*Marbles.

†Con man (i.e., a swindler through "bubbles" such as the South Sea Scheme).

Even with birth and polish few ladies could mix with the gentlemen as their equals. If nothing else, they lacked the educational background. Oxford and Cambridge had no places for girls. While self-taught blue-stockings were increasingly to be met with, they aroused suspicion. The most famous of these was Lady Mary Wortley Montagu. When very young she was a Kit-Cat toast. Later—vivacious and married and still beautiful—she went with her husband on an ambassadorial mission to Turkey. She was one of the first of many English authoresses of travel books. Her achievements would have done credit to any man. Yet as late as 1753 she wrote:

> There is no part of the world where our sex is treated with so much contempt as in England. I do not complain of men having engrossed the government . . . but I think it the highest injustice . . . that the same studies that raise the character of a man should hurt that of a woman.

Ladies were expected to conceal, not use, anything they did learn.

Hence even the literary woman tended to exist in relation to literary men, or at least literate ones. Lady Mary herself had to endure advances (and afterward vindictiveness) from the impossible Alexander Pope. Another, who reflected the female plight more fully, was Martha Fowke. A fluent writer, Martha composed a series of verse love letters, *The Epistles of Clio and Strephon,* purportedly between an English couple in France. Her book went through several editions. But instead of putting her name on it, she called herself "Clio" and added a self-description detailing her large blue eyes; white, regular teeth; dark brown hair; small fingers; et cetera . . . physical items only, with almost nothing of her life or interests. In the 1720s and 1730s she had affairs, real or pretended, with most of the male poets in currency—John Dyer, Richard Savage, David Mallet, James Thomson, and others, most of them younger than herself. She continued to be Clio (or sometimes, for a change, Mira) and they addressed amorous verses to her. Marriage to a Leicestershire squire made no difference. As a Victorian author delicately puts it, Martha Fowke "appears to have troubled the peace of mind of small poets to the last."

Whatever the distresses of the nondominant sex, England professed to be more righteous than the Continent. Yet for any young gentleman of spirit, England had its native unsettling factors quite apart from any *vices anglais*. Oddly important and easy to underrate was the fact that his education involved reading Milton. *Paradise Lost* might not seem to come down on the rakish side. But one of Milton's achievements in it (affected, perhaps, by his study of the *Zohar* as well as his Roundhead politics) was to give the arch-rebel Satan an unprecedented allure, and thereby undermine God. Satan's pride and self-will, his building of Pandemonium as a sort of Thélème in Hell, his maxim "Evil, be thou my good" were much more fascinating than the poet intended.

Such a literary influence many sound remote from the rake's world, even when he retained his education. Yet we do not have to delve far into the eighteenth-century undergrowth to find reading matter such as *The Fruit-Shop* or *A Companion to St James's Street*. In this curious work, long, would-be titillating discourses on sex and modish harlotry are mingled with equally long discourses on *Paradise Lost* and what it implies. The author suggests that Milton's attempt to "justify the ways of God to men" is so counterproductive that we can take it as justifying the ways of men to women: the Christian poet is the supreme debunker of Christian principles, and the Devil comes off best.

OF CLUBS AND COFFEE HOUSES

If *rake* is a key word, *club* is another. In the period of change from Stuart to Hanover, it became plain that a city the size of London—its population was over 600,000—could put almost any mode of living on an organized social basis. Even apart from size, London was more likely to do so than, say, Paris. The English capital was witnessing a new trend that was to be very much its own. The Kit-Cat was not isolated; the club, in a more formal sense than any Mohock fraternity, was growing from the coffeehouse.

It was not a total novelty. Elizabethans such as Raleigh and Ben Jonson had belonged to groups that met periodically in taverns. But the eighteenth-century development went much further, leading to results that are still solidly with us. Toward 1700 each coffeehouse and chocolate house had begun to attract a recognized clientele, often sharing a common interest. There were Whig and Tory coffeehouses, poets' coffeehouses, and so on. The regulars took to using the place for reading and writing, exchanging news, and holding meetings and parties. A practice grew up of pooling or "clubbing" expenses. Presently a point might be reached where a group of regulars had a secretary, a dues-paying membership, its own room, eventually separate quarters—and a true club was born. This was how White's originated, a very early instance founded before the turn of the century. Foreigners were impressed by English gentlemen's clubability, which was hard to parallel abroad.

Once the pattern was established, clubs took shape without the same unofficial buildup. Ned Ward, in a somewhat overwrought *Secret History of Clubs* published in 1709, describes thirty-one. His definition is loose, and most of them seem to have been informal tavern coteries that soon faded out, but some clubs lasted. At one point London had four for politicians alone: the October (Tory), the Saturday (headed by Bolingbroke), the Green Ribbon, and the Hanover. Other clubs pursued other concerns. The Golden Fleece was a convivial social body with members known by facetious assumed names. The Wet Paper (an allusion to fresh printer's ink) was for those who wanted the latest publications. The Mollies catered to male homosexuals and transvestites. There were eccentric clubs such as the Ugly and the Lying, and pretentious ones such as the Ace of Clubs, which aspired to be the most exclusive, and was so much so that it survived less than a year.

Among all the rest, clubs were launched for gentlemen of Mohockish outlook, but with greater wealth and education and less overt lawlessness: clubs in fact for rakes, on the new, more cultured pattern. Among them—worth mentioning because (on and off) it has continued—was the Beefsteak Club, founded in some form about 1707 and reincarnated in 1735 as the Sublime Society of Beefsteaks, which met on Saturdays in a room over Covent Garden Theatre. In its later guise it slowly became respectable, but it did not begin so.

Rumor accused these riotous fellowships of blasphemy and pacts with Satan . . . a charge that brings us back to the Devil Tavern, where, allegedly, the Mohock emperor held court. This was an old hostelry near Temple Bar. The Apollo Club, to which Ben Jonson belonged, had gathered there a century earlier. By 1712 its name was acquiring a point that it had lacked in Jonson's day. A diabolic rake legend was already just beginning to form. Probably unfounded at the Mohock level, it was soon to become reality among the club gentry who relished Milton's Fiend and exchanged irreverent notions on things in general.

It was in this milieu that the first hints appeared of a Thélème for the opposition minded—including malcontent Whigs stifled by the masses of Walpole Whigs. "Do what you will" was not destined to be proclaimed as a slogan again, in plain terms, till 1748. But we can trace a well-defined run-up to its reinstatement that is all part of the same story. The blinkered complacency of the age of Walpole, that age that suffocated most forms of revolt, ironically encouraged revolt-through-outrageousness. If Leibniz and Bolingbroke and Pope were right; if Nature was benign and the rational way to live was to obey her; if enlightened Man was good, if all was for the best and nothing was fundamentally wrong . . . then why *not* be wicked, if that was your own way of obeying Nature? If that was how Nature prompted you to assert your freedom, what right had the sourpuss of Respectability to complain?

4

A DUKEDOM IN HELL

THE PURSUIT OF BLASPHEMY

On April 28, 1721, George I issued an Order-in-Council proposed by Baron Macclesfield, the lord chancellor. Its avowed aim was to suppress "immorality and profaneness." Its chief target was a body known as the Hell-Fire Club.

Trustworthy details, sadly enough, are scarce. However, the royal Order itself supplies us with a few pointers. These can be eked out a little from a would-be-poetic pamphlet entitled *The Hell-Fire Club Kept by a Society of Blasphemers,* dedicated by its unnamed author to Macclesfield, and applauding his action. Its shocked piety does at least disclose what the Club's special attraction was.

Hell-Fire devotees had three meeting places: at houses in Westminster and in Conduit Street near Hanover Square, and at Somerset House, once the residence of dowager queens, but since converted into cheap apartments for courtiers and minor nobles. Either there were three distinct societies—the Hell-Fire Club itself and two others like it—or there was a single Club comprising three groups. Total membership known to the authorities amounted to forty-odd "persons of quality" of both sexes. The admission of women is interesting, since most clubs excluded them. At Somerset House, it was alleged, everybody met for orgies. But the Order-in-Council and the pamphlet both witness that this was not the reason for the ban. Plenty of persons of quality held orgies. The Hell-Fire Club's main pursuit was blasphemy; in other words, spitting in the eye of the Church and the official morality it stood for.

The proceedings sound comic rather than evil. As at modern gatherings of the Dickens Fellowship and the Baker Street Irregulars, the members came to meetings in assumed characters. But instead of being Mr. Micawber or Dr. Watson, they turned up as revered figures from the Bible, or saints, and played them for laughs. They staged mock rituals making fun of Christian dogmas such as the Trinity. When the company sat down to dinner, the menu included a drink called Hell-Fire Punch and dishes with such names as Holy Ghost Pie, Devil's Loins, and Breast of Venus. A Holy Ghost Pie was an imitation Host made with angelica root. Breast of Venus was constructed out of small chickens, with cherries for nipples. This fitted into the general scheme as a heathen touch.

Why did the lord chancellor bother? Even on the assumption that one club did embrace all three groups, it was still quite small and, we might conclude, just a rather immature joke. But an *organized* display of aristocratic scorn toward Christianity, meaning the Church of England, was more seditious and heavily charged than might appear. The Church was supposed to be a mainstay of the Revolution settlement, and the Hell-Fire Club had come into being at a time when it was vulnerable and touchy.

Anglicanism was just recovering—or failing to recover—from what was described as the Bangorian Controversy. In 1717 Benjamin Hoadly, Bishop of Bangor, preached a sermon in George I's presence denying that the Church had any special divine status in the earthly scheme of things. "The Kingdom of Christ," he said, "is not of this world"—giving that text as much weight as it would bear. The Government approved. It printed thousands of copies of Hoadly's sermon, which implied in practice that the clergy had no right to take political stands, and that their only duty in public affairs was to serve the state unquestioningly as moral policemen. When this theory was disputed (notably by Bishop

Atterbury of Rochester, one of the most distinguished prelates) the Government clamped down. It forbade the Convocation of the Church of England to meet. The Church, cowed, submitted to the facts of a power relationship, hardly even retaining the dignity of a department of state. Henceforth it was increasingly staffed by clergy whose "safe" views took priority over character and scholarship.

This in fact was the actual process by which the Christianity of the Walpole era became what it was. The Hell Fire Club arose when the thing had just happened, at a juncture where more people than hitherto were looking upon the Church as discredited, and fair game. From Macclesfield's standpoint as lord chancellor, the Club was subversive because it guyed the religion that the Government still valued as a prop for its own structure. It sapped what was left of the moral policemen's prestige.

A membership of forty-odd does not sound formidable. Forty, however, was then a vastly bigger proportion of upper-crust London than it is now. Furthermore, the antics of "persons of quality" were liable to become public and set a fashion. The closest modern parallels to the Hell-Fire charades would not be the activities of any private club, but the sketches on television satire shows in the 1960s—which, when they satirized religion, drew furious complaints that the BBC was threatening the basis of Christian society.

In 1721 official action was fairly prompt. At the time when Hell-Fire performances were banned, they had probably not been going on for more than a year. The anonymous poem hailed the Club's downfall with much bombast about divine judgment and very few facts. Perhaps the author was one of those self-appointed censors who know very little about the things they denounce.

A LEADER, A LEGEND

A second reason that the Club caused disquiet emerges when we realize who its president was: a brilliant young peer who had been built up as a pillar of the Establishment and could start untold trouble if he should walk out from under it. Philip, Duke of Wharton, was more than a common rake. His career epitomizes so much, and foreshadows so much, that the future growth of the scandalous seeds he planted cannot be understood without him. In more ways than one he is a key figure of his age and an unacknowledged immortal.

His father, Thomas, first Marquis of Wharton, was one of several emancipated sons of puritan fathers who had laid the groundwork of Whiggism under Charles II. This first marquis was a champion of the Revolution and wrote its hit campaign song "Lilliburlero," boasting afterward that he had sung King James out of three kingdoms. He married the charming Lucy Loftus. In 1698 she was a toast of the Kit-Cat Club, and shortly before Christmas of the same year she gave birth to her husband's heir, Philip. William III and the Princess Anne, later queen, agreed to stand as godparents.

Wharton Senior tried to force the boy into Whig statesmanship by intensive education. Philip absorbed it all—classical literature, Shakespeare, mathematics, metaphysics, French, Spanish, Italian. He learned to recite speeches in front of his father's guests. Unfortunately he also learned to mimic the guests.

His father sought to steady him under the tutelage of an older companion, Edward Young, a Fellow of All Souls. But before he attained his seventeenth birthday, Philip made a runaway marriage with the daughter of a mere major-general. The bride, a protégé of Lady Wharton's, came blithely to the wedding in a dress the Whartons had given her to wear on the queen's birthday. Thomas hunted the couple out at midnight, with the attorney general and a posse; but although he parted them for a while, he failed to get the marriage annulled and died of the blow a few weeks later.

Philip inherited the title. In the spring of 1716 he set off on the Grand Tour, without his wife, but with several footmen, a valet, two sets of coach horses, and a French Protestant tutor. His father's trustees allowed him £1,000 a year, then a good income. He left the tutor in

Geneva, bequeathing him a bear cub that he had bought and didn't know what to do with. The rest of his entourage stayed with him . . . for a time.

Revolt against the paternal system was fermenting rapidly. Perhaps Philip had heard the old man whistle "Lilliburlero" once too often. In Paris he made contact with Jacobite exiles. One, an Irishman named Gwynne, received him in an attic. Philip said he hoped the stairs didn't lead up to Heaven, because if they did he would go down again, and invited Gwynne to join him in Hell, where he was to be the Devil's Lord of the Bedchamber. Gwynne was shocked, but not so deeply as to fail to see the young lord's potential value to the Pretender.

Philip met "James III" and accepted a meaningless Knighthood of the Garter from him, and an equally meaningless promise of the Dukedom of Northumberland. Next he talked the Pretender's mother out of £2,000 with vague undertakings to help their cause. Lord Stair, British ambassador in Paris, and an astute anti-Jacobite operator, warned him to be careful. The advice was poorly received. When an English medical student broke some of the Embassy windows and was arrested, Philip tried to collect a party to march on the Embassy and break more of the windows.

Early in 1717 he seemed to be settling down. He crossed over to Ireland, taking Edward Young as his secretary, and sat in the Irish House of Lords, then separate though English-controlled. He supported the government, spoke well, and attended committees conscientiously. But he was already in trouble over money and drink. Dean Swift, who had loathed the father but liked the son, warned him in vain.

In 1718 George I made Philip a duke. No other nonroyal minor had ever been honored thus. George hoped to cement his loyalty, but the plan went awry. Wharton was now in England again and showing an unwelcome acumen. He saw through the South Sea Bubble and denounced ministerial conduct so trenchantly that Lord Stanhope, struggling to answer him, collapsed with a cerebral hemorrhage on the floor of the House. Meanwhile Wharton had acquired a reputation for brawling in public; raced horses at Newmarket; and had nearly broken the priceless and talismanic goblet of the Musgrave family, the "Luck of Edenhall," by tossing it up and not quite catching it.

Also he had showered cash and gifts, which he couldn't afford, on Edward Young. The duke, who possessed a mild talent for verse, admired the ability in others, and Young was now showing it. One of Wharton's gifts to the poet was a human skull made into a candle holder, to write tragedies by. He attempted without success to get Young elected an MP and then made a donation to All Souls, his college.

Wharton's Hell-Fire Club venture probably began in 1720. Given his slide toward rebellion, it was a logical result of his upbringing. In the puritan folklore that lingered on with the earlier Whigs, the Devil was an inescapable character. Cartoonists put him in their pictures surprisingly often.* No amount of skepticism could entirely exorcise him as a focus for dangerous thoughts. He was all the easier to turn to because of that new grandeur and attractiveness that one of the greatest Roundheads of all had given him in *Paradise Lost*. It is uncertain whether Wharton—or whoever did start the Hell-Fire Club—picked up the idea from any earlier body. Ned Ward, in his *Secret History,* has a tale of an Atheistical Club in the reign of Anne. He describes it as a coterie of half-baked intellectuals and libertines, who sneered at religion, "asserted the Devil's cause," and talked loudly of social emancipation, till they were put to shame by a practical joker dressing up as the Devil and throwing them into a panic. This may be mainly a figment of Ward's imagination, but even so, his book came out in 1709 and could have supplied a hint.

Whatever the Hell-Fire Club's antecedents, it ended as we saw. When the ban fell in 1721 Wharton made a speech in the Lords denying that he was a patron of blasphemy. To prove his point he produced a Bible. But outside the House he assailed the interfering lord chancel-

---

*On this and other aspects of the "satanic opposition" mentality, see John Carswell, *The Old Cause,* 132–33.

lor in a verse satire, bracketing him with Jack Sheppard and Jonathan Wild, noted criminals of the day. (Not too unfairly: Macclesfield was later convicted of corruption and forced out of public life.) The following year Bishop Atterbury—the same who had fought for the dignity of the Church against Hoadly and his backers—was charged with treason as a Jacobite. Wharton defended him in a well-argued speech. Atterbury, however, had to leave England.

Wharton was now the most able spokesman of the dissentient Whigs who resisted, or wanted to resist, Sir Robert Walpole. But he quickly became the first object lesson in the difficulty of finding any firm ground for an opposition to stand on. His later vagaries seemed, in his own time, to have little to do with the defunct Hell-Fire Club. In the sequel the connection is clearer. They sketched a pattern and launched a legend . . . several legends. From the Duke of Wharton there is a continuity that is psychological and political at once.

DISSENT IN THE NAME OF LIBERTY

The first move in Philip's attempted campaign was to plunge into a dispute over the election of sheriffs in London. He endorsed two Jacobite candidates, and secured his right to a voice in the city's affairs by getting himself elected to the Wax Chandlers' Company. At meetings he charmed everybody, yet the move led nowhere. It was the first in a series of dead ends.

As his own platform he started a twice-weekly paper, the *True Briton*. It ran from June 3, 1723, to February 17, 1724, and was largely written by himself, in person or under various pseudonyms. Circulation rose into thousands. This was an achievement that no lightweight (or incipient alcoholic) would have been capable of.

The *True Briton's* purpose was to indict the Walpole regime. It did this in a roundabout way, often through hints that a reader was expected to decipher himself. Sometimes Wharton wrote essays on corrupt ministers in general, leaving the reader to make the cap fit.

Sometimes he criticized the governing clique by discussing historical cases that were implied to be parallel, or by giving invented accounts of foreign affairs that were really English. Thus Walpole figured in a pseudo-Spanish narrative as "Don Ferdinando." There were no dissenting forms. Wharton professed loyalty to the Church of England while denouncing its actual clergy as political puppets.

Where, a reader may ask, does all this lead? Wharton declares for LIBERTY (in capitals) on the first page of his first issue. Elsewhere he reaffirms the stand that the men of 1688 took: that Liberty goes with Property.

> The two great Essentials, requisite for the well ordering of Society, are, To be allowed the full Extent of our Liberties, and To be protected in our respective Properties.

Wharton claims, however, that the 1688 settlement has been subverted by the ambition and avarice of "grandees." Walpole's regime is a corrupt oligarchy. Britain needs a further installment of revolution.

Here is a major part of Wharton's importance. It is he, Philip, the apostle of blasphemy and uninhibited living, who sets in motion the only distinct idea that opposition politics ever do acquire under the first two Georges: that the Whig magnates' stranglehold must be broken, so that true Liberty can revive through a free parliament, no longer controlled by patronage. Wharton's theme is "the Revolution betrayed"— that is, the 1688 Revolution—and his restless temper makes him the Trotsky who dares to say it.

His weakness, like Trotsky's, is that he has no clear notion of what to do after exposing the betrayers. The only force that seems independent enough to shake Walpole and his skillfully managed Hanoverian sovereign is Jacobitism . . . but that can't be aired in print. Later we shall find Wharton's main idea being linked with a conception of patriotism (the word began to be current about 1726) and with the dream, or mirage, of a Patriot King who will reform the system from above:

all of this, most strangely, in a continuing Hell-Fire glow. But the duke himself never gets that far.

In the eight months of the *True Briton* he never did get far, either with his idea or with his journalism. Trouble began when only six issues had appeared. His first printer, Samuel Richardson, prudently withdrew. Wharton contrived to carry on, still shakily protected by his father's name, as far as No. 74. Then he gave up.

Since early 1723 he had been living at Twickenham, trying, not very hard, to keep his outgoings within £2,000 a year. His neighbors included Alexander Pope and Lady Mary Wortley Montagu. At Twickenham he ran a second club on permissive lines, though the bias this time was amorous rather than blasphemous. Lady Mary described it in a letter to her sister:

> Twenty very pretty fellows (the Duke of Wharton being president and chief director) have formed themselves into a committee of gallantry, who call themselves "Schemers," and meet regularly three times a week to consult on gallant schemes for the advancement and advantage of that branch of happiness.

The renown of the Schemers, she added with enthusiasm, "ought to be spread wherever men can sigh, or women can wish."

> 'Tis true they have the envy and the curses of the old and ugly of both sexes, and a general persecution from all old women; but this is no more than all reformations must expect in their beginning.

Pope, debarred by physique and temperament from such amusements, and jealous of Philip's success with the lovely Mary, was much colder. In his eyes, Wharton squandered rare talents on frivolities because of a craving for the wrong kind of esteem. Some years afterward Pope wrote a venomous description of him. It is said to have been toned down for publication. One wonders what it was like before.

Wharton, the scorn and wonder of our days,
Whose ruling passion was the lust of praise:
Born with whate'er could win it from the wise,
Women and fools must like him, or he dies:
Though wondering senates hung on all he spoke,
The club must hail him master of the joke. . . .
Thus with each gift of Nature and of Art,
And wanting nothing but an honest heart;
Grown all to all; from no one vice exempt;
And most contemptible to shun contempt;
His passion still to covet general praise;
His life, to forfeit it a thousand ways;
A constant bounty which no friend has made;
An angel tongue, which no man can persuade;
A fool, with more of wit than half mankind;
Too rash for thought, for action too refined. . . .
Ask you why Wharton broke through every rule?
'Twas all for fear the knaves should call him fool.

But Pope made too much of the sillier side of the Hell-Fire Club and the Schemers. He was not equipped to appreciate either.

The cost of bringing out the *True Briton* landed Wharton in deeper money difficulties. His Irish estates had to be sold for £62,000; his English ones were put in the hands of trustees. His pictures were also sold, the van Dycks and Lelys being picked up cheap by the hated Walpole. In 1725, still with debts of £70,000, and with an allowance of only £1,200 a year, which he soon overspent, Wharton left the country. He went to Vienna—the unbridled Duc de Richelieu, who was then French ambassador, must have been a congenial contact—and out-shone the diplomats. He went to Madrid and did the same. The British ambassador, finding himself eclipsed at the Spanish court by an ama-teur, persuaded London to order Wharton's return. The duke received the order while in a coach and tossed it out of the window.

Disintegration was setting in. His deserted wife died in April 1726. He fell in love with one of the Spanish queen's maids of honor, a dark-eyed Irish girl (who, to do him justice, brought no dowry), and became a Catholic to marry her. Also he committed himself finally to the House of Stuart. In his public statement announcing this move, he recalled his father's part in the Revolution but reiterated that the Revolution had been betrayed. England was saddled with a permanent army, a press censorship, a corrupted Parliament, and a servile Church and was in bondage to outsiders from Hanover who "trampled on the ancient nobility." It was none too plain what the Pretender could do about it if he did become king, but presumably he could do something. The statement was at least dignified; the duke was not. An English traveler who met him in Spain wrote home that he was drinking and smoking far too heavily and assuring anyone who would listen that James III had made him provisional prime minister.

When the king of Spain besieged Gibraltar, Wharton volunteered to serve in the Spanish army. He strolled toward the British lines, made himself known, and was allowed by his bewildered fellow countrymen to walk away. Though the siege was called off, he did manage, before the end, to get a minor wound in the foot, and returned hobbling to Madrid as a Jacobite hero. The king decided to give him a permanent commission. The Spanish army included a regiment of Irish exiles, and Wharton, already allied to them by marriage, became a colonel in it.

Again he drifted to France. The Pretender, who was in Rome, sent him money—never enough—but preferred to keep him at a distance. A long-delayed indictment for high treason closed England to the duke for good. However, we go on getting grotesque glimpses of him.

In 1728 he parked his new duchess with a relative near the Jacobites' palace of St. Germain and flitted backward and forward himself between there and Paris. One evening, while at St. Germain, he met a young peer—yet another Irishman—and hustled him off to Paris on "important business," borrowing his coach for the purpose. The peer stood by in growing mystification as Wharton engaged a second coach, drove to the stage door of the Opera, hired six musicians from the orchestra (it was well past midnight), and took the whole party back to St. Germain. At five in the morning the secret began to be revealed. Wharton led his musicians into the palace, to a staircase below the bedrooms of some ladies, and told them to play a serenade.

Even this uproar in the small hours was not the end. He took his improvised band to Poissy, increasing its volume with drums and brass, and began a second performance for an English gentleman living there. The gentleman, after a moment of panic, invited the party in to breakfast. But the musicians were restive. Arrangements for their fees remained nebulous, and if they failed to report back at the theater for their normal duties, they would be fined. At this juncture Wharton explained to the Irishman that he hadn't any cash on him and asked him to settle up, promising to return the favor when opportunity served. The victim doubted whether a parallel case would ever arise, but he settled up.

Later the same year, a knight of the Portuguese order of chivalry invited Wharton to a banquet. As the duke's only costume seemed to be his threadbare Spanish uniform, the knight advised him to have a black velvet suit made in the style of the order and recommended a tailor for the job. Wharton got the suit and wore it. When the tailor presented the bill, England's self-styled Prime Minister in Exile passed it on to the knight, on the ground that he was wearing his livery and therefore counted as one of his household. Meanwhile he showed himself around Paris in his expensive suit, getting credit on the strength of it.

Early in 1729 Wharton displayed symptoms of taking his new religion seriously. He stayed at a French monastery and charmed the monks with his conversation, wide reading, and air of repentance. But creditors were closing in. That May he fled to Spain and fell back on his last resource, his Spanish army commission. At least it gave him living quarters and a small income. Between spells of military duty he turned to literature again, beginning a translation from French and a play about Mary Queen of Scots, but finishing neither.

By now Wharton was sick, subject to fits and stomach trouble. The waters of a Catalan spa gave him some relief. In May 1731 he set out for this place but had one of his fits while riding through a village. After a week of nursing at a Benedictine monastery he died. The monks assured everybody that the strange English Milord had "made a very penitent and Christian exit" and buried him at Reus, near Tarragona. His family became extinct. He left no surviving children.

That should have been the end of the Duke of Wharton. Yet he went on haunting eighteenth-century minds for many years. Because of his odd flair for seeing through the current complacencies, combined with his naughty libertine temperament, he initiated a protest that he could never follow through himself but that later protesters could and did. After the demise of the *True Briton,* another paper, the *Craftsman,* took up his anti-Walpole campaign in much the same half-radical, half-Tory spirit. The brilliant, tricky Bolingbroke was behind this. A further sequel was more ironic. The legal document settling the remnant of the duke's estates was authorized by the signature of a lord of the treasury named George Dodington. And this same Dodington was destined to try out Wharton's ideas in practical politics; to sponsor a research project aimed at proving him right about 1688 and its aftermath; and also to carry out the Hell-Fire tradition as part, so to speak, of a package deal.

Meanwhile, the memory of the duke's general conduct did him good as well as harm. His unrestrained sex life, his flouting of Protestant respectability, his crazy spending, his seriocomic Jacobitism, all resulted quite naturally from the state of affairs where the only way to be rebellious was to be shocking. Even these set a trend and gave him a posthumous fascination. Forty years afterward a far greater political leader, Charles James Fox, could still look at him as a model. Fox felt no qualms about living scandalously while asserting high principles. Wharton's story convinced him that a public figure who had it both ways would project a more striking image than one who didn't.

Wharton lingered on also in literary disguise, as a minor Satan, thanks to two men he had employed.

One was Edward Young. After parting company with the duke, Young took holy orders and wrote more poetry. During the 1740s he produced his major work, *Night Thoughts.* This is a massive blank-verse tract in defense of the doctrine of immortality. The poet addresses himself throughout to an unbeliever, Lorenzo. Apart from his unbelief Lorenzo is shadowy. His only clear attribute is patience; he is never allowed to get a word in edgewise. However, in picturing this listener and his likely reactions, Young is known to have had Wharton in mind—not the Catholic convert of the last phase, but the Hell-Fire freethinker. *Night Thoughts* went through many editions and became a classic. (For some reason it was the favorite bedside reading of Robespierre.) Under the mask of Lorenzo, Wharton was reborn as a prototype "infidel."

His second immortalizer was Samuel Richardson, the cautious printer of the *True Briton.* While Young was working on *Night Thoughts,* Richardson was belatedly finding that he had a talent for fiction. He virtually invented the novel as we now know it. His masterpiece *Clarissa Harlowe*—a book that had an enormous vogue and influence—is the tragedy of a young lady's sufferings at the hands of a rake named Lovelace. Richardson's acquaintance with rakes was limited, and he was generally assumed to have created his villain by drawing on memories of Wharton.

Lovelace is not a portrait. He is colder and steadier, with less of the genius-gone-astray. But contemporaries were probably right about his origin. Lorenzo and Lovelace, the age's pattern Infidel and pattern Gentleman-Libertine, can both be tracked back to the president of the first Hell-Fire Club.

BROTHERS OF BLASPHEMY

The *first* Hell-Fire Club; not the only one. Wharton's society was in no danger of passing into limbo without successors. It filled a need. The Order-in-Council of 1721 was effective for a while. But it did not apply in George I's other kingdom, and in Ireland, where both Whartons were well remembered, the flames began flickering again. Presently they did more than flicker. A wave of blasphemy swept over the small, close-knit world of the Anglo-Irish.

Among these, direct baiting of the Establishment was even more difficult. Swift had the ability and the will, but he worked alone as a pamphleteer, not as one of a party that others could join. However, if revolt through serious protest was a nonstarter, revolt through outrage was easier than in England. The Protestant gentry had to keep up a front against the conquered, watchful papists around them. Misconduct before the natives was peculiarly piquant. Quite apart from being fun in itself, it was letting the side down and therefore a powerful irritant.

The Irish Hell-Fire groups are hard to sort out. The name shows that their founders took a hint from Wharton. But they tended to be more frankly wicked, and sometimes more overtly harmful. Their members flirted with crime, and with an ill-informed kind of black magic and devil worship. Some hardly did more than revive the London Mohock violence at a higher social level.

Limerick had a Hell-Fire Club, and a picture in the Council Room of the Corporation is said to portray members of it. The actual name, however, was not always adopted. One band of rakes was called the "Dublin Blasters." This was still active in March 1737 when it was the subject of a report to the Irish Parliament, stressing "blasphemy" in much the same tone as the denunciations of Wharton's club. The founder of the Blasters was Peter Lens, a painter, who boasted of being a Satanist and praying to the Devil. Another Blaster, a young nobleman, received a caller completely naked. According to the shocked visitor's story, he said: "Worthy Dr. Madden, I am glad to see you, how do you do?" and went on as if the situation were normal, standing in the doorway "as a show to the people passing by."

But a more notorious Dublin fraternity did use the old name. It flourished in and around the capital from about 1735. As in London, there may be room for doubt as to whether the records refer to a single club with several branches and meeting places or to several distinct clubs. If—as is supposed—Dublin had only the one Hell-Fire Club, it was an urban body with country retreats, and possibly offshoots.

Its founders were Richard Parsons, first Earl of Rosse (of the first creation), and Colonel Jack St. Leger. The colonel was related to the originator of the annual horse race bearing his name, which is properly pronounced Sillinger. Another relative of his, the Hon. Elizabeth St. Leger, was—according to tradition—the only woman ever admitted as a Freemason: she hid in an empty clock case during a Lodge meeting and was forced, when caught, to undergo initiation and swear secrecy. Colonel Jack himself lived at Grangemellon near Athy, in County Kildare, where his ghost still rides at night in a spectral coach with a headless driver.

A picture by James Worsdale in the Irish National Gallery shows five members of the Club. They are Lord Santry; Simon Luttrell, afterward first Earl of Carhampton, nicknamed the Wicked Madman; and Colonels Clements, Ponsonby, and St. George. Santry, then in his twenties, had a penchant for cruel practical jokes. He encouraged dueling, with his colleagues' approval. Every member who killed his man was presented with a badge of honor. Santry himself notched the barrel of his pistol to mark each "deed of blood." He went too far in 1739 when he murdered a footman and his peerage was extinguished.

The Dublin Hell-Fire brethren held orgies at the Eagle Tavern on Cork Hill, at Daly's Club on College Green, and at a hunting lodge on Montpelier Hill, in the range south of the city. The lodge was let to them by its owner, William Connolly. Connolly's son refused to renew the lease, and the lodge was burned down, but the Club apparently shifted its activities to the Killakee Dower House farther down the same hill. Here and elsewhere the members assembled to drink hot scaltheen, a mixture of whiskey and butter laced with brimstone. They toasted Satan and addressed each other by sinister names, such as Old Dragon and Lady Gomorrah. It was whispered that they held mock crucifixions, and that their meetings were chaired by a huge black cat. Once a curate gate-crashed a meeting and exorcised the cat, who vanished with a whiff of sulfur.

A potent aura still surrounds the Killakee Dower House, now rebuilt as an art center. For a couple of years it was one of the most aggressively haunted houses in Ireland. In 1968, when the rebuilding began, several people saw the celebrated black cat. He was as big as an Airedale, with red-flecked amber eyes, and he came and went through locked doors, growling. An artist painted his portrait.

Among many ghostly happenings at the Dower House was an apparition of two nuns—allegedly pseudonuns called Blessed Margaret and Holy Mary, who had taken part in Black Masses on Montpelier Hill. A more solid and ghastly find occurred in the garden. Tradition accused the Club members of torturing and suffocating a deformed youth. During the 1968 work, a grave was unearthed containing a small skeleton with an oversized skull. But the murder story may have been a lurid rumor that grew round an accident.

Blessed Margaret and Holy Mary, the bogus nuns, belong to a class that now begins to recur. Women—with the exception of a Mrs. Blennerhasset of Limerick—were not admitted to full membership of these Irish clubs. The person who passed as Lady Gomorrah may have been a male transvestite (accompanied by a Lord Sodom?). Women did attend, however, as orgy partners, and sometimes also because they were needed for satanic rites. In the Wharton phase such exercises are not mentioned. Soon afterward they appear.

Why the change? Secret ritual was coming into fashion at this time because of Freemasonry. The Grand Lodge of England had been founded in 1717. Wharton himself was Grand Master in 1722–23. Though he seems to have regarded the post as mainly honorary, he took and kept enough interest to found the first foreign Lodge during his time in Madrid. Throughout the 1720s and 1730s a rapid growth was under way, extending as far as Boston and Philadelphia. But in the Hell-Fire field the strongest ritual influence may have been Continental. Black magic was enjoying a vogue beyond the Channel, especially in Italy, with a widespread impact in other countries. Alongside the Masonic movement, young gentlemen on the Grand

Tour were learning modish occultism and bringing it back to the British Isles.

Furthermore, magical pursuits went with the sexual kind, if only because of the presumed value of love potions and spells. The Duc de Richelieu himself, France's arch-womanizer, was accused of fearful practices when ambassador in Vienna in 1727. According to one rumor, somebody saw him after dark riding in his coach of state with a black lamb, which he intended to sacrifice at full moon to increase his virility (though one has the impression that he hardly needed to). According to a rival rumor he had two sacrificial victims, a black goat and a white goat, and fed them with consecrated wafers before killing them. A third story said that two evil Franciscans performed the ceremony for him; and a fourth said that he sacrificed one of the Franciscans.

Whatever the extent of Richelieu's sorcery, this sort of thing was in the air. As the memoirs of Casanova prove, that enlightened century was very credulous indeed; an age not merely of magic but of peculiarly suspect magic, sadly debased since Paracelsus and Dee, and expounded by characters like the Comte de St-Germain, who convinced many intelligent people that he was two thousand years old. Magic, at any rate, did spread to the rakish set in Britain and Ireland, taking a dark tinge. Traces of the Hell-Fire revival in Britain are scanty, but such as they are, they carry a more satanic stamp than before.

Edinburgh had at least one club that arranged pacts with the Devil. Meetings occurred in Jack's Close, Canongate; in Allan's Close, Carrider's Close, and Halkerston's Wynd. There are traces of activity in much the same style at both English universities. An Oxford Hell-Fire Club is supposed to have flourished for several decades. A pamphlet published in 1763 refers back to this as a reproach against a clergyman named John Kidgell, who is accused of membership—perhaps as an undergraduate in the 1740s—and whom we shall meet again. At Jesus College, Cambridge, a tradition that Quiller-Couch used to relish tells of an "Appalling Club" started in 1738. Its founder and president was the Hon. Alan Dermot, son of an Irish peer; it sounds like an imitation of the club in Dublin. The alleged minute book, a small volume bound in red leather, was formerly in the possession of the Masters of Jesus. Around it a superb ghost story grew up, connected with a haunted room at the top of one of the College stairs nicknamed Cow Lane—a room kept vacant for many years and used only for storage.

This is the tale. The Appalling Club had seven members. They called themselves the Everlastings. After Dermot the most important was Charles Bellasis, a Fellow of the College. The rules prescribed that there were to be no resignations and no recruitments. A member would remain a member forever, whether he was corporeal or incorporeal (i.e., alive or dead). The main annual event was fixed for November 2, All Souls Night. At 10 p.m. on that date they were to meet for supper at the residence of a corporeal member, in keeping with a rota. They were to sign the minute book and give their places of abode and could be fined for absence. However, if four or more met in October and resolved that the November meeting should be canceled, it was.

For six years the Appalling Club was active, to the scandal of the University. College authorities sent down such Everlastings as they had power to, but the seven still gathered for the annual meeting . . . until 1743, when a double disaster hit them.

On November 2, six assembled and signed the book. One, Henry Davenport, did not. He had been killed overseas in battle, but the news had not reached them. His chair stood empty, and the president recorded a fine. The decanter passed round. When it came to the empty place, Davenport's ghost appeared like Banquo's and picked it up. He was the first incorporeal member and had reported as such. The next day his change of status was duly noted in the book.

Worse was to follow. The president had signed with the rest, giving his place of abode. People who afterward read the book saw it written there in his own hand: "Alan Dermot, President, at the Court of His Royal Highness"—meaning the Young Pretender, Prince Charles Edward, Dermot being a Jacobite. Now Dermot actually had been living in Paris with the Prince's court-in-exile. But he had been killed in a duel on October 28. His colleagues heard and recorded this on November 10. But in that case, they realized, the figure that had presided and signed was another incorporeal! Their founder's ghost had been playing a ghastly trick on them.

With a revulsion of feeling, the secretary wrote, "The Good God shield us from ill" and closed the book. From then on the five survivors simply met every October and canceled the All Souls supper. One of them died, and in 1766 three more died, leaving Charles Bellasis alone with no procedure for cancellation. He was still a Fellow of Jesus, occupying the room at the head of Cow Lane stair. On November 2 he retired to it and locked himself in. At 10 p.m. the College heard yells, oaths, and a noise of shattering glass.

In the morning the Master knocked and got no reply. He had the door broken down. Bellasis was seated at the table, dead, covering his eyes. Six other chairs were drawn up. Broken glass littered the room. The minute book lay open. All seven Everlastings had signed—though the six dead ones had not written their place of abode. With Bellasis dead too, there were no corporeal members left on the rota. Therefore, in theory, the Appalling Club could hold no more annual meetings. But according to legend the seven ghosts did continue to gather in the room in Jesus, shouting and blaspheming.*

The other English club of this type, the only one in the 1730s actually adopting the Hell-Fire name, has no such detailed legend. It met in London at the George and Vulture Inn, Cornhill, better known for its link with Mr. Pickwick. The George and Vulture was formerly the George pure and simple. An eighteenth-century landlord, however, bought "a most noble and extraordinary cock vulture" at Peckham Fair, kept it in the yard, scared customers with tales of its supernatural powers, and added it to his sign after its death. He is also said to have lit the cellar with an Everlasting Rosicrucian Lamp in the ceiling. A guide-

---

*The more obvious University records do not contain the names of any of the characters in this story . . . alas.

book describes this as "a large globe of crystal, encircled by a serpent of pure gold, with its tail in its mouth—a symbol of eternity." Suspended below it, the guide adds, are "chains of twisted snakes," and "crowning the globe is a pair of silver doves' wings."

These English and Scottish clubs remain obscure. But a few Hell-Fire stories resembling the Dublin ones probably refer to the George and Vulture club. One that was put on record by Thomas De Quincey concerned a lord (unnamed) who tied a man to the spit in the kitchen and "proceeded to roast him." Another mentions a Black Mass, complete with a naked girl as altar, stretched out on a table in the bar . . . presumably after closing time. Hogarth's picture *Charity in the Cellar,* painted about 1739, has been construed as giving a glimpse of the same club. But the case is weak. All we see is a drinking bout in a dark room, without even a Rosicrucian lamp. The sole evidence is that the five drinkers are identifiable and can be connected in other ways with two alleged members of the club, and the membership even of these is dubious.

Yet however phantasmal the two members may appear at this point, they have their interest. One was a future first lord of the admiralty, the young Earl of Sandwich. The other was a future chancellor of the Exchequer, a baronet a few years older than Sandwich—Sir Francis Dashwood.

5

WHATEVER IS, IS RIGHT

TRICKS OF THE TRADE

Throughout those first Hanoverian decades, rakish imaginations found more and more to feed on. England sprouted a whole new undergrowth of shady and dirty reading matter. Its fertility spirit, so to speak, was a figure whom historians are shy of discussing: the publisher and bookseller Edmund Curll.

He was a strange portent. Within his limits he foreshadowed the twentieth century. Haldeman-Julius, that mail-order paperback pioneer who flooded America with "little blue books," had a touch of Curll about him. Haldeman-Julius, however, was a model of rectitude by comparison. Curll himself could only have happened when he did.

His age of glory coincides, more or less, with the lifetime of the Hell-Fire groups surveyed in the last chapter. But he laid its foundations in the reign of Queen Anne (while young Philip Wharton was still undergoing his hothouse training for statesmanship) by exploiting the nature of the book trade. Publishers then had several advantages over their modern successors. They were usually booksellers as well. They kept their own shops, made money from distribution, which helped to finance productions, and were not at the mercy of separate retailers demanding a bigger cut or making conditions. Also, England had no copyright law till 1710, and the Act that became law in that year protected the publisher rather than the author. A publisher could cash in on an author's popularity by bringing out pirated editions, especially cheap reprints, without asking the victim's leave or paying him royalties.

Piracy was a source of profit in more ways than one. Writers who lacked other means of livelihood—private income or a patron—were rendered so poor and insecure that publishers could virtually buy their services and employ them to churn out books to order at minimal cost, or even to fake books by established authors. Over the years a growing mob of hacks drifted into cheap lodgings along what is now Milton Street, near Moorgate, but was then Grub Street.

Edmund Curll came into this scene from the West Country. In January 1706 he set up shop near St. Clement's, in the Strand, under the sign of the Peacock. He was then in his twenties or early thirties. Till almost the middle of the century he was successfully publishing books of many kinds, as well as selling them. A large part of his list was always beyond reproach. However, it was the reproachable part that kept the business flourishing and gave Curll his reputation.

He soon hit on what was to be a staple source of income: popular rehashing of spicy lawsuits and trials. *The Case of Sodomy,* dealing with the scandal over a certain Lord Audley, appeared in 1707. But he did not follow this up at once. His first major coup, trendsetting in several ways, occurred in another field.

As anybody can see from a glance at some of the newspapers of the time—and as Curll did see—a thriving market existed for alleged medicines and remedies; especially, of course, cures for the Pox. In April 1708 Curll published *The Charitable Surgeon,* a do-it-yourself handbook on venereal disease, by "T. C." He gave it a splendid blurb, printed, as was then the custom, on the title page of the book itself.

The Charitable Surgeon: Or, the best Remedies for the Worst Maladies Reveal'd. Being a new and true way of Curing (without Mercury) the several degrees of the Venereal Distemper in both Sexes, whereby all Persons, even the meanest Capacities, may, for an Inconsiderable Charge, without Confinement or Knowledge of the nearest Relation, cure themselves easily, speedily, and safely, by the Method prescrib'd, without the help of any Physician, Surgeon, or Apothecary, or being expos'd to the hazardous attempts of Quacks and Pretenders. With a new discovery of the true seat of Claps in Men and Women, different from the commonly receiv'd Opinions of Authors. And a peculiar Method of Curing their Gleets and Weaknesses, whether Venereal, Seminal, or otherwise; with some pertinent Observations relating thereto, never before taken notice of. Likewise the certain easy way to escape Infection, tho' never so often accompanying with the most polluted Companion.

At a shilling *The Charitable Surgeon* was an obvious bargain. But it didn't stop at therapeutic and prophylactic advice. It boldly named an outstanding specimen of the "Quack and Pretender," John Spinke. Spinke retorted with a pamphlet, *Quackery Unmask'd,* exposing the author's own incompetence. A war of abuse broke out. Where some publishers might have been distressed, Curll stayed calm. He was among the first to make the discovery that any publicity is better than no publicity. When the fuss died down, he was better known than he had been before, and ready to expand.

Moving to the Dial and Bible, beside St. Dunstan's Church within Temple Bar, he blamelessly issued a volume of Shakespeare's poems. This he followed up with an account of the seventeenth-century Bishop Atherton, "who" (in the words of his advertisement) "was Convicted of the Sin of Uncleanliness with a Cow and other Creatures, for which he was Hang'd at Dublin." Soon Curll was able to open a branch in Tunbridge Wells.

He was also able, from about 1712 onward, to build up his own team of writers and translators and keep them on call. Enemies charged him with exploiting them, and even causing the death of one by starvation. He seems in fact to have dealt with them honestly and paid them fairly. His honesty, however, did not extend to all the jobs he paid them to do. Some of his books consisted of a few lines from a well-known author, reproduced without permission, plus a mass of hack-written material. The book came out with the celebrity's name on it, not the hack's.

Curll even gave his writers deceptive pen names. One became "J. Addison," two in succession became "J. Gay." The real Joseph Addison and John Gay could do nothing about it. When Curll published a book as by the diplomat-poet Matthew Prior, Prior inserted a notice in the papers disowning it; whereupon Curll inserted a notice explaining that Prior's notice was the work of an unknown person taking an inexcusable liberty with Prior's name.

He went on bringing out serious books of quality, including a few of his own on current affairs. Yet sometimes he did not put his name on his better publications, while he did put it on the other sort. The stream of his long-term best sellers began flowing in 1714 with the first of a series of *Cases of Impotency and Divorce.* By publishing these, and the pornographic stories and scandal books that presently joined them, Curll laid himself open to a risk of prosecution. Yet in practice it was hard to touch him. He was too successful in supplying an evident demand. As a versifier commented:

> *Can Statutes keep the British Press in awe,*
> *When that sells best, that's most against the Law?*

We get a direct glimpse of Curll from Thomas Amory, an Irish memoir writer. The publisher was "very tall and thin, an ungainly, awkward, white-faced man." He had large gray eyes. He was fond of the theater, with many backstage contacts, and he was also "intimate with all the high whores in town," who bought his more improper books. They often dined with him, but he was not, in general, a lavish host or bon viveur. According to Amory he seldom drank except when somebody else was paying.

He could scarcely complain when his activities did get him into trouble. He caused special resentment by cashing in on the deaths of public persons with instant biographies. As biographies they were almost worthless. His sole object was to be first. He would tell his hacks to collect whatever information they could—which, at short notice, was usually not much—and eke it out with speeches or writings of the deceased that had already been printed. The result was published as a "Life." Occasionally he managed to get hold of a copy of the will. After one or two such scoops, Dr. John Arbuthnot, the court physician, remarked that Curll's biographies had added a new terror to death.

Curll pressed on through several nasty experiences. When he brought out an illicit text of a speech given at Westminster School, the boys invited him to visit the school, and then (seemingly with the masters' connivance) tossed him in a blanket, flogged him, and forced him to beg forgiveness. Here more especially a modern publisher might pause to reflect on the changes that his profession has undergone. Curll endured a more savage and sustained attack from Pope, who accused him, rightly, of "carrying the trade many lengths beyond what it ever before had arrived at." The assault was not confined to words. Pope stood Curll a glass of sack at the Swan in Fleet Street and slipped an emetic into it. He also wrote skits on him, including one that told—quite fictitiously—how Curll had pretended to be converted to Judaism so that the Jews would help him to get richer and had then run into difficulties over the rabbi's insistence on circumcision.

A second eminent critic was Daniel Defoe, who denounced the obscenity of a Curll book entitled *Eunuchism Display'd*—or to give its full title, *Eunuchism Display'd: Describing all the different Sorts of Eunuchs; Occasion'd by a young Lady's falling in Love with Nicolini, who sung in the Opera at the Hay-Market, and to whom she had like to have been Married.* Curll replied to Defoe. He said that he was simply being open and frank and warning the young against the perils besetting them—a reasonable defense, in view of the young lady's dreadful mistake, though he weakened it by rushing out a sequel entitled *Onanism Display'd.*

The law caught up with him at last in 1724. That October he published a story translated from the French, *Venus in the Cloister; or, the*

Nun in her Smock. His advertisement promised amatory scenes "not to be parallel'd for their agreeable Entertainment in any Romance or Novel hitherto extant." Learning that a prosecution was being prepared, Curll printed a plea on his own behalf. In it he mentioned another of his books, Meibomius's *Treatise of Flogging in Venereal Affairs,* with an added *Treatise of Hermaphrodites.* Nobody had suggested that this work would be included in the indictment, but Curll thought he might as well draw the public's attention to it, while stressing, of course, for the judge's benefit, that it was an innocent medical manual. (As a matter of fact Meibomius is a genuine classic, the first to treat flagellation openly and objectively. The author bases his study partly on observations of the effects of religious scourging on the sexual state of the penitent.)

Curll's trial at the King's Bench was inconclusive. The prosecution had trouble framing the charge. Was *The Nun in her Smock* a libel? Did it tend to corrupt? Curll was found guilty, given a suspended sentence, then jailed after all for several months. He issued a public statement announcing his retirement from business. The statement, however, explained that before doing so he just wanted to see two more books through the press, and that one of these was *The Case of Seduction, being the late proceedings at Paris against the Rev. Abbe des Rues, for committing rapes upon 133 virgins. Written by himself.* As for Curll's withdrawal from publishing, all it actually meant was that the same business was carried on in the name of his son Henry. Three years later Edmund was back.

He had no more trouble from the law, except for a single fine and a few hours in the pillory facing a sympathetic crowd. The feud with Pope, however, dragged on. When Pope gave him an undignified role in his satire *The Dunciad,* Curll counterattacked in characteristic style. He published a "key" to *The Dunciad* itself, spelling out Pope's meaning, in case any reader might miss the point. For good measure the key contained an advertisement for *The Nun in her Smock.* Also he threatened to bring out a "Life" of Pope.

In the end the poet scored after a fashion, by planting some of his letters on Curll and tricking him into publishing an unauthorized edition, whereupon Pope pounced on him, got his stock confiscated, and then issued an authorized edition himself. But it was a mean triumph, reflecting no credit on the victor. Curll outlived Pope and most of his other critics, publishing and selling books to the last, and died in December 1747. An alley off the Strand used to be known as Curll's Court.

His more notorious output falls roughly into six classes. Prices ranged from sixpence to ten shillings but were mostly nearer the cheap end of the scale. The authors—that is, the real authors—were nearly always anonymous or obscure.

The accounts of scabrous trials and lawsuits were always popular. With a sure instinct, Curll drew most of his cases from high society. He also gave a few well-placed slaps in other sensitive quarters, as with the story of the priest's multiple misconduct, and with two books advertised as *The Backsliding Teacher* and *Boarding School Rapes*.

Allied with these were several volumes of social exposé in general, such as *Court Tales; or, a History of the Amours of the Present Nobility, with a Compleat Key* and *The Natural History of Both Sexes . . . with an Account of the Present State of Whoring in these Kingdoms*.

The medical books, beside those already mentioned, include the classic *Syphilis* by Fracastoro, which gave the disease its name. In Curll's remarks on the Meibomius flagellation study there is a tragicomic link with an earlier world. He says that the English version was prompted in 1718 by the untimely death of Peter Motteux, "who lost his life in a brothel through an act of unnatural lewdness." This is the Motteux who finished Urquhart's translation of Rabelais.

Alongside the medical works we may place a few that deal, in a sense, with conduct. There is *Pancharis, Queen of Love; or, Woman Unveil'd . . . the whole Art of Kissing*. There is *The Praise of Drunkenness*, "written by a Person of Honour (who is a Freemason). Author of *Eunuchism Display'd*." There is *The Pleasures and Mysteries of the Marriage Bed modestly unveil'd*, for young brides. There is even *The Benefit of Pissing;*

or, the whole Art of exercising that Engine of Nature in Both Sexes, a bargain at sixpence.

Pornographic fiction, verse, and fantasy are not as plentiful as might be expected. Curll was in business for twelve years before he published any at all. Besides *The Nun in her Smock,* however, he produced various risqué tales and poems, and he did well in his later years with a series under the general title *Merryland.* He also brought out an edition of Martha Fowke's *Epistles of Clio and Strephon,* a work that was inoffensive, but written by a lady whose reputation might arouse hopes.

One further theme is significant, though it was never a major interest of his, and he published only a few relevant titles himself. This was magic. Its attraction for the more turbulent spirits, in and out of Hell-Fire circles, remained at a high level. Edmund Curll did a little to nourish it and handled the books of other publishers who did more.

THE NATURE OF SEX

How far did the wave of twilight literature reflect a real shift in moral ideas? To gauge the progress of a more or less reasoned permissiveness under George II, preparing the way for the next outright proclamation of the Rule of Thélème, we must turn from Curll's underworld and take a look at a few books of the same type but higher quality.

Three will be enough to reveal all that needs revealing. First, a poem. Hanoverian verse writers had a touching faith in their ability to make poetry out of anything—anything whatever. The literature of the day includes metrical handbooks on the wool industry, sugarcane, and the breeds of dogs. One stalwart in this manner was John Armstrong, a Scottish doctor who practiced in London.

Dr. Armstrong's major work is *The Art of Preserving Health,* which deploys his medical expertise in four books of blank verse. Its outstanding feature is, in the words of a modern anthologist, its "relentless analysis of the workings of the human stomach." But Armstrong made a briefer poetic venture of the same kind, with livelier results. This ran to a mere 612 lines. It was called "The Oeconomy of Love." (*Oeconomy* means "management.") He brought out the first edition in 1736. Afterward, losing nerve under censure, he decided to leave it out of his Collected Works and tried to laugh it off as a juvenile trifle or parody. It passed, nevertheless, through several more editions and was still being reprinted in the following century.

"The Oeconomy of Love" has never commended itself to compilers of Golden Treasuries. Standard reference books dismiss it with a shudder as "nauseous." Nauseous or not, it deserves a second glance. It is quite simply a sex manual such as the 1960s and 1970s have made familiar . . . only it is dressed up, with absurd yet disarming sham-Miltonic pomposity, as a poem.

The doctor concerns himself chiefly with advice to the young. But he changes focus at intervals and covers a fair range of topics. Sometimes he lectures, clinically and impersonally; sometimes he speaks to an imagined boy; sometimes to an imagined girl; once, to the copulating public at large.

At what age (Armstrong asks after a short prologue) does practical sex begin? At fifteen, he replies, to give a round figure. But adolescents don't all mature equally fast. The symptoms of a dawning power to perform are easy to recognize. With the male, wet dreams. This is how Armstrong puts it:

> *The boy may wrestle, when*
> *Night-working fancy steals him to the arms*
> *Of nymph oft wish'd awake, and, 'mid the rage*
> *Of the soft tumult, every turgid cell*
> *Spontaneous disembogues its lucid store,*
> *Bland and of azure tinct.*

With a girl there is menstruation, of course, and also a sign more obvious to male eyes:

> *The maid demands*
> *The dues of Venus, when the parting breasts*
> *Wanton exhuberant and tempt the touch.*

With both sexes, moreover, there is the growth of pubic hair as a protection.

> *The rising down*
> *Then too begins to skirt the hallow'd bounds*
> *Of Venus' blest domain. In either sex*
> *This sign obtains . . .*
> *But for this,*
> *Excoriate oft the tender parts would rue*
> *The close encounter.*

Dr. Armstrong now advises the boy directly. If you hope in due course to raise a family, he says, go easy with your trial spins. Don't overdo it. But don't be backward either. Petting is always good, at least to the extent of fondling the breasts; beyond that, be careful. Avoid masturbation. It will pall and weaken your response to the real thing.

If pressures grow too strong to control, then, rather than masturbate, go to prostitutes. But this of course can be expensive. Also it lacks privacy and quiet. Other customers are liable to get impatient and interrupt.

> *Oft, to crush*
> *Thy slacken'd manhood, in the mid career*
> *Of puissant deed, untimely rushes in*
> *A forward boist'rous wight, and from thy arms*
> *The passive spouse of all the town demands.*

Anyhow, you may catch VD. Armstrong adds a few words about the treatments but has a low opinion of them.

So (he continues, still addressing the boy) it's wiser to find a nice girl of your own, who likes you and will comply. Learn the technique of unwrapping, and the icebreaking effectiveness—in Dr. Armstrong's opinion—of letting her see and handle the erect male organ.

> *Forthwith discover to her dazzled sight*
> *The stately novelty, and to her hand*
> *Usher the new acquaintance. She perhaps,*
> *Averse, will coldly chide, and half afraid,*
> *Blushing, half pleas'd, the tumid wonder view*
> *With neck retorted and oblique regard;*
> *Not quite her curious eyes indulging, nor*
> *Refraining quite.*

When it comes to the crunch, the doctor asks, can you tell whether she's a virgin or not? Be cautious, either way. There are tricks for tightening the orifice even after deflowering. On the other hand, if she seems suspiciously easy to penetrate . . . well, realize that they vary.

Next comes a most interesting passage. Modern sex counselors in print have felt obliged until lately to pretend that their advice is for married couples. Armstrong doesn't. While he respects matrimony, he is talking to the unmarried, and he makes that clear.

> *Now hear me, lovers! ye whose roving hearts*
> *No sacred nuptial chains have yet confin'd . . .*

What about morality? In comes "Nature"—that blessed Nature of the first half of the eighteenth century—guaranteeing (as Pope put it) that "whatever is, is right." Since Nature is good, all her promptings are good. *And if morality says otherwise, then so much the worse for morality.*

In 1736 this was a bold step for anyone to take in plain terms.

Rabelais himself was hardly so explicit. But Armstrong is saying what many educated contemporaries were willing to think. He insists that sex is right because it is natural. People who preach abstention usually do so because they are soured by repressed passions of their own.

> *What Nature bids*
> *Is good, is wise; and faultless we obey.*
> *We must obey; howe'er hard stoic dreams*
> *Of apathy, much vaunted, seldom prov'd:*
> *For ofte beneath the philosophic gloom*
> *Sly lewdness lurks. . . .*

Not only lewdness. Resentment, too, and a vengeful wish to hurt those who are happier. Bounteous, all creative Nature knows best.

> *For wisest ends this universal power*
> *Gave appetites: from whose quick impulse life*
> *Subsists.*

Still, society's mores being what they are, Armstrong advises the youth to be discreet. Don't boast about a conquest, he says; this is unpleasant for the girl. If the secret leaks out, then consider marriage. If you can't marry her, at any rate see that she is taken care of. He has his own rather significant way of putting it.

> *Let wedlock's holy tie*
> *Legitimate th' indissoluble flames.*
> *If abject birth, dishonourable, and mind*
> *Incultivate or vicious, to that height*
> *Forbid her hopes to climb: at least secure*
> *From penury her humble state.*

Otherwise she may slide into prostitution or a loveless marriage for the sake of support.

The same advice applies to an illegitimate child. (We are still in a precontraception era.) Provide for it. Many such have risen to greatness, so, apart from anything else, you have a social duty to rear a potential leader or genius. Above all, don't let your child fall into the clutches of a church orphanage.

Finally, what about the long term? Sex is good, but don't get carried away. Cultivate a wide range of interests. They will enrich sex itself, and survive it. It is a sad fate to wear yourself out, get past it, and then find you have no other resources. The elderly satyr perversely struggling to recapture lost ardors is a dismal spectacle.

> *Him all the Nymphs despise, and the young Loves*
> *With leering scorn behold; while vigorous heat*
> *Has fled his shaken limbs, surviving still*
> *In his green fancy. Thence what desperate toil*
> *By flagellation, and the rage of blows,*
> *To rouse the Venus loitering in his veins!*
> *Fruitless, for Venus unsolicited*
> *The kindest smiles, abhorring painful rites.*

Don't imagine, either, that you can restore potency with aphrodisiacs. Armstrong lists a few, including Spanish fly ("fell Cantharides") but has as low an opinion of these as of VD remedies.

Having urged moderation on the male, he urges it on the female. Be a bit restrained, he says, not a pushover. That advice might seem to conclude the lesson. It doesn't. The last word is about Nature again.

Nature blesses some things, not everything. In "these vicious days," he explains, Nature's laws are defied, and at fashionable sex deviation he does draw the line. Such behavior is not only unnatural but unpatriotic.

> *For man with man,*
> *And man with woman (monstrous to relate!)*
> *Leaving the natural road themselves debase*
> *With deeds unseemly, and dishonour foul.*

Britons, for shame! Be male and female still.
Banish this foreign vice.

So permissiveness is not total. But whatever is "natural" is right, at least for anyone likely to read the poem. Armstrong's ethic still has more than a touch of Thelemic aristocracy. He takes it for granted that his young gentleman belongs to a class that can take care of its girlfriends and their children, even if the girlfriends themselves may not always belong to it.

Many gentlemen of that class, so far as they rationalized their habits at all, were undoubtedly finding the same handy support in "Nature" as Armstrong. It was a fair inference from the optimists of the Age of Reason, from Leibniz and Bolingbroke and Pope, with Thélème hovering in the background for those whose reading extended to Rabelais. Armstrong's distinction was that he spelt it out in print. Pundits of the Establishment, who wanted to keep philosophers and churchmen in a united front, still liked to maintain (in public at least) that Nature underwrote Anglican morality. They preferred not to face the issue of what would happen if the two clashed. Armstrong did face it and gave a logical early-Hanoverian answer. Obey Nature, it's the only rational course; do what comes naturally; don't be afraid to defy the moralists, who are mostly frustrated sourpusses anyhow.

This rule of life, adopted by others as well as Armstrong, and applied in practice, was a time fuse. Much later the spark would reach the explosives and set off a detonation that we are still feeling, though few realize the long-unmentionable cause. Meanwhile, in the buoyant days of "The Oeconomy of Love," we can trace attitudes more exactly by considering a couple of novels.

NAUGHTY BY NATURE

After more than two centuries of large-scale fiction—after Jane Austen and Scott, Flaubert and Dostoevsky and Proust and Joyce—it is not easy to see the beginnings of it all through the eyes of contemporaries. We think of The Novel as a major form of literature, dealing with human life in a broad sweep. So indeed it was already conceived by Henry Fielding, one of the English pioneers, who admired Cervantes and, in the late 1740s, produced *Tom Jones*. But Fielding was ahead of his time. A more normal impression, drawn from the rather few so-called novels that had found a wide readership, was that such books were high-class erotica: decked out with plots and adventures and stylistic graces, but still mainly about sex relations. That is what Curll had in mind when he used the word *novel* in his advertisement for *The Nun in her Smock*. Decades afterward, when the chief justice impounded some copies of an improper best seller, Horace Walpole described it in his memoirs as "a work that simplified novels to their original intention."

The best seller in question was the most famous of English erotic books, *Fanny Hill*. It came out in the same year as *Tom Jones* but has never been so widely studied in courses on English literature.

Novelists of standing were still very few. Samuel Richardson, the Duke of Wharton's former printer, dominated such field as there was. Both the stories he had published were about the predicaments of young women. *Pamela; or, Virtue Rewarded* dealt with a maidservant's resistance to her employer's attempts at seduction. Virtue's distinctly down-to-earth "reward" was that he gave up and married her. *Clarissa Harlowe,* published in 1747, was the one with the good and beautiful girl persecuted by the lustful Lovelace, Wharton's fictional ghost.

Now Richardson's intentions were highly moral. He was far more sincerely Christian than most of his contemporaries. But he induced thrills of the wrong sort. Clarissa's sufferings appeal to emotions only partly understood by the author himself. Not only is she harassed by Lovelace, she is hounded by her parents and thrown into a debtors' prison; she has a Freudian nightmare of being stabbed and pushed into a grave; and in waking reality Lovelace traps her in a brothel, drugs her, and rapes her. At the end she dies in a scene that is meant to be edifying but becomes morbid, using her coffin as a writing desk.

Richardson opened doors that he never meant to open, onto realms of fantasy that he failed to reckon with. Whartonian Hell-Fire was burning too close for safety. He was shocked—yet he ought not to have been—when Fielding took up some of his more direct amorous motifs and exploited them in cheerful plots that he disapproved of.

This by way of preface. *Pamela* and *Clarissa* made, or revealed, a market for book-length fiction with a sexual orientation still, but also with literary quality. *Fanny Hill* followed in 1749. Curll did not quite live to see it. *Fanny* was the climax of the trend he had done so much to promote. The new art of the novelist and the older art of the pornographer converged. The result, after its fashion, was a minor masterpiece.

Its original title (now printed as the subtitle) was *Memoirs of a Woman of Pleasure.* The author of this first-person narrative was a man: John Cleland, a well-read, intelligent misfit, the son of a Scotsman who, like Armstrong, migrated south. Born in 1709, Cleland worked for the East India Company and the British consular service but quarreled with his superiors and returned to England empty handed. He wrote *Fanny Hill* to stave off creditors. A publisher bought it outright for twenty guineas, then published it at three shillings a copy and made, it is said, £10,000.

Whether or not that figure is correct, the sales were prodigious. *Fanny* was especially popular with the clergy. For that reason, perhaps, a number of bishops tried to get it suppressed. Cleland was summoned before the Privy Council and reprimanded, but no ban ensued, and Lord Granville, a member of the council, found him a government job as an information officer. With £100 a year, and duties that left him plenty of spare time, Cleland went on writing until his death in 1790. But his other works were stillborn. In *Chambers's Biographical Dictionary* a hundred years later, Cleland was still simply "best forgotten as the author of *Fanny Hill.*"

His novel did eventually vanish from open circulation, but it remained an under-the-counter favorite. It was still getting expurgated and having trouble with the law as late as 1964 when it reappeared in paperback. Though now easy to obtain, it is more familiar as a joke than as book actually read, having been swamped by competition and eclipsed by changes in taste. Hence it is worth taking a little trouble to grasp the essential character of what Fanny says, the milieu she implies, and the point of view she expresses.

Her story is not offered as an exposé of London vice in the manner of a Sunday paper. To its more innocent readers it may have been, but the tone implies a fairly sophisticated audience, reading for amusement rather than surprise or shock. Fanny's importance is not that she reveals anything unfamiliar to her public, but that she flaunts so much that has not been flaunted before. Her entry on the scene in 1749 marks a shedding of inhibitions as to what can be aired in more or less reputable print. The watchword is perhaps not "Do what you will" but certainly "Write what you will," with only one criterion, truth. To quote Fanny's apt phrasing on the first page:

> Truth! stark, naked truth, is the word; and I will not so much as take the pains to bestow the strip of a gauzewrapper on it, but paint situations such as they actually rose to me in nature, careless of violating those laws of decency that were never made for such unreserved intimacies as ours. . . . The greatest men, those of the first and most leading taste, will not scruple adorning their private closets with nudities, though, in compliance with vulgar prejudices, they may not think them decent decorations of the staircase, or saloon.

The actual story is slight. A Liverpudlian, orphaned at fifteen, Fanny is persuaded to go to London and seek her fortune. There she registers naively with a bogus domestic agency and is caught. Her employer at first keeps up the pretence that she is being taken on as a servant. But another member of the household, a young woman of lesbian tendencies, goes to bed with Fanny and embarks on a stirring-up exercise that strikes her as being beyond the call of duty.

Fanny realizes what kind of house she is in and finds herself exposed to a customer, an old, ugly, and semi-impotent merchant. She resists him but accepts her position. Training proceeds by way of demonstrations without action. She is not actually deflowered till a handsome young man named Charles visits the house. Fanny falls in love with him. He contrives her escape and keeps her for a while, but his father sends him overseas. Resigned to losing him, she goes on as she has begun, joining a select establishment and living in comfort. At last an elderly client dies, leaving her his money, and Charles turns up again and marries her. . . . End of story.

The appeal of *Fanny Hill*—which has a definite charm, though it lasts too long—is largely voyeuristic. There are careful descriptions of people, both dressed and undressed, and of places. One of Cleland's merits is that you can always picture the scene, piece together the layout of a house, follow the characters from room to room. There are detailed blow-by-blow narratives of sexual encounters, mostly normal, though the postures vary, but also including flagellation and other modes of kinkiness.

It is difficult to give samples, because so much of the effect depends on a leisurely piling up of minute particulars. Here, however, is the beginning of one of the early observation scenes, when the trainee Fanny watches an Italian client.

At five in the morning, next day, Phoebe, punctual to her promise, came to me as I sat alone in my own room, and beckon'd me to follow her.

We went down the back-stairs very softly, and opening the door of a dark closet, where there was some old furniture kept, and some cases of liquor, she drew me in after her, and fastening the door upon us, we had no light but what came through a long crevice in the partition between ours and the light closet, where the scene of action lay; so that sitting on those low cases, we could, with the greatest ease, as well as clearness, see all objects (ourselves unseen), only by applying our eyes close to the crevice, where the moulding of a panel had warped, or started a little on the other side.

The young gentleman was the first person I saw, with his back directly towards me, looking at a print. Polly was not yet come: in less than a minute tho', the door opened, and she came in; and at the noise the door made he turned about, and came to meet her, with an air of the greatest tenderness and satisfaction.

It is like good television.

Much later, when Fanny is expert, she joins in a party where four couples perform successively in the same room, each watched by the others.

The first that stood up, to open the ball, were a cornet of horse, and that sweetest of olive-beauties, the soft and amorous Louisa. He led her to the couch "nothing loath,"* on which he gave her the fall, and extended her at her length with an air of roughness and vigour, relishing high of amorous eagerness and impatience. The girl, spreading herself to the best advantage, with her head upon the pillow, was so concentered in what she was about, that our presence seemed the least of her care and concern. Her pettitcoats, thrown up with her shift, discovered to the company the finest turn'd legs and thighs that could be imagined, and in broad display, that gave us a full view of that delicious cleft of flesh; into which the pleasing hairgrown mount over it, parted and presented a most inviting entrance, between two close-hedges, delicately soft and pouting. Her gallant was now ready, having disencumber'd himself from his clothes, overloaded with lace, and presently, his shirt removed, shew'd us his forces in high plight, bandied and ready for action. But giving us no time to consider the dimensions, he threw himself instantly over his charming antagonist.

*Note the phrase from the recurrent Milton—even here. The allusion is to *Paradise Lost* ix. 1037–39:

Her hand he seiz'd, and to a shady bank,
Thick overhead with verdant roof embower'd,
He led her nothing loath; flowers were the couch . . .

The cool clinicality of a flagellation passage goes on for nine pages and can be suggested only by a few scattered excerpts.

I was then, by Mrs. Cole, brought in, and presented to him, in a loose *dishabille* fitted, by her direction, to the exercise I was to go through, all in the finest linen, and a thorough white uniform: gown, petticoat, stockings, and satin slippers, like a victim led to sacrifice; whilst my dark auburn hair, falling in drop-curls over my neck, created a pleasing distinction of colour from the rest of my dress.

As soon as Mr. Barville saw me, he got up, with a visible air of pleasure and surprise, and saluting me, asked Mrs. Cole if it was possible that so fine and delicate a creature would voluntarily submit to such sufferings and rigours. . . .

As soon as Mrs. Cole was gone, he seated me near him, when now his face turned upon me, into an expression of the most pleasing sweetness and good humour. . . .

He stood up near the fire, whilst I went to fetch the instruments of discipline out of a closet hard by: these were several rods, made each of two or three strong twigs of birch tied together, which he took, handled, and view'd with as much pleasure as I did with a kind of shuddering presage. . . .

I led him then to the bench, and according to my cue, play'd at forcing him to lie down; which, after some little show of reluctance, for form's sake, he submitted to; he was straightway extended flat upon his belly, on the bench, with a pillow under his face; and as he thus tamely lay, I tied him tightly, hand and foot, to the legs of it; which done, his shirt remained truss's up over the small of his back, I drew his breeches quite down to his knees; and now he lay, in all the fairest, broadest display of that part of the back-view. . . .

Seizing now one of the rods, I stood over him, and according to his direction, gave him, in one breath, ten lashes with much good-will and the utmost nerve and vigour of arm that I could put into them, so as to make those fleshy orbs quiver again under them.

After protracted efforts Mr. Barville has an orgasm. When they exchange roles, Fanny doesn't enjoy it at the time. They have supper together, and then she is startled by a fierce onset of excitement. Mr. Barville obliges as best he can, though the process is a little complicated, he being tired and she being too sore to lie down. On reflection she compares the effects of being flogged to "a dose of Spanish flies; with more pain perhaps, but less danger." Mrs. Cole, who set up the meeting, is delighted with her.

One observes a lack of privacy in all this. The select establishment, like Thélème, has a strong flavor of *group* activity. It is almost a mini-community. Fanny and her friends spend hours watching as well as doing and comparing notes. Usually the watching is fun, inside the house and elsewhere. She has one nasty jolt when she spies on a couple in the next room at an inn and finds that both are male. Even then she keeps her eye to the peephole and has her excuse ready:

> The criminal scene, I had the patience to see to an end, purely that I might gather more facts and certainly against them in my design to do their deserts instant justice.

Though in fact they get away, and she never does report them. Mrs. Cole hears all about it and is very properly indignant at such depraved conduct.

Exaggerations occur, of a type well known in erotica. The potency of some of the male characters is improbably great. Their equipment is improbably large. Yet one seldom feels too remote from reality. Female readers who ought to know have praised Cleland's insight into the sexual feelings of women. A modern reader can find further interest, if incidentally, in many details on social habits, clothes, and so forth. Where Fanny gives glimpses of the moral atmosphere and attitude that apply in her world, something authentic is certainly coming through. It is an ambivalent something. She doesn't moralize much, or take stands. But she has implications, and they face both ways. She is harder to pin down mentally than physically.

Fanny accepts most of what happens, approves of most of the clients, and often enjoys her dealings with them. So do her colleagues. When together, without male company, they swap reminiscences. Like Dr. Armstrong she detests sodomy and is disgusted by the gay couple at the inn. Nothing else seems to upset her much. Her reference to "nature" at the beginning is never pursued philosophically, but she gives the same impression as Armstrong, most of the time—that all "natural" sex is good in her eyes, and copy-book morality is beside the point.

This, however, is only one aspect. Fanny is not really antimoral or even emancipated. Sodomy isn't the only thing she draws the line at. She also draws the line at plain language. Throughout the story, with all its visual vividness, she uses no four-letter words and not many anatomically precise ones. Instead she has an amazing repertoire of euphemisms and circumlocutions. She can refer to the same things in endless different ways, with a pseudocoyness meant to tease as plain language wouldn't.

> The soft silky down, that had but a few months before put forth and garnish'd the mount-pleasant of those parts, and promised to spread a grateful shelter over the seat of the most exquisite sensation . . .

> She, with the greatest effrontery imaginable, unbuttons his breeches, and removing his shirt, draws out his affair, so shrunk and diminish'd that I could not but remember the difference.

> Then his grand movement, which seem'd to rise out of a thicket of curling hair . . . stood stiff and upright, but of a size to frighten me, by sympathy, for the small tender part which was the object of its fury.

> He made me feel the proud distinction of his sex from mine.

> Then gently removing her hand, which in the first emotion of

natural modesty, she had carried thither, he gave us rather a glimpse than a view of that soft narrow chink running its little length downwards and hiding the remains of it between her thighs.

This of course becomes a joke between Fanny and the reader. How is she going to put it next? To sum up—her language is never dirty. It is naughty, a very different matter, and it presupposes conventions . . . that, therefore, she hasn't really broken with.

At the close she performs what she has never performed before in all her career: a somersault. Well off, safely married to her dear Charles, she ends in the tone of the pious Richardson.

> Thus, at length, I got snug into port, where, in the bosom of virtue, I gather'd the only uncorrupt sweets: where, looking back on the course of vice I had run, and comparing its infamous blandishments with the infinitely superior joys of innocence, I could not help pitying, even in point of taste, those who, immers'd in gross sensuality, are insensible to the so delicate charms of VIRTUE. . . .
>
> If I have painted Vice in all its gayest colours, if I have deck'd it with flowers, it has been solely in order to make the worthier, the solemner sacrifice of it to Virtue.

These sentiments, sprouting abruptly and comically on the last pages, are in tune with the vocabulary. They preserve the book's naughtiness. Vice turns out to have been forbidden fruit after all. Cleland, and his readers, can have it both ways.

The fact that *Fanny Hill* was written, and published, and widely read, shows how the tide was flowing. Yet the novel itself never fully lets go.

A TREND TOWARD COARSE FICTION

However, while Fanny opts for respectability, the heroine of another novel does not. She is French, and her name is Thérèse.

The reign of Louis XV was marked by a good deal of showy "libertinage," and as in England, it sometimes went with a restlessness— even among the rich and powerful—that lacked a constructive outlet. The Duc de Richelieu was not the only great noble who dabbled in magic like the Hell-Fire brethren. But in France the restlessness developed into a more serious probing of values, a more thoughtful rejection of the Christian scheme and Christian-derived ethics. Voltaire, Diderot, and the rest of the philosophes began pushing this trend to un-English lengths. Meanwhile the less gifted could make hay while the philosophic sun shone—and, having made it, could roll in it.

In 1748, between *Clarissa* and *Fanny Hill,* a story appeared entitled *Thérèse Philosophe.* The author may have been d'Arles de Montigny. It has been called "a coarse piece of pornographic fiction," as "The Oeconomy of Love" has been called "nauseous." Yet it was highly thought of at the time, and indeed later, by no less a judge than Dostoevsky. Leaders of the intelligensia praised it in all sincerity as a novel of ideas.

Thérèse begins morally where Fanny ends, in a conventional stance. As a girl, she was educated with pious care . . .

> "You will only be happy," people told me, "as long as you practise the Christian and moral virtues. Every departure from these is vice. Vice brings us into contempt, with shame and remorse as the consequences." Convinced of the soundness of these lessons, I tried in good faith, until I was twenty-five, to live by the principles they laid down. We shall see with what success.

The answer is, with no success whatsoever. Virtue leads Thérèse into frustration and grief. Slowly, however, she makes Dr. Armstrong's discovery and pursues it further. Nature (under God) has given us passions. How can it be wrong to indulge them? Wherever the "Christian and moral virtues" obstruct, they should be set aside.

What lunacy to believe that God has created us to act in ways which go against Nature, and make us miserable in this world! That he wants us to deny ourselves everything which satisfies the senses and appetites he has *given* us!

Sexually at least, then, no holds are barred. Thérèse switches over from virtue to vice, enjoys herself, and does very well out of it, free from qualms of conscience. "All is good, all is from God."

Ideas like Thérèse's, with or without religious trimmings, were current during the 1730s and 1740s. Anti-morality in sex was only the most obvious type. The vogue for questionable magic was gaining ground too, and here too the appeal to Nature was possible, if not so easy. Hadn't Agrippa and Paracelsus claimed to be unraveling Nature's secrets, and seeking harmony with her laws? If Nature *is* benign, such activities must be benign also. Once that was conceded, it was hard to draw a boundary between *white* magic and black, between natural magic and satanism; just as it was hard to draw a boundary between natural sex and perversion, though Armstrong and *Fanny Hill* thought they could.

No one in England was prepared—yet—to condone stealing or murder also, on the ground that "natural" promptings can inspire crime as well as fornication. Still, Fielding had an enthusiastic public for his *Jonathan Wild,* which portrayed that real arch-crook, hanged in 1725, in terms that amounted to a reasoned if ironic defense of his profession.

If we assemble all the clues, we shall get a fairly distinct image of a kind of Englishman whom we shall expect to find flourishing from about 1730 onward. He is socially a gentleman, and a womanizer in the manner of Wharton's Schemers, Armstrong's carefree seducers, and Fanny's gallants. Comfortably off, fairly cultured, fairly well read, he has absorbed a trendy optimism and believes that Nature is on his side and he can do pretty much as he pleases. He dislikes the smug, philistine, corrupt Whig Establishment, and in that spirit may favor ill-defined schemes of opposition, even parlor Jacobitism. In that spirit also he is willing and even eager to shock. He flirts with blasphemy and magic. Yet he may still be glad to see the conventions upheld, as at the end of *Fanny Hill,* so that he can have pleasure in flouting them.

And surely too we shall find Englishmen of this sort clubbing together in a common pursuit, even a common program, taking up where the Duke of Wharton left off.

6

BUBB AND FRED

A LIFE OF ABSURDITIES

About 1722, when Wharton's money troubles were cutting into his bounty, his poetic companion Edward Young began looking around for a new patron. The future author of *Night Thoughts* was not in downright want like the Grub Street brigade, but, in common with many writers of the time, he needed at least one friend with resources and influence. He found the person he wanted—the same who, as a lord of the treasury, was destined to sign the papers for the disposal of Wharton's last assets: George Dodington.

This was the Dorset magnate usually, inaccurately, but irresistibly known as George *Bubb* Dodington, the target of a poem by Browning. In spite of all ridicule then and since, he has been described by a modern historian as "the key to the Whig cipher of the mid century, its Rosetta stone." To take a close look at him, at the setting he moved in and the company he kept, is not to wander down a bypath but to follow a highway leading into the heart of public affairs.

He was christened in 1691 as plain George Bubb, the son of Jeremiah Bubb. According to report, Jeremiah was a Weymouth apothecary. He married, however, above his station. His wife was a Dodington, and her brother George was a Somerset gentleman who profited by the Glorious Revolution, holding a governorship of the Bank of England and several other lucrative posts. In 1709 this elder Dodington bought an estate at Eastbury, near Blandford Forum in Dorset, and planned to build a palace almost if not quite rivaling Blenheim. Having no children, he adopted his nephew George Bubb as its future occupant. The heir's improved status involved taking on the Dodington name, and officially the Bubb disappeared, but in practice he never managed to shed it.

He went to Oxford, he went on an extended version of the Grand Tour, he picked up foreign languages and Italian contacts and tastes. In the first parliament of George I he took over his uncle's seat and was then sent to Spain as ambassador. Though still only twenty-four, he successfully negotiated an Anglo-Spanish trade treaty. Home, and master of Eastbury, he planted himself there in the summer of 1721 and watched his palace as it took shape. Designed by Vanbrugh, it stood (a fragment stands to this day) at the top of a slope commanding a wide, agreeable prospect. It had a frontage of nearly 600 feet around the courtyard; a huge Doric portico with pillars 46 feet high; an octagon room with a painted ceiling; a long vista; an artificial lake. The inside was tawdry and seldom comfortable, and no complete driveway was ever made, so carriages approached over grass. But it realized the grandiose dreams of the rich uncle. Its eventual cost was £140,000.

Here George Dodington played the grand host and literary patron. Edward Young was his first catch, and a valued one. Another Eastbury guest addressed verses to Young as senior incumbent:

> *While with your Dodington retir'd you sit*
> *Charmed with his flowing burgundy and wit . . .*

The wit was not often very witty, but in Bubb's house his feeblest pun would get a laugh, and he was genuinely a fluent talker, a good reader aloud, a genial personality. In London he frequented a Pall Mall Club called "The World" and took Young to it.

Though not yet in office, he was close—at this point—to Walpole. According to Lady Mary Wortley Montagu, the great minister invited him (with a strange foreshadowing) to a tongue-in-cheek "secret committee" debating a proposal to amend the Ten Commandments by deleting the word "not." Dodington remarked that if adultery were made obligatory it would be less popular.

He now sat as MP for Bridgewater, with various West Country interests that enabled him to fill half a dozen other seats with friends and relations. That fact commended him to the prime minister and explains his appointment in 1724 as a lord of the treasury, with extensive control over the patronage that kept Parliament docile. He still accepted Robinocracy and did not go along with the Wharton contention that the Revolution was being betrayed. His approval of Whig constitutional monarchy, and its freedom under the law, had one far-reaching result. In 1727 Voltaire, visiting England, spent the summer at Eastbury; and it was from Dodington, the only member of the government with whom he talked closely at length, that he acquired his knowledge of the English political structure and the admiration for it that, through his writings, prepared the way for revolution in France.

In the light of this and later events, Dodington had (and still has) a right to be taken seriously as a Whig who reflected on Liberty to some purpose. His frequent failure to get himself taken so was due partly to the "Bubb," partly to his own unhelpful development. He became—unfortunately—grotesque, a gift to caricaturists. He had always been short and dumpy with a snub nose, and after he was forty or so, his lavish eating and drinking made him gross. His clothes were expensive but old-fashioned. Until almost the end of his life he wore the heavy wigs of his youth when most gentlemen wore smaller ones. His coats were full skirted with much lace and embroidery. His rings and snuff-box were ostentatious. He favored lilac waistcoats and breeches and is said to have split a pair of the latter while bowing to the queen. When the waistcoats could no longer be worn he set them aside, and a large number were finally reassembled to make a bedroom rug in which the buttonholes still showed.

But through all parvenu absurdities he retained his energy, his acuteness, his zest for literature, and a degree of public spirit. When the neighboring town of Blandford Forum was burned down, he arranged a treasury grant to aid in rebuilding. Young continued to be welcome at Eastbury and wrote some of his best poems there. Voltaire met Young during the 1727 visit, and also another rising poet whom, through Young, Bubb had acquired. This was James Thomson. In the upshot it was Thomson—not "Oeconomy" Armstrong, though they were friends, nor *Fanny Hill* Cleland—who was to revive the Rule of Thélème. He also wrote "Rule Britannia." He might be described as the victim, the not too deeply distressed victim, of a conflict of Rules.

Thomson was a son of the Manse, with much the same Scottish roots as Armstrong and Cleland. He was born in 1700, the fourth child in the large family of a minister, the Reverend Thomas Thomson. When James was eighteen his father met disaster performing an exorcism. A ghost had been reported from a place called Woolie, near Southdean, where the Thomsons were living. The minister made his way to Woolie and began saying appropriate prayers. Before he had finished, a "ball of fire" struck him on the head and stunned him. He recovered enough to blame diabolic agency and then expired. James, deeply shaken, acquired an awe of the supernatural and a visible nervousness about sleeping alone. He remained, however, a bachelor.

His father intended him for the Kirk, but he was incompletely educated and never ordained. His student days were convivial rather than debauched. Migrating to London, he maintained a pinched existence tutoring children of the nobility. He was initiated into Sassenach sins by David Mallet, yet another transplanted Scotsman and versifier, who introduced him to Martha Fowke, with the usual result. Meanwhile Thomson was composing a long and rather original poem of his own, *Winter,* in blank verse instead of the predominant couplets. It found a publisher through Mallet's good offices and came out in 1726 with complimentary lines by Martha. After a faltering start it sold well. Thomson's theme had the advantage of immediately suggesting three sequels. In 1727 he produced *Summer.* Dodington had already expressed interest in him, and Young had brought him to Eastbury, where the meeting with Voltaire took place. Thomson wrote *Spring* in 1728, and *Autumn* in 1730, staying with Dodington and working on it during the appropriate time of year. That final effort finished the cycle known ever after as "Thomson's *Seasons*." His host subscribed twenty guineas to the collected edition.

But his most remarkable work was still some way off.

IN THE SHADOW OF THE PRINCE

Walpole's system continued to prevent the rise of a political opposition in the modern sense. Cliques could be formed to oppose him on particular measures. Journalists could assail and lampoon him, as in the post-Whartonian paper the *Craftsman*. Beyond that, his web of patronage was too strong. It had only a single major weakness—a long-term weakness without definite political bearings, but, over the years, an important one. Where politics meant chiefly sharing the spoils of office, those who were not satisfied would look elsewhere. And however firm Walpole's grip, however close his collaboration with the sovereign, there was an "elsewhere" that remained outside his control. The sovereign was mortal. Therefore the heir to the throne could hold out prospects, and the dissatisfied could gather round him, hoping for their reward when he became king—as, in a world of sudden disease and poor medical science, he might do at any moment.

Once this trend emerged, it would channel unrest of other kinds, even if it offered nothing better immediately than marking time while the sovereign lived. Whatever shadow court gathered round the Prince of Wales would attract those who wanted policies changed or the system broken but could achieve nothing via Walpole's controlled parliaments. There was, for instance, an aggrieved feeling that the Hanoverians were neglecting England's commercial interests because they cared more about Hanover, and that for this reason Walpole submitted too tamely to Spanish restraint on trade in America. Britannia should rule the waves and didn't. There was also the more radical critique started by

Wharton and elaborated in the *Craftsman* and the anti-Walpole propaganda of Bolingbroke, who carried on the claim that the Revolution had been subverted by Whig grandees. He was building up his theory that the cause of Liberty demanded a Patriot King who would smash through oligarchic corruption and choose his ministers for talent alone. The word *patriotism* began its life with this flavor of radicalism attached to it.

Wherever Whartonian ideas found entry, Whartonian rakishness might well follow—a nose-thumbing, disreputable assertion of freedom by civilized and frustrated men. The accession of George II in 1727 ensured that any group rallying to his heir would include a cultured element. The second of England's German kings was a philistine: he refused the dedication of a picture by Hogarth, snapping that he hated "bainting and boetry." Pope, still supreme among the boets, poured scorn on the Establishment and saluted Bolingbroke in his *Essay on Man*.

True, the actual heir—the prospective Next King who would reshuffle the pack—was unpromising material. Frederick, the son of King George II and Queen Caroline, was shipped over from Hanover, after long delay, in December 1728. His father did not want him in England. Public opinion, however, clamored for a resident Prince of Wales, and there had been rumors of plans for a secret marriage. Frederick landed at Harwich with no official welcome and arrived at St. James's Palace—then the main royal residence—in a hired coach. He was proclaimed Prince of Wales, unavoidably, the following month.

Known as Fred, or (to his family) Fritz, he was a short, vacant-looking, swarthy young man with a big, flattish nose and a weak chin. His English was shaky; so was his education. He could be both timid and vain. He was also a shameless liar. Back in Hanover he had at least one discarded mistress—he preferred his women plain—and a load of debts. In spite of debts, English as well as Hanoverian, he gambled. There is a story that he joined a Hell-Fire Club, presumably the one at the George and Vulture. Still, at his best he was an affable, generous person, and he had two assets. One was a veneer of culture: he played the cello and sang French songs to his own accompaniment, and he had a passion for theatricals, with a gift of mimicry himself. His other and greater asset was a knack for public relations. When he exerted himself to be popular, he was.

For a while Fred seemed passive. Though his parents were never cordial, no quarrel blew up immediately. He also kept on good terms with Walpole, who managed him with Lord Hervey as an intermediary. But in 1731 began the long run-up for a general election, and toward the end of that year, George Bubb Dodington detached Fred from Hervey and got the princely ear himself. At first there was little more to this than a careerist attempt to woo the rising star. A congenial attempt; Bubb was a snob (whenever he mentions royal personages in his diary, he enlarges his handwriting). Opponents accused him of already plotting to set up a rival show in defection from Walpole, and certainly he was growing unhappy, as others were, over Walpole's supine policy abroad. But whatever his precise original motives, he was giving an impulse that was bound to go further. Under Bubb's tutelage the prince gradually learned to think ahead and to cast himself in the role marked out for him, as potential convener of a new regime in the making.

He experimented with royal images. He tried, feebly, to model himself on Charles XII of Sweden. He even showed a sneaking fondness for Jacobitism. As a provisional mini-palace he bought Carlton House in Pall Mall, "borrowing" £6,000 from Dodington and afterward treating the polite swindle as a joke. Dodington, who was still rich and bore no grudge, had a house built for himself next door, with a private entry to Frederick's back stairs. According to rumor the prince treated him as a court jester rather than a counselor, on one occasion rolling him down the stairs in a blanket.

Serious issues underlay the horseplay nevertheless. In 1733 a parliamentary move against Walpole defeated one of his measures, but it failed to depose him, and in 1734 the general election left him as firmly entrenched as ever. Far from cracking, the oligarchic facade was growing stronger; the scope for change was shrinking still further. This was the time when the leading clubs became exclusive. White's rules were amended in 1736 to provide that a candidate could be debarred by a single blackball anonymously dropped in the ballot box.

The hardening of Robinocratic respectability acted as a spur toward the growth of a Prince of Wales faction. Frederick developed on self-assertive lines that stemmed from Dodington's promptings. His own difficulties were pushing him on to a collision course. To pay his debts he very nearly contracted a marriage that the king would never approve, undertaking to the aged and spiky Sarah, Duchess of Marlborough, that he would espouse her granddaughter for £100,000 a year. To disengage the prince from this deal, Walpole had to find money for him from other sources. But the difficulties were not resolved. Fred's income consisted of revenues from the Duchy of Cornwall, plus an allowance from the king. The total was over £30,000, but it was not enough. He went on pressing for a suitable marriage and an independent establishment to go with it.

Temporarily cooling toward Dodington (who was still in the government), he changed the locks in Carlton House so that the adviser next door could no longer drop in when he chose and turned to less cautious politicians. He did succeed in making his matrimonial point. In April 1736 his father returned from a trip to Hanover with a bride for him—Augusta of Saxe-Gotha, a tall, gauche, but docile princess of seventeen who spoke no English. The couple, however, were still not permitted to break away. They were simply installed in a wing of St. James's Palace. After the wedding, guests were ushered in to inspect them in bed, where, as a memoir writer records, "there was nothing remarkable but the Prince's nightcap, which was some inches higher than any grenadier's cap in the whole army."

Whatever family warmth the marriage had brought, a cooling off rapidly ensued. King George—or Queen Caroline, reports differ—was heard to describe Frederick as "the greatest ass, the greatest liar, and the greatest *canaille,* and the greatest beast in the whole world," adding, "I heartily wish he were out of it." Fred had recourse to literature, composing a fairy tale about a handsome and gentle prince with cruel, mean parents. But he also courted popularity, taking advantage of his father's long absences abroad. He staged distributions of beer and beef for "the poor" and personally helped to put out a fire in the Temple. As he toiled beside the firemen, shouts of "Crown him!" were heard. His friends took up a scheme of Bolingbroke's and campaigned for extra funds for the prince out of the Civil List—in other words, government money, a measure that would have ripped open Walpole's patronage system and laid the basis for a paid opposition. The project failed because Dodington was not yet ready to back it in the Commons. But the personal stresses had gone too far for appeasement.

The crisis came in July 1737 over Augusta's first child. The prince did not tell his parents that she was pregnant till almost the last moment (female fashions then made concealment easier). They were all staying at Hampton Court, and George decreed that the birth should take place there. Accordingly, when Augusta was in labor, Frederick hustled her away to St. James's, where his mistress Lady Archibald Hamilton helped to deliver the baby, a girl "about the bigness of a good large toothpick-case." The king and queen arrived, furious, a few minutes later. Fred, in a nightshirt, gave his mother a round-by-round description of the birth, which upset her. When he had left she said, "I hope in God I shall never see the monster's face again" . . . and she never did.

Fred now proceeded openly with a rival court. After some uneasy moving about, he rented Leicester House, on the north side of the present Leicester Square, as a meeting place for his adherents. He also acquired Cliveden House near Cookham, a square, white building on a hill with a spacious lawn. He began dreaming up shadow cabinets and promising rewards for his hangers-on when he came to the throne. So far as his court had any policy, it was on the Patriot King pattern sketched by Bolingbroke. Walpole nicknamed the political intriguers who gathered round him the "Patriot Boys." The prince could exert a little pressure by influencing elections in his Duchy of Cornwall, and fitfully, he did. The father-son rift ran through society. Whoever was received at the king's court was excluded from the prince's, and vice versa. There was a King's Theatre in Haymarket and a Prince's Theatre in Lincoln's Inn Fields. George liked Handel's music; Frederick refused to listen to it and favored rival composers.

The prince was strengthened by the death of his mother, which occurred late in 1737, without reconciliation. George was more deeply shocked than anyone had expected, and Walpole, who had owed much of his power to the queen's support, was less secure. He tried to influence George through a mistress, but she was no substitute. Several leading Whigs drifted away from him, including Dodington, who, in 1740, attached himself less hesitantly to the prince. Another of Frederick's shadow courtiers blossomed as a critic of Walpole in the House—the young and rising William Pitt. The prince backed a fresh campaign to drag Walpole down. It began with the War of Jenkins' Ear, when Pitt mobilized anti-Spanish feeling to defeat Walpole's policy of peace; the imperialism of the commercial interests, hungry for overseas opportunities through sea power, was getting too vigorous to contain. Walpole struggled on till February 1742 and then resigned.

At last . . . and yet it did not seem, after all, to have made much difference. The system ground on—Robinocracy without Robin. The king remained firmly on his throne, and though he still disowned his son, Frederick had an air of being bored with the quarrel. He even offered (unsuccessfully) to serve in the army. He lived in an easygoing style, writing verses to his wife and mistresses, playing cricket and rounders with his children, organizing family concerts, and reviving the royal patronage of horse racing, which the two Georges had neglected. Rebellious politicians frequented his town houses and Cliveden as before, but when they got there they were apt to be pressured into attending plays, or worse. Fred once insisted on an entire house party going out to work in the garden in a February east wind, and regaled them afterward with a cold dinner and a performance of *Macbeth*.

Fred being thus, it was the old story: *how* to oppose? While Walpole was still in office, though waning, Dodington had begun trying to take the situation in hand. The disgruntled characters around the prince should be given a real policy. There was no point left in the moth-eaten distinction of Whig and Tory; the new opposition would be a body of new, critical Whigs; and noting the prince's flirtation with the Patriot King notion, Dodington set out to give this more substance by—in effect—a full-blown reinstatement of Philip Wharton. The Glorious Revolution had been sold out, so the opposition's job was to prepare the way for a sovereign who would restore it in its uncorrupt glory.

This vision had implications—for instance, that the future sovereign should acquiesce in disentangling England from Hanover and attendant commitments. Frederick realized that the aim was to cut him down in some ways while building him up in others. He accused one of Bubb's friends of wanting to demote him from a real monarch into a "Stadtholder" or president. However, he played along, even to the point of standing aloof from his own dynasty. During the Forty-Five, when his brother Cumberland was out fighting the Jacobites, he gave a party in which the centerpiece was an iced cake representing the fortifications of Carlisle, and a team of girls broke it down by pelting it with miniature cannonballs.

Dodington was still a patron of authors, and he made use of the fact. One of his protegés was Henry Fielding, who had not yet achieved *Tom Jones*. Fielding's *Jonathan Wild,* with its ironic subversion of morality, was dedicated to Bubb, who enjoyed reading it aloud to elderly ladies, unexpurgated, with theatrical gestures. Fielding agreed to edit a paper for the new opposition, the *Champion*. After he had put this on its feet, it was taken over by another Dodington man, an American and friend of Benjamin Franklin, James Ralph. Dodington commissioned Ralph to write a partisan *History of England* from 1660 to 1715 showing just how the betrayal of the Revolution had happened. The thesis of the book was Wharton's, and it urged that the same arguments that justified kicking out James II would justify a further installment of revolution. (At about the same time, Young published his *Night Thoughts,* where Wharton's ghost walked in another guise as Lorenzo;

and Richardson was at work on *Clarissa Harlowe* with Lovelace in it. The Hell-Fire duke was haunting people in the 1740s.)

For some years Dodington was still oscillating, still office seeking at intervals, and it was not till 1749 that he became finally and irrevocably Fred's shadow prime minister. But from the last phase of Walpole onward, his ideas of how Parliament should be reformed were taking shape. He laid stress on "independent gentlemen." In the House of Commons sense, an "independent" meant a member who was outside the net of patronage and apt to disapprove of it. There were always 150 or so of these. In the nature of things they could not combine, but they could be drawn together to check ministerial power, to resist the growth of the bloc of officeholders, to demand elections. And one such independent whom Dodington ushered into the new opposition, with strange but wholly appropriate results, was Sir Francis Dashwood.

THE DEEDS OF DASHWOOD

Dashwood, the future realizer (in a way) of Thélème, was the man to whom the prince made his "Stadtholder" complaint. But although an MP, he did not rank constitutional theory very high among his interests.

The Dashwoods were connected by marriage with the descendants of Milton. However, there was nothing Roundhead about them. They were old-fashioned Tories, and such rebelliousness as they showed took the shape of mild Jacobite leanings. At sixteen (he was born in 1708) Francis succeeded his father's baronetcy and estate at West Wycombe in Buckinghamshire, with a great deal of money. He appeared on the London scene too late for the original Hell-Fire Club, but the general rakish milieu suited him well. In 1726 he made the Grand Tour with a tutor. The outcome was a legend to rival Wharton's, which, in this case, the hero lived to enjoy and exploit.

His tutor—at least according to the received story—was a Catholic Jacobite, chosen by senior relations for political motives. Francis himself was ready and eager to sample anything, including Catholicism and Jacobitism. In later life he used to say, "Taste the sweets of all things." But his notion of sampling was to fling himself into a role, to strike an attitude rather than to explore an idea. The pair of them moved across Europe in an atmosphere of charades, crises, demonstrations, and fornications.

The tour ran to a second installment during 1729–31. In Rome Francis's companion exposed him to the holiest shrines in the hope of converting him. His usual reaction was to laugh. On Good Friday he did more than laugh. It was customary on that day for penitents to go into the Sistine Chapel. An attendant handed each a miniature scourge, a priest put out the candles, and the congregation bared their shoulders and symbolically beat themselves, chanting prayers and lamentations. Francis, more impressed by the chapel than by its occupants, decided to test them with a proper penance. Returning muffled in a long cloak, he waited till the chapel was dark again and the holy exercises were in full swing, then produced a real horsewhip and strode up and down, giving the penitents a real flogging. Amid yells of "Il diavolo! il diavolo!" they jumped up and fled to the door. It was some time before they were all convinced that the Devil had not appeared in person.

On the face of it this was hardly more than a lark. It has a sequel, however, that makes Dashwood himself the butt and raises queries about him. Like other portions of his legend the story is not well attested, but it may at least be ben trovato. One night the tutor was woken up by cries of alarm and found his young baronet staring in terror at four green eyes gleaming in an eerie uproar. They belonged to a couple of squalling cats; Francis insisted that a four-eyed devil was after him. The tutor knew better but foolishly did not say so, and for a while Francis was a Catholic convert. Disillusionment, when the tutor betrayed the secret to a friend, and it came back to him, revived his old scorn so violently that he never recovered from it.

Certainly this impression of a willing demibelief, ready to shoot off in different directions, fits in with some of his other activities abroad.

For instance, he seems to have gone further than most Grand Tourists in picking up the occultish interests that Italians catered to. But he also had less shady pursuits. It was in Italy that he met the Milanese painter Giuseppe Borgnis, whom he later set to work in England, with flamboyant results.

Sir Francis wavered homeward, displaying a mixed bag of characteristics. He had the sexuality of the rake carried even further than it usually was: in the words of Walpole's son Horace, "the staying power of a stallion and the impetuosity of a bull." He had an erratic restlessness and, in particular, a fixed contempt for most religion—not in the spirit of skeptics such as Voltaire, but with a continued adolescent fondness for mockery and blasphemy, which helped to nourish a continued flirtation with the black arts. Also he had fair artistic taste, with an Italian bias, and a penchant for (so to speak) *being* art as well as looking at it, which took the form of dressing up, role playing, forming live tableaux, and being painted.

With all his quirks Dashwood exuded a warmth and a good-fellowship that were not bogus. When he grew to be better known and entered politics, hostile critics such as Horace Walpole accused him of "cultivating a roughness of speech" and generally setting up as a plain blunt man, in the style of Shakespeare's Mark Antony. But this was not as much of a pose as they imputed. In some respects he actually was a plain blunt man. His coarse language in Parliament shocked his colleagues, and when he grappled with a problem requiring close thought, he was apt to become bewildered. Mathematics defeated him: he confessed his inability to do a sum with more than five figures. Nor could he manage a set speech explaining any subject that was at all complex. Armed with these last two qualifications, he was eventually to become chancellor of the Exchequer.

During the 1730s that apogee was far off. Sir Francis was still traveling for much of the time. In 1733 he went to Russia. He turned up at the Court of St. Petersburg disguised as Charles XII of Sweden, Peter the Great's arch-enemy, who had been dead for fourteen years. Under this oddly chosen mask he paid court to the tsarina. She encouraged his attentions and was rumored to have slept with him several times. He returned by way of Copenhagen, writing a valuable account of the city. Later in the 1730s he visited, and relished, Turkey.

At home he was digging himself in at West Wycombe and exploring London. His town house was 18 Hanover Square. He bought erotic and magical books from Edmund Curll. He may have joined the Hell-Fire Club at the George and Vulture. He did join the Sublime Society of Beefsteaks when it was started, or rather reconstituted, in 1735. But he had already taken a more important step. Noting how an emancipated mode of life, a philistine-baiting love of art, and a spirit of political disaffiliation were all tending to flow together and appear in the same people, he took the lead in forming a new fraternity (members were forbidden to call it a club) where such people could combine.

A FRATERNITY FOR AESTHETICS

This was the Society of Dilettanti. It was launched in 1732 with about forty members. Most were young. Some, a little older, were perhaps veterans of the Hell-Fire Club of Wharton. They met on the first Sunday of the month at the Bedford Head Tavern in Covent Garden—and later at another tavern, in Palace Yard—with unfettered conviviality and a part-comic, part-magic ritual probably devised by Sir Francis himself. The books were kept in a casket called "Bacchus' tomb," and an officer known as the Very High Steward carried a silver image of the god round his neck. The president wore a scarlet toga and sat in a curule chair. The arch-master of ceremonies had a "long crimson taffeta robe full pleated with a rich Hungarian cap and a long Spanish Toledo." At initiations an "Imp" played an important part. He too wore a red robe, and he carried two lighted tapers and had a tail stuck on behind. The secretary was always dressed as Machiavelli. The seal of the society was a staff with coiled serpents.

Socially the chief members, besides Dashwood, were three young peers—Lords Middlesex, Harcourt, and Ponsonby. They were adherents of the Prince of Wales and struck the society's political keynote, which persisted as Frederick's opposition stance grew more marked. The serious business of the Dilettanti was art, especially Italian art; one requirement for membership was to have visited Italy. The business genuinely was serious. By 1740 the society was a body with high prestige, bringing together connoisseurs who influenced aesthetic fashion. The Dilettanti fostered an anticlassic reaction, a vogue for "savage" landscape painters such as Salvator Rosa, and for "picturesque" gardens with rocks, artificial ruins, and kindred irregularities.

One rule prescribed that every member must have his picture painted in costume. The pictures were hung permanently in the room where they met. The first of the society's portrait painters was George Knapton. His definitive version of Sir Francis Dashwood (seemingly not the first, since it was painted as late as 1742) marked a stage in the growth of both a fresh legend and a reality. It was already known that Dashwood favored a clerical style of dressing up, guying the Catholic Church. About 1738 an artist named Carpentiers had depicted him as *Pope Innocent* in full vestments before an altar. Knapton portrayed him in a Franciscan habit, at his devotions. Around his tonsured head was a halo with the words "San Francisco di Wycombo." He held a silver chalice engraved "Matti Sanctorum"—To the Mother of Saints. But the image of the lady in question was a small replica of the Medici Venus. The pseudofriar was gazing rapt at her body, and from behind her modest lower hand a stream of glory was shining on him.

This picture was adapted by a greater artist, William Hogarth, chronicler of the Rake in his less endearing aspects. Hogarth was never close to the Dilettanti as such, but he knew Dashwood through the Society of Beefsteaks, of which he was a founder-member. His own *Sir Francis Dashwood at his Devotions* was commissioned by Viscount Boyne, a Dilettante who appears himself in Hogarth's *A Night Encounter*. Doubtless he relished the Knapton portrait and wanted one like it for his private collection. Hogarth's portrays Dashwood in his

Franciscan habit again, kneeling in a grotto, with wine glasses and an upset dish of fruit on the ground, and an inaccurate rosary hanging from a peg. In his right hand is a cross-marked imitation Host, probably a Holy Ghost Pie such as the first Hell-Fire Club consumed. On a ledge in front of him lie an open book and what ought to be a crucifix but is in fact a figurine of a nude woman, reclining voluptuously.

The halo over the head of her adorer encircles a face in profile, looking down. This is the face of one of his young Dilettanti cronies, John Montagu, fourth Earl of Sandwich. Sandwich is immortalized (it seems too obvious to be true) by the fact that he invented sandwiches. His object was to concoct a meal that could be eaten without leaving the gaming table . . . or according to a more charitable view, his writing desk. He was an unamiable, ugly young man; a tireless seducer, with a nervous or muscular defect that gave him a weaving walk: people said he went down both sides of the street at once. The satirist Charles Churchill compared him to the ubiquitous Wharton:

> *Nature design'd him, in a rage,*
> *To be the Wharton of his age,*
> *But having given all the sin,*
> *Forgot to put the virtues in.*

Nevertheless he did have several rakish virtues—wit and taste; a talent for cricket that he exploited socially (his runs must have been nerve-racking to watch); a vast reserve of energy when he cared to use it; and a total disregard for others' opinion of him. A feature that commended him to Sir Francis more than most was a vocal scorn for religion. He was said to have held a parody of divine service in his village church, preaching to a congregation of cats.

Like Dashwood, Sandwich is named unreliably as a member of the Hell-Fire Club at the George and Vulture. Like Dashwood, he visited Turkey and found Turkish ways congenial. At Constantinople his traveling companion, Jean Liotard, painted him in green and crimson robes and a turban. Back in England in 1740, he and Sir Francis were similarly painted; and in 1744 they founded another society, the Divan Club, with an oriental motif. This was a small, intimate affair and lasted only a couple of years, but it cemented a significant partnership.

As you could not join the Dilettanti unless you had been in Italy, so you could not join the Divan unless you had been in Turkey. The club met every two weeks at the Thatched Tavern in St. James's Street. Members were expected to wear blue turbans and colorful robes and to carry daggers. The master of ceremonies, whose office passed from one to another by rota, was called the Reis Effendi, and his minute book was called (but was not) the Koran. A second functionary was the Hasnadar. Sir Francis was "El Faquir Dashwood Pacha" or "Dashwood Effendi." The standing toast was "The Harem."

Dressing up had, for eighteenth-century minds, a link with the idea of emancipation. The ritual masquerader was getting outside the established order by becoming exotically "other," like an actor wearing a mask. This motif survived into the French Revolution. Even those who at first felt it to be absurd and embarrassing were apt to get caught in the spirit of the thing: Sandwich, as arch-master of the Dilettanti, tried to excuse himself from wearing the outfit, yet we find him playing the Turk at the Divan. Once again the clue lies in the rigid consensus of a society where it remained difficult to rebel, difficult to assert freedom or dissent, except by eccentricity.

Sir Francis himself, an extreme example of the age in this way as in several, revealed the converse as well. Politically independent, not an officeholder, he wanted to oppose, yet at first he did not know how. His family Toryism was moribund. Sometimes he toyed with a near-republican radicalism but found no party to identify with; and sometimes he swung toward the Jacobites.

In 1739–41 he was much in Italy. During the summer of 1740 he lived in Florence, meeting—perhaps—Lady Mary Wortley Montagu, and holding concerts every Wednesday. Jacobitism was then reviving slightly as Prince Charles Edward grew up in Rome. Sir Horace

Mann, the British envoy in Florence, was sending back secret reports to London. An appointee of Sir Robert Walpole, he was zealously aided by Horace Walpole. From Rome the younger Walpole informed him on the activities of "Mr. Stuart" and his two sons, of whom Prince Charles Edward was the elder; and from Florence, Mann passed the information on, with his own warnings against such dangerous English sojourners as Sir Francis Dashwood. When Horace came to Florence himself, he kept an eye on Sir Francis personally. Sir Francis did correspond with the Young Pretender, giving him not very useful news of England. But he was never deeply enough involved to run risks, and he was deterred by the Stuarts' Catholicism. "I am at one with this gallant Prince," he told Sandwich. "He has all the gifts of a true leader and above all he is honest. But I detest most heartily the fripperies of Rome which emanate from his entourage. . . . Should the Prince truly come into his own, it is difficult to see how he could keep away from their influence."

Drawing back from the Jacobite abyss, he accepted the position of an MP and was returned for New Romney in 1741. Marriage to a rich Buckinghamshire widow, Sarah, Lady Ellis, enhanced his status and political value. Sarah gave no trouble. According to Horace Walpole she was a "poor, forlorn Presbyterian prude," and her husband, however physically unfaithful, was always kind and affectionate toward her. In view of his general outlook, and the bias of the Dilettanti, he had only one possible political haven—the shadow court of Prince Frederick. George Bubb Dodington held the key of the door. In 1742 Dashwood secured Bubb's election to the Dilettanti, and they began to cooperate. From then onward, so far as Dashwood was anyone's politically, he was Frederick's.

Dodington had brought in a momentous recruit.

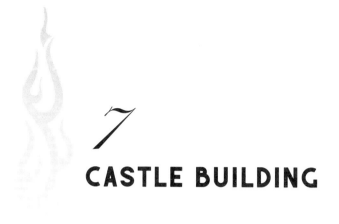

7

CASTLE BUILDING

THE PRINCE'S BARD

Meanwhile Dodington's second poet, James Thomson of the *Seasons,* had been moving on a convergent course. His role in the opposition was to bear out an opinion of Freud; that an author's function is to dream other people's dreams for them better than they can do it themselves.

After his last long visit to Eastbury, he lost direction. He convoyed a lord's son on the Grand Tour, picked up sinecure jobs, courted patrons. But he kept in touch with Dodington and gravitated toward the Prince of Wales. In a poem called "Britannia" he had already denounced Walpole's failure to protect British commerce from Spanish interference. Britannia's destiny, he said, was to rule the waves—though he didn't yet put it in exactly those words. The poem included a salute to the prince. During 1734–36 Thomson composed a longer poem, *Liberty.* This he dedicated outright to Frederick, who, on setting up his shadow court, gave the poet a pension of £100 a year. *Liberty* does not preach revolt in any really unsettling sense. It extols a "respectable" liberty based on Protestantism, Virtue, politics without deep party divisions, constructive labor. These, it implies, will flourish under Frederick more brightly than under George II. Politically the protest is very mild indeed.

But Thomson realized that this was not quite his proper line anyhow. He tried other media. Several attempts to break into the theater were apathetically received. He wrote only a single phrase that caught the public ear. One of his characters exclaimed in blank verse, "O Sophonisba! Sophonisba! O!"—a line genially parodied by Fielding with fatal effect, and soon altered.

Thomson had more successes as a patriotic bard. In 1740, by the prince's command, he collaborated with his old crony Mallet (now in the same opposition circle, and soon to become Frederick's undersecretary) on a *Masque of Alfred* for a select audience at Cliveden. This included "Rule Britannia," virtually a singable digest of part of his earlier "Britannia" poem, and was greeted with applause. Incidentally the National Anthem originated in its present form in the same year, as a hymn "God Save the King" arranged by Henry Carey for the birthday of George II. Britain's possession of two more or less official anthems is the most durable result of the rivalry of George and his son.

Thanks to Dodington, the shadow court had acquired its own Laureate. King George's was the actor-dramatist Cibber; Fred got the better bargain, a partial counterpoise to his father's annexation of Handel. Yet there was a flaw. Thomson had an un-Laureatish side to him. Fat and pleasure loving, probably a latent homosexual, he could never quite square his inclinations with his own rhetoric about Industry and Public Spiritedness and that version of the Good Life that his political friends were obliged, publicly, to seem to be in favor of.

Sometimes he foreshadowed the hippiedom of a later age in what was then to be described as "rejection of the work ethic." He was slovenly about clothes, though he took great care with his wig. Staying with Bubb at Eastbury he would lie in bed till noon and then stroll out into the garden, where, when the peaches were ripe, he took bites at the sunny side of them without removing his hands from his pockets. He liked going for walks to nowhere in particular.

He was a connoisseur of wine, maintaining a good cellar when he could afford it, at his house in Richmond; guests noticed that after a few glasses his conversation and manner became quite different. The failed minister of the Kirk would relax and chat with male friends in an irreverent atmosphere . . . feeling guilty afterward. Those friends included John Armstrong, who had written "The Oeconomy of Love" but not yet disowned it; Lord Lyttelton, a political and poetic hanger-on of Frederick's, another of the group introduced to the prince by Dodington; and the actor Quin, whose generosity once kept Thomson out of a debtor's prison.

As W. B. Yeats said: "We make out of the quarrel with others, rhetoric, but of the quarrel with ourselves, poetry." In "Britannia" and *Liberty,* Thomson had pamphletized on the prince's behalf. But in his last work, *The Castle of Indolence,* he allegorized his inner disquiets. The result (patchily at least) was poetry on a level that his verse pamphlets had never approached. Published in 1748 after long gestation, it was an attempt at exorcism. Like his father's at Woolie it was none too successful, and like his father he did not long survive it. In August of the same year he caught a chill boating on the Thames, went into a fever, and died.

The Castle of Indolence is oddly unlike the rest of Thomson. It had an instant success that, on the whole, it deserved. In spite of a professed moral intent it is deeply subversive, even poetically. Rejecting not only the approved heroic couplet, but also the blank verse of his own *Seasons,* Thomson imitates Spenser's *Faerie Queene.* He adopts its nine-line stanza. He catches, often, its dreamy music and atmosphere. *The Castle of Indolence* expresses its author's epicurean side, in an imaginary setting that is close to being the Abbey of Thélème over again. It reproclaims the Rule of Thélème. And this time, chiefly because of the Dilettanti element in the shadow court, fiction is followed by a partial realization in fact.

FICTION AND REALITY

Thomson's allegory is in two cantos. It begins firmly enough with the ostensible moral: that while we may not enjoy work, the consequences of taking things easy are worse. But having made this not very inspiring point, Thomson launches himself and the reader into a warmly conceived mini-Utopia for privileged dropouts, which has no precedent in English literature.

The Castle of his fantasy stands among trees beside a river, in a beautiful, secluded, somnolent valley. Its owner is Indolence personified, an "enchanting wizard." He attracts visitors and invites them to stay, rather as the heads of religious communities attract lay pilgrims to retreats. Indolence, indeed, addresses the visitors as "pilgrims." But his Castle is more seductive than most retreat houses.

The prospectus is tempting. The first specific delight it offers is that Indolence's guests don't have to get up early. There are no noisy workshops or markets within earshot; there are not even any farms with cocks crowing. All is peace, harmony, mutual tolerance.

> *Here nought but candour reigns, indulgent ease,*
> *Good-natured lounging, sauntering up and down:*
> *They who are pleased themselves must always please;*
> *On others' ways they never squint a frown.*

The wizard adds that residents need not feel any qualms of conscience.

> *Why, what is virtue, but repose of mind,*
> *A pure ethereal calm, that knows no storm;*
> *Above the reach of wild Ambition's wind,*
> *Above those passions that this world deform?*

Anyhow, life in the Castle is not mere idleness. It offers scope for all sorts of activities: literary meetings in pleasant surroundings; gardening; fishing.

> *But if a little exercise you choose,*
> *Some zest for ease, 'tis not forbidden here.*
> *Amid the groves you may indulge the Muse,*
> *Or tend the blooms, and deck the vernal year;*

> *Or, softly stealing, with your watery gear,*
> *Along the brooks, the crimson-spotted fry*
> *You may delude . . .*

Pilgrims pour in, among them (as it transpires) Thomson himself, with various friends—Armstrong, Lyttelton, and several of less interest. He continues with an eyewitness account of the guests' reception. As each intake arrives, the wizard casts a spell that weakens their will to leave; Thomson compares the change in them to a sexual surrender. Passing through the entrance hall, the new inmates change their tight clothing for cosy slippers and flowing epicene gowns. They are then served a drugged drink that makes them carefree. A member of the staff gives them the Rabelaisian watchword:

> *Ye sons of Indolence, do what you will.*

After which, they disperse to their rooms.

Here Thomson reminds himself sternly that he ought to be singing of nobler themes, and then, with an almost audible gasp of relief, plunges back into his daydream narrative. The Castle takes shape as a kind of ten-star hotel. Thick Persian carpets, couches, and cushions make every room a potential bedroom. The doors have no bells or knockers. Buffet tables stand everywhere laden with exotic food. In some rooms, tapestries on the walls portray scenes from the mythical golden age. In others hang pictures by landscape painters approved by the Dilettanti.

> *Whate'er Lorraine light-touch'd with softening hue,*
> *Or savage Rosa dash'd, or learned Poussin drew.*

Soft music, without visible players, comes and goes directly. And—again—this establishment has only the one rule:

> *Here freedom reign'd, without the least alloy;*

> *Nor gossip's tale, nor ancient maiden's gall,*
> *Nor saintly spleen durst murmur at our joy,*
> *And with envenom'd tongue our pleasures pall.*
> *For why? There was but one great rule for all:*
> *To wit, that each should work his own desire,*
> *And eat, drink, study, sleep, as it may fall,*
> *Or melt the time in love, or wake the lyre,*
> *And carol what, unbid, the Muses might inspire.*

This Castle has two further features, with no parallel in Rabelais. The first is a television lounge.

> *One great amusement of our household was,*
> *In a huge crystal magic globe to spy,*
> *Still as you turn'd it, all things that do pass*
> *Upon this ant-hill earth.*

The residents sit and watch this for hours. One program shows social butterflies disporting themselves and losing money; the next, authors at work, looking frustrated. Or there may be a documentary on urban life and traffic problems:

> *Then would a splendid city rise to view,*
> *With carts, and cars, and coaches roaring all:*
> *Wide-pour'd abroad behold the giddy crew;*
> *See how they dash along from wall to wall!*

After that, a political program:

> *The puzzling sons of party next appear'd,*
> *In dark cabals and nightly juntas met;*
> *And now they whisper'd close, now shrugging rear'd*
> *Th' important shoulder.*

And newsreels of war, which make the Castle's guests especially glad to be inside and not out:

> But, what most show'd the vanity of life,
> Was, to behold the nations all on fire,
> In cruel broils engaged, and deadly strife:
> Most Christian kings, inflamed by black desire,
> With honourable ruffians in their hire . . .

Thomson goes on to sketch some of his own companions. They are real people, all male—the poet's tastes deny us any account of what must have been a major amenity of the Castle. This canto ends with an un-Rabelaisian glimpse of the darker side. It mentions residents who have become bores, or bored—aging men, veterans of the place, with no zest left for anything but political gossip; lazy upper-class women (the only women described at any length), languid from lack of occupation. When inmates become sick or unattractive, and cease to please the rest, they are swept out of sight to live in a basement, with nothing to do but fret over their symptoms.

In this passage Thomson faces an issue that Rabelais evades. We feel for a moment that he is seriously thinking about the Thelemic dream instead of reveling in it. If he had developed the idea, criticizing his dropout community through its own self-deception and heartlessness, *The Castle of Indolence* would have been a profound poem. Unfortunately his public side demanded a cruder rebuttal. The second canto brings in a new character. He is "Sir Industry" (in the broad prefactory sense of "hard work"), a dreadful prig who has gone about the world fostering arts and crafts, and come to Britain, where the climate of constitutional Liberty suits him. Virtue, he insists like *Fanny Hill* on the last page, is the only source of true joy.

Hearing of the Castle of Indolence, he rides there with an attendant bard and subdues the wizard. The bewildered residents gather around, and the bard exhorts them in painfully predictable language. Nothing is achieved without effort. The "toiling swain" is "perhaps the happiest of the sons of men." Work keeps you fit, and what's the use of anything without health?

The "better sort," including Thomson, are stirred. They walk out with renewed vigor into the busy world. The majority, however, resent Sir Industry. "Is happiness a crime?" they ask. He produces a wand with "anti-magic" power and waves it. The old people's infirmary below the Castle bursts open, they emerge rejoicing, and the knight conjures up a proper residence for them. Meanwhile the beguiling landscape has revealed its true spiritual ugliness and has turned into a sub-Miltonic Hell, a wilderness of desert and swamp, full of snakes and toads and ravens, with corpses dangling from lightning-blasted trees. Sir Industry hands over the most stubborn dropouts to fiends, who hustle them off to a long penitential exile.

Here the poem ends, a little abruptly. But Thomson has laid his soul bare enough. The wizard Indolence and the knight Industry, as their matching names show, are psychological twins, the two aspects of his nature. One says, "Do what you will," urging this as the way to freedom, beauty, delight. The other says sternly, "Do your duty," and dismisses Thelemic freedom in the name of a duller Liberty with a capital *L*. We are meant to conclude that beauty and delight on these terms are mirages, falsifying a wasteland of subconscious evil.

In practice, though, the conscience-figure Industry is no real match for the wizard. Even if the place where the Castle stands is Hell, we feel, like Aucassin, that there is plenty to be said for Hell, so long as the company holds together and the spell is unbroken. Thomson's second canto fails to undo the first. Some of his readers, both among the Dilettanti (corresponding to Indolence) and among the more positive political heretics (corresponding to Industry), were surely left suspecting that the right answer would be to find a method of having it both ways. At any rate, the one man who was prominently active in both fields decided to try. A first edition of Thomson's poem is in the library of his house to this day, as well as the works of Rabelais.

MYSTERIES AND MEDDLING

Sir Francis Dashwood's scandalous Permissive Society at Medmenham is one of the most intriguing of eighteenth-century puzzles. Its origins, its activities, even its existence, have been subjects of dispute and the wildest guesswork. Today it is commonly referred to by a name borrowed from its Whartonian ancestry and never used at the time, either by members or by outsiders. It is remembered not only as a Hell-Fire Club but as *the* Hell-Fire Club, eclipsing the rest. This is a kind of question begging that disguises a mystery. Some historians survey the club's career and see nothing but harmless jollifications. Others see devil worship and gilded vice. Others scent a conspiracy that tried to take over the government and, briefly, succeeded—a conspiracy supplying keys to major events, such as the American War of Independence.

Its full and correct title in its heyday seems to have been "The Order (or Brotherhood) of the Friars of St. Francis of Wycombe." "St. Francis," of course, was Dashwood himself, as in Knapton's portrait. The false name arose later through secrecy and confusion. A society that was at least thought to do what the previous Hell-Fire clubs had done, and to carry it further with more effect, was bound to attract the tradition to itself; even though its members were of a different type—older, weightier—and certainly had intentions going beyond group naughtiness. The Hell-Fire label bears witness to the strength of the legend and mystique handed down by Wharton. It is not a safe guide.

The extreme theory about this pseudo-Franciscan Brotherhood is that it never existed. Because of the destruction of records, there is a case for believing that the whole thing was invented as a political smear. A case, yes. But not a case that will stand up convincingly. There are letters, such as a couple to Dashwood from John Tucker, one of Dodington's political proteges, that mention the Brotherhood and establish that the writer belonged to it. Even without those, a total denial is untenable. Some of the stories are too full, vivid, and detailed to have been made up by busy politicians who had no talent for fiction and would not have wasted their days churning it out at pointless length. The reports might be suspect if they all came from an imaginative author, but only one of them does. Also—and this is crucial—at the height of a political crisis neither Sir Francis nor his colleagues refuted the stories, or even contested them, damaging though they were. Instead they retorted with a counter smear drawn from the same source.

Hence, the Order existed. But having settled that, we plunge into problems. Though the association with the old abbey of Medmenham (pronounced Mednam) is firmly rooted and amply proved, whence that other popular name "the Monks of Medmenham," the Order was not born there. Nobody does know where or when. A certain Sir Miles Stapylton, who died in 1752, has been claimed as a member, a belief that argues that its origins cannot have been later than that year. Scanty clues suggest that it may have begun informally in the junketings of Prince Frederick's circle. Several of his adherents besides Dashwood turn up afterward in accounts of the Brotherhood, and a vague rumor makes out that the prince himself was a member, in what must have been an early phase—for reasons that will become apparent. Rumor attributes membership to Lyttelton, who was not only a companion of Thomson in his Castle of Indolence but a courtier of Frederick's. On the other hand, rumor omits the name of Thomson himself, and if the Order had been in existence before his death in 1748, he would almost certainly have come into the story somehow. There are indications that the Order was taking shape a year or two after that. It may be significant that around 1749–50 the prince was dabbling in magic. Not of a very profound kind: he frequented palmists and kindred fortune-tellers. But still, magic.

George Bubb Dodington's diary attests to this fact among others and supplies a few negative hints about the Order's beginnings. Bubb is generally assumed to have been a member, very likely a founder-member. From early March 1749 to early October 1754 his diary has an entry of some sort for nearly every day, and from 1755 onward it still accounts for a good deal of his time. Here and there, however, a meeting with

Dashwood is followed by an odd little gap. The diary's modern editors argue, no doubt rightly, that these gaps correspond to activities in Sir Francis's company that Bubb prefers not to record: in other words, the pseudo-Franciscan meetings. This happens first on May 20, 1750, and next on September 13 of the same year. In the latter case Dodington goes to Dashwood's house at West Wycombe on September 10 for a political consultation and remains as his guest on the eleventh. On the twelfth they visit Cliveden together to see the prince, and seemingly stay the night. The thirteenth is the blank day, and on the fourteenth "Sir Francis and I return'd to Wycombe, by ten in the morning." So if the Brotherhood did meet on that empty thirteenth, the meeting would appear to have taken place at Cliveden under Frederick's auspices.

This diary entry need not go against the main probability—that Dashwood formed a libertine mock-religious body among his friends in the opposition, and that West Wycombe House was, or quickly became, its normal rendezvous till other quarters were found. He had launched the Dilettanti and the Divan, but these were not on his premises or under his control. The bogus Order of Franciscans was to be his very own.

Most certainly he was working on his estate, making West Wycombe a fit place for eccentric and lavish gatherings, a strange classical-Italianate improvisation. To the two-story house he added extensions and embellishments—colonnades, loggias, statuary. His chief designers were John Donowell and Nicholas Revett, whom he brought into the Dilettanti. He also imported his old acquaintance Giuseppe Borgnis from Italy. Borgnis covered the ceilings of the long saloon and other main rooms with Olympian amours and feasts, with cherubs and gods and voluptuous cloud-home goddesses. Most of the pictures on the walls were Italian; the one that faced visitors on the main staircase portrayed "a maid stealing to her master's bed, laying at the same time a finger on her lips." The dining room was gorgeous in gold and pale red. Sir Francis's private room was hung with Brussels tapestry.

Outside, the baronet gave equal attention to his park. The river Wye flowed through it and broadened into a lake with an island, on which (predictably) he projected a sham temple, though this was not finished till much later. Instead of the formal gardens, which might have been expected to go with classicism, he aimed at a scene of planned wildness and innuendo. Clumps of bush interrupted the lawn. A controlled cascade gushed over grouped rocks. A sculptured Neptune surveyed his element from a demigrotto. A carefully disposed wood masked another temple dedicated to Venus. Urns and columns stood everywhere, with riddling words on them. There were shrines of Daphne and Flora and the Four Winds; there was an image of Priapus, the outstandingly phallic garden-god. One of the temples had an entrance shaded with bushes, an adjacent stone pillar, and urns inscribed to Potiphar's wife and the "Matron of Ephesus." Elsewhere, satyrs and erotic emblems flourished in stone. Legend has improved on these hints. Near the lake, it is said, Sir Francis had a garden with a perplexing layout of hillocks, hedges, and water channels. Looked at from a point higher up, it composed a female figure complete with nipples (clusters of red flowers on top of two mounds) and pubic hair (a triangular shrubbery). Alas, there is no real evidence that this garden existed, though Sir Francis did set up twenty-five small statues in front of his temple of Venus in what may have been a suggestive pattern.

He was popular in the village, where his activities gave work during a slack time. In consultation with the villagers he built a new road connecting West and High Wycombe, starting at the Bird in Hand Inn. The roadbed was made of chalk dug out of the hill under West Wycombe church. Dashwood's laborers penetrated the hill through a cave, which their quarrying and tunneling greatly enlarged, with results still to be seen. The road was finished in 1752. Sir Francis commemorated its building with an obelisk surmounted by a stone wall, costing £27 7s. 8d., and inscribed with his own name and the mileages to various places.

Whatever the nature of the parties he held in his domain, the names of one or two members of his eventual Medmenham setup emerge to view in the opposition intrigues of this period. From 1749 to 1751 Dodington's campaign through the prince was at its height. Events were moving in his favor. George II and his ministers were growing old and paying the price of Walpole's skill in holding down rivals—few younger men had been groomed sufficiently to take over. Bolingbroke's *Idea of a Patriot King,* expounding his theory in full, came out in 1749. Early in March of that year, by invitation, Dodington committed himself finally to Frederick as a salaried shadow minister. The princely finances were in healthier shape, and he was able to sponsor a paid opposition out of his revenue. Dodington was given a nominal job as "Treasurer of the Chambers" with £2,000 a year and obtained appointments for Dashwood and others, his "very few most efficient friends," with promises of office in the approaching new reign.

Averse to mere cabal forming, but still with no tangible program beyond the nebulous Patriot King idea, Dodington urged Frederick to conceive opposition in terms of creating a fresh atmosphere around himself as heir apparent. Frederick should not seem to be backing a group of Outs to replace a group of interchangeable Ins. He should try to convince the public that he was above faction, devoted impartially to the good of all his people, and so forth, and that his followers stood for a real alternative regime. Frederick, alas, was now past forty and ill equipped to convince anybody. His popularity had faded. But his shadow ministers did their best with him. Dodington and Dashwood conferred about plans, and Dodington kept a small personal staff who came in as advisers and go-betweens. They included his historical propagandist James Ralph. They also included a doctor, Thomas Thompson (who lived in his house), and yet another poet, or at any rate versifier, Paul Whitehead. Whitehead certainly was one of the pseudo-Franciscans, and Thompson almost certainly.

For two years their attempt to give the opposition a meaning struggled on . . . and then, abruptly, it collapsed. The constitutional fact that had supplied its only basis vanished. On March 5, 1751, the prince caught a cold. It turned to pleurisy. The doctors, Thompson among them, disagreed. On the eighteenth he recovered enough to drink coffee and eat rolls. Less than forty-eight hours later he died, with a dancing master and political spy named Desnoyers playing the fiddle at his bedside. Someone brought a note to his father, at the card table with Lady Yarmouth. "Fritz ist tot," said the king, barely disguising his relief. Frederick's wife Princess Augusta was genuinely sorry, and so were his children. But the best comment on the campaign to give Frederick a strong public image is his famous, anonymous mock epitaph.

> *Here lies Fred,*
> *Who was alive and is dead:*
> *Had it been his father,*
> *I had much rather;*
> *Had it been his brother,*
> *Still better than another;*
> *Had it been his sister,*
> *No one would have missed her;*
> *Had it been the whole generation,*
> *Still better for the nation:*
> *But since 'tis only Fred,*
> *Who was alive and is dead,—*
> *There's no more to be said.*

Fred was preferred to the rest of the Hanoverian family, but when you'd said that, you still hadn't said anything.

Dodington, of course, was plunged in despair. The new heir apparent, Frederick's son George, was too young to be made a leader or even a figurehead. Bubb's schemes fell to pieces. He was still an MP, but his support for the prince ruled out an early return to favor. On April 17, 1754, he even lost his seat in the Commons. He had represented Bridgewater for over thirty years, but in the general election of 1754 he was opposed by the ambitious if silly Lord Egmont. The campaign was distasteful. To quote his diary, Egmont arrived "with trumpets, noise

&c," and Bubb himself had to spend his time in "infamous and dis-
agreeable compliance with the low habits of venal wretches." Egmont
won "by the injustice of the Returning Officer," who rejected fifteen
good Dodington votes and allowed eight bad ones for Egmont, thereby
reversing the result in a close poll of only 338. So Bubb was out. Yet
as a politician he achieved immortality in spite of it. In 1754 Hogarth
painted his "Election" series. The constituency is not Bridgewater, but
in the picture *Chairing the Member* the defeated Bubb—with some
irony—is the model for the member being unsteadily chaired.

BUILD WHAT YOU WILL

With no shadow court for the opposition to gather in, and no political
goals to pursue, very little was left of it but the Dilettantism and the
rakishness. That being so, Dashwood came into his own.

West Wycombe was not a satisfactory center for the full-blown
Brotherhood he envisaged. After all it was his private residence, where
his wife and servants lived, and his more ordinary pursuits went on.
Further, the Italianate and classical styles were out of key with his
notions of a burlesque monasticism. What was needed was a special
locale with a special atmosphere, a true Castle of Indolence; and it
ought to be Gothic.

That was no novelty. He had already planted sham medieval ruins
in his own grounds. Other men of property had gone further. During
the first half of the eighteenth century, antiquaries were rediscovering
a forgotten England. There were then no guidebooks to the decaying
monasteries and castles. They had to be reached, often with difficulty,
and explored and described. But once described, they appealed to many
imaginations. From about 1750 onward, poets and artists—James
Thomson and Edward Young among them—were flirting with "melancholy" and crumbling ivy-clad arches, tombs, and owls and ravens;
and thanks partly to the Dilettanti, their imagery was translated into
architecture and horticulture.

The landowners who went in for this were mostly rich parvenus. They met with a good deal of ridicule, and by 1750 Gothic style was no longer trendy, was thought in fact to be finished. It was rescued at the right moment to interest Dashwood by someone who never liked him yet crossed his path a number of times, Horace Walpole. Sir Robert's son (not heir, at least not principal heir—he was the third) had a seat in Parliament but was not yet politically active. Instead he spent his share of the Walpole fortune on a house he bought at Strawberry Hill, by the Thames near Twickenham, in 1747. The original property was small, hardly more than a cottage. Walpole built it up, slowly and conscientiously and with much loving research, into a little castle that gave Gothicism "class" and a fresh prestige. Following up ideas that sometimes came to him in dreams, he constructed a great hall, a gallery, a chapel. The most important phase of the work was in the four years from 1749 to 1753.

Inside this private sub-Thélème Walpole did what he would, though he probably never put it like that. He wrote memoirs of his time and kept up a voluminous correspondence, planned with the memoir writing in view. On a private press he printed expensive books by himself and his friend Gray, the poet. Around him a hoard of curios grew steadily. In due course visitors were shown James I's gloves, William III's spurs, Admiral van Tromp's tortoiseshell pipe case, and, an amazing link, one of Dee's scrying stones.

Dashwood had no wish to create another Strawberry Hill. But a charmed enclosure of Gothic fantasy was clearly what he needed himself, and thanks to Walpole it would no longer be incorrect for a gentleman of taste. His chance came through his friendship with Francis Duffield of Medmenham. There—in a grove of elms on a peaceful stretch of the Thames, six miles from West Wycombe—stood the remains of an actual monastery. It was a Cistercian house, founded in the twelfth century. At the time of the dissolution of the monasteries it had been acquired by Henry VIII. Early in the reign of Elizabeth I it had passed into private hands. The new owner, James Duffield, turned it into a three-story dwelling house in the shape of an E for Elizabeth. In 1751 his descendant Francis, a soldier and amateur painter of some talent, was finding it inconvenient. Part of the house was derelict. Hardly anything recognizable was left of the monastery except a few gray pillars. Still, the site was Gothic, undeniably Gothic. At some date not precisely known, Dashwood signed a lease; the Duffields moved out; and Medmenham Abbey underwent its second conversion.

Workmen were brought daily from London and returned at night so that they would not gossip to the locals. Under Sir Francis's direction, the team stuck on a cloister (with ivy trained over it), and a pointed arch, and buttresses, and a carefully ruined tower at the southeast corner. They found a worn stone Madonna in the genuine ruins and set it in a niche in the tower for verisimilitude. They replaced the plain windows with stained glass. And at the east porch they inscribed the motto of Thélème in slightly revised Renaissance French, above a real doorway after two centuries: *Fay ce que voudras.* Do what you will.

The Order of the Friars of St. Francis of Wycombe had its place of assembly.

8

MEDMENHAM

INCONTESTABLE BRETHREN

Who were they, these Franciscans, and what did they do in their unique riverside clubhouse?

The Order has no documented history. If its members were not actually sworn to secrecy, they at least had a gentlemen's agreement about it. Records such as the minute book did exist, and some of them may have existed into the nineteenth century, but nearly all were destroyed sooner or later as irreligious, indecent, or incriminating. We must piece the story together from a few hostile accounts written in the 1760s, one of them frankly fictionalized; from assorted clues in letters, poems, and so forth; and from a mass of rumor shading off into legend.

It seems, however, that things were well under way at Medmenham by March 1753, because of a joke of Dodington's to be noted in due course. The revamped Abbey was probably not completed so soon. But meetings in 1752, even with work still in progress, are consistent with what is known of the Duffields' moving out.

So far as we can reconstruct the original membership, it reflected the founder's friendships and contacts. Political opposition was the point of departure, and no one in George II's ruling bloc ever joined. But quite a number of Dashwood's recruits were only marginally politi-cal. Some of the Friars were country neighbors of his. Some were veterans of the Dilettanti or the Divan. Some were Beefsteaks. One or two may have belonged to the defunct George and Vulture Hell-Fire Club.

When they gathered at Medmenham they used quasi-religious names. It is hard to compile a trustworthy membership list. The best single source does not take us back to the beginning. This is a fragmentary series of pages from the Abbey's cellar books, covering portions of several years from 1760 onward, and now preserved at West Wycombe. It records bottles of wine issued to various brethren for their "private devotion" when they were using the Abbey as a club. The drinkers were noted down by their pseudonyms, but most can be identified from other sources, and most of those can be assumed with fair confidence to have belonged from the early days.

The cellar-book names are Francis of Wycombe, John of Aylesbury, Francis of Cookham, Thomas de Greys (or "of Greys" on the pattern of the rest), John of Henley, John of Melcombe, John of Chequers, Thomas of London, John of Magdalen, and John of London. It is a little daunting to find only three different Christian names among ten members, but the majority can be sorted out.

Francis of Wycombe is, as ever, Dashwood himself. Of the others, John of Aylesbury is the most famous: he is the turbulent politician John Wilkes. However, Wilkes must be set aside at this point because he is known to have been a latecomer. All or nearly all of the rest were probably founder-members. Francis of Cookham is Francis Duffield, the Abbey's landlord. Thomas de Greys is Sir Thomas Stapleton, a squire with a cousinly relation to Dashwood; he helped to pay the rent and enjoyed his membership largely because of the banquets that were served. John of Henley is a Mr. Clarke, otherwise obscure. John of Melcombe is John Tucker. Tucker was an MP who sat for Weymouth under Dodington's aegis and was mayor of the town in 1754. Politically he was a close ally of his patron, not a servile one, but not very lively either. He has usually escaped notice in the Medmenham context, yet his letters to Dashwood are among the very few direct proofs from within that the Order did exist as described.

John of Chequers is almost certainly Sir John Dashwood-King, a half brother of the founder. His membership is confirmed elsewhere by a letter. Thomas of London is likely to be Dr. Thomas Thompson, Dodington's resident physician, who was turning into a notorious "character" and eccentric, renowned for his slovenliness and his prejudice against muffins. John of Magdalen and John of London are more doubtful. Other lists give one further member named John who could fit in here, Sir John D'Aubrey, a magistrate; though D'Aubrey may not have belonged in the early phase.

Two members who are not in the cellar-book fragments but can be proved, like Dashwood-King, by letters under their own hand, are Sir William Stanhope and Dodgington's assistant Paul Whitehead. Stanhope, a brother of Lord Chesterfield, was a minor figure among the Franciscans. Whitehead—"Paul the Aged" or "Paul of Twickenham"— was a major one and appears in various contexts as Sir Francis's right-hand man, high steward and secretary-treasurer of the Order.

A tailor's son, born in 1710, Whitehead passed as a poet and was undoubtedly facile in the making of verse. Dr. Johnson alludes to him, though only with scorn. An early spell in a debtors' prison embittered him, and he began pouring out satires and diatribes against Walpole, Freemasons, boxers, and other assorted targets. He made a constant noise about Liberty with a capital *L,* sometimes verging (like Dashwood) on republicanism, and was drawn into Prince Frederick's circle as a paid agent and propagandist. His conversation was described by Sir John Hawkins as "desultory, vociferous, and profane." His face was gaunt and sneering, his general moral repute was low; a rival satirist called him a "disgrace to manhood." But sexually he was a late developer, more or less faithful to his ugly, half-witted but rich wife till she died, then blowing up in his forties at just the right time to make a Dashwood-type secret society interesting to him.

Whitehead is said to have been the first to draw attention to the Medmenham site, perhaps because its hallowed associations appealed to his atheism. He planned most of the Brotherhood's ritual, superintended the wine supply, and collected the subscriptions—which were equal, but augmented by subsidies from the wealthier brethren. His outlook commended him to Sir Francis, and so did his ideas of humor. He once organized a procession of tramps and beggars in fancy dress, to parade through London travestying an annual Masonic march. He is alleged to have based the Medmenham ritual on a handbook of sorcery obtained by Sir Francis from a bookseller named Coustance, who had fallen heir to part of Curll's clientele.

Not established by quite such solid proof, but beyond serious doubt, is Lord Sandwich—in religion, John of Hinchingbrooke. Sandwich, whom we met as a Dilettante, was involved in the opposition during the onslaught on Walpole, but aloof from it during the final phase of Frederick's life. He was then first lord of the admiralty—a post in which he displayed startling energy and public spirit. When he exposed the corrupt inefficiency of the dockyards, he could hardly have hoped to keep his job for long, and he did not. His enemies intrigued against him, and on June 12, 1751, King George dismissed him. Fred being dead, Sandwich found himself on the discard pile too late for a political riposte, but he was glad to join Sir Francis in a new and perhaps more congenial species of Establishment baiting.

Last of the incontestable brethren who fit into the pre-Wilkes phase is Thomas Potter. His Franciscan pseudonym is unknown; the date of his death rules out his being Thomas of London. A younger son of the late archbishop of Canterbury, he was Frederick's secretary during his last years. As an MP he was a pioneer in urging a national census. The Lords threw out his Bill and there was no census till 1801. Hogarth portrayed him as the rival candidate in the Election series.

Rich, handsome, and witty, Potter was also madly extravagant and famous for his sexual adventures. One of these was the seduction of the wife of Bishop Warburton, whose writings in defense of the Christian religion excluded him from Potter's respect. He paid the price of his activities (and admitted that he was paying it) with gout, scurvy, and palsy, a "petty triumvirate" that "shook him to atoms," and he responded with alternations of cynical amusement and black morbidity. His pastimes included watching executions and copulating in graveyards. Like Whitehead he had a talent for verse, but chiefly for derivative verse, distorting others' material rather as Lewis Carroll does in "How doth the little crocodile," but (of course) obscenely. He composed dirty versions of the Psalms and—a delayed-action bomb—a pornographic parody of Pope's *Essay on Man* entitled *Essay on Woman*.

So we arrive at ten early Franciscans who are certain and identified. The most prominent are Dashwood, Whitehead, Sandwich, Potter, and Tucker. Besides these five public or semipublic figures there are five less conspicuous—Duffield, Stapleton, Clarke, Dashwood-King, and Stanhope. We also have "Thomas of London" who is probably Thompson (the doctor was a great friend of Whitehead's and was buried in Dashwood's mausoleum at West Wycombe), and two further Johns, one of whom may be D'Aubrey. Thirteen proved members, with Wilkes subsequently making a fourteenth.

But several others were reasonably sure. George Bubb Dodington himself was certainly in the secret, and almost certainly belonged. At the very least he attended as a guest. We can add three brothers, real brothers, of the Vansittart family of Shottesbrook in Berkshire, Arthur, Robert, and Henry. All were young when the Abbey started. Arthur Vansittart was a country gentleman who became an MP and vice-lieutenant of the county. Robert was a tall, thin scholar, a Fellow of All Souls. Henry, born in 1732, worked in India for the East India Company as a youth. He returned home in 1751 with substantial savings, which he ran through. In 1754 he went to India again, where he knew Clive, quarreled with him, and became governor of Bengal. A son of his was later to be president of the Bible Society, but Henry himself introduced *Kama Sutra* to England as a textbook for Medmenham.

Robert Vansittart was a friend of Whitehead and also knew Hogarth well. At Shottesbrook House there are Hogarth portraits of all three brothers painted in 1753. They depict the Vansittarts wearing blue hats like tam o' shanters, which are believed to have been part of their Franciscan regalia and have the motto "Love and Friendship" around the brim.

Another Friar who seems fairly well attested is George Selwyn, a society wit and man-about-town, who had been sent down from Oxford for ostentatiously using a communion chalice at a party: he cut his arm, let his blood drip into the chalice, and told his companions to "drink this in memory of me." Selwyn was a rabid anti-Catholic and, like Potter, a lover of executions, sometimes attending them in female disguise. He also had necrophilic leanings.

Dodington, the Vansittarts, Selwyn . . . five more. Beyond, the list of alleged brethren trails off into vagueness. We get at least thirty further names. Sometimes a link can be demonstrated, but it is hard even to guess what it amounted to in Medmenham terms. Plenty of men may have gone to the place as guests who were never members. Hogarth himself is among the may-have-beens. If he had nothing to do with the Brotherhood at all, it is strange that he should have taken the models for both his Election candidates from that quarter. Later we find him backing Dashwood in politics when this was an unpopular line to take. His role as public moralist does not accord very well with the Medmenham atmosphere, but he may have been attracted there by personal friendships (he was close to Whitehead as well as Robert Vansittart) and by artistic interests. Other artists who are credited or debited with membership are two employed by Sir Francis, Giuseppe Borgnis and Nicholas Revett.

More or less believable lists name the Lord Lyttelton already mentioned; the Earl of Orford, Horace Walpole's unbalanced nephew; Henry Lovibond Collins, another minor poet; and William Douglas, Earl of March, afterward Duke of Queensberry and known as Old Q, a notorious racing figure and womanizer and a crony of Selwyn's.

This was by no means a club of youthful rakes sowing wild oats. Most of the brethren were past thirty, and most were gentlemen of status. In some sense or other the Order was, and remains, a phenomenon to take fairly seriously. Full membership is said to have been kept to thirteen, an inner circle comprising the founder plus twelve apostles. In a few cases, such as that of D'Aubrey, we are told that somebody was never admitted to this. When a vacancy occurred in it, any of the lesser Friars could apply, and the applicant who got the most votes from the full members was elected. There must have been a turnover, and one gets the impression of a distinct second generation drifting in after 1757, which included not only Wilkes but his literary satellites Charles Churchill and Robert Lloyd, and a Dr. Benjamin Bates of Aylesbury who became Dashwood's personal physician.

The fringe members never entirely knew what went on in the inner circle, and Dr. Bates, who remained on the fringe, insisted in his old age that the wild tales about the Order were "scandalous and sarcastic fabrications." But he seems to have been the only Medmenhamite who ever did attempt a denial. None of the full members did.

RITUAL MOCKERY

Medmenham was visited by people who had no connection with it at all, and notably by Horace Walpole, though at a late date in the Order's career. His description is helpful. Only a small part of the Abbey was barred to outsiders. Two of its best rooms were reached by a staircase hung with lurid pictures and overlooked by an alabaster group of the Holy Trinity. Everywhere Sir Francis's stained glass dimmed the light. The drawing room was decorated in Roman style and furnished with ornate sofas upholstered in green damask. Adjacent was a room housing the Order's library, an array of occult and pornographic volumes, some with false bindings suggesting that they were prayer books or collections of sermons . . . though a Bible and an old book of Saints' Lives were genuine. This room also contained musical instruments and equipment for games. High on the walls were a great many small portraits—of the brethren, of their girlfriends, and of the kings of England, with a paper sticker over Henry VIII as a reproof for dissolving the monasteries.

Under the pictures ran a long row of pegs, each labeled with a brother's name and address. On these the ceremonial costumes were hung. Most of those seen by Walpole consisted of white cloaks, jackets, and trousers, and round white hats—a kind of Pierrot outfit. The blue Vansittart bonnets may have been the insignia of the inner circle, and the abbot wore a red one trimmed with rabbit's fur.

On the right of the main entrance was a refectory. At one end of it (or possibly of the drawing room, the accounts are a shade confused) was a statue of the Egyptian child-god Horus or Harpocrates as a god of silence, his finger to his lips. At the other end was a statue of Angerona, a Roman goddess with the same notion attaching to her, making the same gesture . . . like the "maid stealing to her master's bed" at West Wycombe.

Behind the tower, private cells were provided, each with a bed (a bizarre story of "wicker cradles" seems to have arisen from a misunderstanding about some old furniture, long afterward). A corridor led to a chapter room. Latin mottoes adorned the walls. Above the entrance to the chapter room was the obscure inscription *Aude, hospes, contemnere opes*—Dare, O guest, to despise wealth. Outside across the lawn was the old family chapel of the house, redecorated with lewd frescoes. Only Friars were admitted to the chapel, and only the superior ones were admitted to the chapter room.

Meetings took place twice a month, and a tremendous Annual General Meeting (AGM) went on for a week or more, allegedly around the last part of June, though most of the surviving letters hint at September. The only meetings that can be dated precisely began on Monday, September 7, 1761, and on Monday, June 21, 1762, the summer solstice. During the fraternal course of the longer gatherings, the full members took it in turns to be "Abbot of the Day" and determine the program. When the brethren dispersed, an abbot was appointed to carry on in that job for the next year; Sir Francis did not hold it in perpetuity, though he always enjoyed special honors as the founder.

When we ask point-blank what the Order did, however, we run into difficulties, owing to the pledges of secrecy and the spread of rumor. It must be stressed that there is wide scope for divergence of opinion.

To begin with the ritual, the heart of the problem lies in those restricted zones, the chapter room and chapel. The whole scheme and background of Sir Francis's conception make it clear that there was some sort of mockery of Christianity in general and popery in particular. But as to what was done by his inner circle in the chapter room, we have no safe information, and our approach has to be indirect.

The chief ceremony of the Brotherhood as a whole was the reception of a new member. So far as can be made out, it was held after dark. A bell tolled from the tower, and the secondary Friars gathered in the cloister while the abbot and the Twelve performed their secret rites in the chapter room. When these were finished, music from the chapel gave the Friars their signal to move. They advanced to the chapel two by two. The leader knocked three times on the door. Sir Francis opened it and ushered them in among the dirty pictures. He retired behind the altar rail where the rest of his apostles stood facing the incoming procession. Wax tapers gave the only light. The congregation went through a parody-Christian service concocted by Paul Whitehead and the archbishop's son Potter, and the neophyte knelt and pattered through the Creed with changes of wording that perverted the meaning. He was then admitted.

The chapel service, on these and other occasions, seems to have involved a good deal of sexual innuendo and double entendre. Sir William Stanhope, writing to Dashwood in September 1758, says he is sending some "pious books" (meaning erotica) for the Abbey, "hoping they will now and then occasion an extraordinary ejaculation to be sent up to heaven." He refers also to "that part of the Litany when I pray the Lord to strengthen them that do stand."

Thus far the procedure sounds like a joke, with less bite, if anything, than the Duke of Wharton's charades. The question is whether there was more—pagan, or actively diabolic, or both. Whitehead's biographer called the Friars "happy disciples of Venus and Bacchus." However, he meant it figuratively. No direct evidence exists that St. Francis of

Wycombe was a literal worshipper of Bacchus, and the Knapton portrait is hardly evidence in itself that he worshipped Venus.

Wilkes eventually asserted—not from firsthand knowledge, he was never in the inner circle—that the rites of the chapter room were "English Eleusinian Mysteries" and libations were poured to the *Bona Dea* or Divine Mother. Today this would savor of neo-witchcraft, its Goddess, fertility cults, and Robert Graves. So would the inner membership of thirteen, a coven.* In George II's England the anthropological theory was lacking. But any good classical scholar (and the Order could draw on such) would have had at least some inkling of the Great Mother with her many shapes and aspects, and sacred orgies and seedtime-and-harvest rites. The main ceremonies of Eleusis were held in mid-September, a time that agrees fairly well with the several indications of important meetings in September . . . including that possible pre-Medmenham one in 1750.

Hence, even the Knapton portrait may be a clue. Anyone with Sir Francis's sexual energies and odd humor might easily have progressed from a comic pose of Venus worship to a ritual centered on a female divinity—however spurious, however synthetic, however debased with occultish hocus-pocus. The first twenty lines of Lucretius would have been hint enough, and every gentleman got at least that far into Lucretius. Or Dashwood could have drawn on more detailed ideas about the Goddess worshipped at Eleusis and elsewhere in Apuleius's *Golden Ass,* a classic Roman tale of witchcraft and mystical religion, improper enough in places to suit Medmenham. A print published in 1763, purporting to blow the gaff, does show Dashwood and Whitehead in their holy of holies with a female image on the altar extremely naked, a book of "evening prayers" open nearby, and "Hymns by Ovid" (author of *The Art of Love*) on the floor.

---

*Believers in Margaret Murray's extension of the witch cult into a history of "divine kingship" and ritually slain English royalties may also care to speculate about the link with Prince Frederick, and the fact that Dr. Thompson, a probable Friar, was accused of causing his patients' death and attended the prince in his fatal illness.

Devil worship, in the chapter room or the chapel, is another matter. Here the confusion between Medmenham and the true Hell-Fire Club has probably helped to foster a legend. The morbid or puerile anti-Christianity that goes in for Black Masses and deliberate evil seems foreign to the Medmenham kind, and there is no hint of it in the more trustworthy materials. Members of a society that carried on where the Dilettanti left off may well have dabbled in Italianate sorcery and may have done so in the free milieu of the Abbey. It is not likely, however, to have been part of the official program. Lurid descriptions published many years later—notably by Nathaniel Wraxall in 1815—speak of "black baptisms, the sprinkling of salt and sulphur, inverted crucifies, black tapers, blood-red triangular wafers" . . . but this is hearsay.

Only a single detail is at all specific, and its meaning has been buried under discrepant anecdotes. The common factor in every version is a baboon. Henry Vansittart brought or sent it from India, and his brother Robert presented it to the Order as a chaplain, a Sandwich-type jest. We are told that Sir Francis gave it the Eucharist, a singularly futile gesture where no priest was present to consecrate the Host. But the whole topic has been bedeviled—in more senses than one—by a later fantasy that must be deferred to its proper place. The tradition of an outright satanic cult, as distinct from occasional Hell-raising seances that may have been staged for fun, has no solid basis but this dimly descried monkey. Though the local people gossiped about the Abbey, they noticed nothing sinister. It never acquired the somber and haunted atmosphere that clings to some of the Hell-Fire sites in Ireland.

What these neighbors did notice is more significant. It was a periodic importation of women and wine; in Horace Walpole's words, "nymphs and hogsheads." The feasting needs little comment—"Epicurean and Ambrosial Banquets at Medmenham," as one participant put it, "beneath a vast canopy under which a refectory table glistens with sparkling silver and the crystalline purity of fine glass; the food of a most exquisite kind and in *gargantuan* portions." A Latin grace was recited first, and they drank (perhaps) from human skulls. Whitehead, as steward, saw to the wine. The cellar-book pages attest to their vast appetite for claret and port.

WOMEN OF THE ABBEY

The wenching is the part of their revelry that is least in dispute, and yet, in a way, it remains the most mysterious. Of course there was nothing novel in a piquant association of sex with monastic forms and ceremonies. The Duc de Richelieu (that recurrent example) had pictures painted of three of his mistresses in religious habits, and sometimes met them dressed as a monk himself. Sir Francis's two "Franciscan" portraits repeat that motif. At Medmenham the orgy partners presented themselves in some sort of religious costume, though they did not keep it on all the evening. In a poem by Charles Churchill, who was there, is the couplet:

> *Whilst Womanhood in habit of a nun*
> *At Medmenham lies, by backward monks undone.*

The Abbot of the Day had first choice. So far as can be made out, the spirit of the Order was heterosexual and normal. Probably the orgies included group action on *Fanny Hill* lines, but each full member could take his playmate to his own private cell and there do what he would. Tradition speaks of pleasure boats, in particular a gondola, and of outlying retreats on secluded Thames islands and stretches of the bank. A hostile author alludes vaguely to "lasciviousness for which proper objects were provided." However, the sole piece of apparatus attested in plain terms is the *idolum tentiginis,* a sort of hobby-horse so that a woman bestriding it could stimulate herself while bouncing around.

But who were the women? Did they count as nuns?

Reports differ. One says they were simply prostitutes ordered from London brothels. This can scarcely be the whole truth, if only because a prostitute would not be "undone." Another speaks of invitations to local women, both single and married. Another asserts that each Friar was allowed to bring "a lady of a cheerful, lively disposition, to improve the general hilarity." Women are stated to have arrived at the Abbey wearing masks, as if afraid of recognition, and to have unmasked only when the whole company was present and seen to be safe. The inference is that they were ladies of fashion. Guests in this class are said to have joined the Order and paired off with the Friars as "wives" during their stay. The same version adds that medical services were provided—a doctor and a midwife, one or both of them perhaps an abortionist—and that the offspring, when offspring came, were reared to be Abbey servants. Such a long-term plan is hard to credit. The Abbey never had a domestic staff, only a resident housekeeper, according to Walpole, plus a gardener. Most of the servants needed for meetings were hired by the day.

Yet in spite of dubious aspects, the idea of the Nuns of Medmenham persists. Edward Thompson, Whitehead's biographer, mentions nuns in his memoir of the poet; and as this was dedicated to Sir Francis and therefore, one presumes, more or less acceptable to him, the word must mean something. There is also a letter from Dashwood-King sending his excuse for not attending a meeting ("paying our adoration" is how he puts it) and wishing "the present standard of Mirth to the Sisterhood." This letter belongs to a very late time in the Order's history, September 1770. Still, it names a Sister—"Curtois Novice"— and in other, though less authoritative contexts, names are named for earlier phases.

Among the supposed nuns are two of Dashwood's reputed mistresses and his half sister Mary Walcott, whom he seems to have brought into the Divan Club also as the Sultana Walcotonia. Lady Mary Wortley Montagu, though past sixty, is said to have been admitted in token of friendship with the founder. As she lived abroad during the 1750s, her membership, as we might infer on more obvious grounds, can only have been honorary. Lady Betty Germain is mentioned; her other title to history's regard (again that weird linkage) is that she claimed to possess a scrying stone of Dee's, the one that Walpole eventually acquired. Slightly better defined is the delectable Fanny Murray. She was the daughter of a musician in Bath and began life as a flower seller, but soon became the mistress of Beau Nash, Lord Sandwich, etc. Sandwich could have introduced her to Medmenham. Potter's salacious *Essay on Woman* was addressed to her.

A circumstantial yet puzzling nun is Agnes Perrault, an Englishwoman who subsequently married a Frenchman and left the country. Her maiden surname is unknown, and her baptismal name was apparently Mary. Perrault family tradition relates that she worked for the bookseller Coustance who took over some of Curll's business, and that Whitehead inducted her at Medmenham as "Sister" or "Saint" Agnes. A poem of his refers to her in passing. She became a kind of hostess, exempt from the women's normal function, and she may have been the midwife.

Finally, Thomas Langley, a historian of the district who died in 1801, interviewed the Medmenham housekeeper in her old age and unfortunately decided that the Order's affairs "might as well be buried in oblivion." Whether this lady belonged herself is not stated. However, Langley elsewhere mentions a Mrs. Edgerley in the neighborhood in 1748–49, the "fine London wife of Richard Edgerley"; and a battered diary kept by a local tailor, discovered and deciphered long afterward, shows that in 1751 or 1754 a Sophia Edgerley "reported to Lady Mary for a situation at the Abbey." The same diary mentions eight ladies' white habits "made to original design" as delivered there. Lady Mary could have been any of several women in Dashwood's circle able to help on the domestic side. Sophia Edgerley herself, possibly, got the situation and was the housekeeper throughout. If she was no ordinary servant but a "fine London wife," she may have taken part in the activities.

Nothing, however, gives the slightest hint of sexual equality. Even if nuns were recognized and received, they were neither first-class nor even second-class members. They were companions for the Friars.

TRENDSETTERS AND IMITATORS

Had Sir Francis any deeper purpose in all this?

Nobody knows. His position as founder and superior, whoever held the post of abbot, gave him a leadership of sorts in the remnant of the opposition. With all the secrecy it was easy to suspect a cover for political scheming, and as time went on, some outsiders probably did. The author of that essay in pedantic indecency *The Fruit-Shop*, published in the 1760s and already mentioned, wrote darkly of "the majority of a certain club that assemble in a house not far from the banks of the Thames, and who have acquired to themselves an universal notoriety (we leave our readers to settle in what sense) for some late proceedings, wherein they let out their understandings, to be the venal and prostituted tools of a single man's ambitious machinations." Even here, though, the implication is that the Order went through a political phase rather than that it was always covertly political; and as will appear, the phase can be identified and the "single man" is probably not Dashwood.

Far from being crypto-parliamentary, the Order's style modified the one major parliamentarian who was connected with it, George Bubb Dodington. During the first years of its existence, with his prince gone and his hopes ebbing, Dodington was devoting much care and money to a villa that he built, or rather remodeled, on the curve of the river below the present Hammersmith Bridge. He employed an Italian designer recommended by the great art patron Cardinal Albani and gave the villa a stucco front and a balustrade and a pillared temple of Venus as a summerhouse and bathing hut. A pattern of white pebbles on the sloping lawn formed a bugle, his family crest. Inside he had a marble chimney piece with sham icicles hanging down, urns and inlaid floors and huge garish frescoes. In opulent rooms the eye encountered gilt leather, tapestries, antiques. His own bedroom—which was much ridiculed—was predominantly purple, with a purple and orange bedspread and a huge sheaf of peacock feathers above. Beside it lay his rug made of old waistcoats. He also had a sculpture gallery 85 feet long, its roof supported by 17-foot pillars of Italian porphyry that were polished under his proud supervision at Ponders End. Besides its statues this gallery had a marble floor . . . yet it was upstairs. When Bubb showed it to the Duke of York, he remarked that some visitors had told him the gallery ought to be on the ground floor. "There is no need to worry, Mr. Dodington," the duke replied. "It soon will be."

Here Bubb held court as at Eastbury, entertaining his literary friends and Dashwood's Franciscans. His wife (so obscure, it is a jolt to come across her at all) hovered on the fringes. But the most interesting thing about this villa is the new name he gave it. From March 1753 onward, as we know from his diary, he was calling it La Trappe in allusion to the parent house of the Trappists; and also, jocosely, "my convent." Dr. Thompson and two other resident companions were his "monks." Even religious costume is hinted at. For the moment, Sir Francis was setting the pace and Bubb was following.

9

THE FAVORITE
AND THE MAVERICK

FRESH MEAT

For several years, grotesquely enough, the opposition's main rendezvous, so far as it had one, was Medmenham. At first—one must stress again—this did not mean much. Dodington's diary underlines the unlikelihood of any serious political purpose. It shows him in frequent contact with Sir Francis in London, where they dined at each other's town houses. If the meetings of the Order had been important politically, he would have gone to them as well, and often. The diary gives no evidence that he did. Admittedly many entries are curt, leaving most of the day unaccounted for. We can fit in unmentioned flying visits to Medmenham, if we care to, and longer ones in the years from October 1754 to October 1760, which the diary does not cover in detail. But this would be guesswork. For the period that it does cover, the guilty-looking breaks when Sir Francis is in the offing are very few. In August 1755, when Bubb reverted for a time to fuller coverage, we get another gap of the same kind. However, there is no positive trace of active membership.

The explanation is ready at hand. At sixty-odd he was getting too old, and too fat, for Sir Francis's kind of fun. Political intrigue would have been the only strong motive to bring him. For part of this time, admittedly, he was veering away from opposition and cherishing hopes of creeping back into office, but never so resolutely as to break with his comrades. If he did not go to Medmenham often, it was because hardly any politics happened there. What did happen was the ritual comedy, which didn't amuse him; the banqueting and drinking, which he could get elsewhere; and the wenching, which he was nearly past, and had never been enthusiastic about. Once when he found himself alone with a Mrs. Strawbridge in her boudoir, he shied away from the impending "conjuncture" and exclaimed: "If only I had you in a wood!" To which she replied: "And what would you do—rob me?"

Medmenham in the earlier years was a freakish remnant of Frederick's shadow court, without the prince. Yet if it was not an active political center, the main reason was not necessarily that the will was lacking—rather, that very little activity was going on anywhere. English politics had settled into an aimless lull. Bolingbroke's death within a few months of Frederick's deprived the opposition of its theorist as well as its titular leader. For the moment there was nothing to theorize about and no one to lead.

Politics had not essentially altered for thirty years. A clique of veterans still clung to power. The king was old, as were his chief ministers, but no replacements were in sight. Frederick's son Prince George, the new heir apparent, was a mediocre boy in his mid-teens. An early succession would mean an unpredictable regency. The Jacobite alternative was at last fading out. Meanwhile, thanks to Sir Robert Walpole's jealousy of junior talent during his long rule, few politicians under sixty were anywhere near the top. William Pitt, Henry Fox, George Grenville were untried figures with doubtful prospects.

Only one personage was left for an opposition to cultivate: Princess Augusta, Frederick's widow, mother of the heir apparent. She lived at Carlton House, and Dodington called on her assiduously. He kept an anxious eye on her health. And presently the lull ended, with portentous results for Sir Francis and his fellowship.

In 1756, Prince George being eighteen, his grandfather the king set him up in an establishment of his own. Augusta hovered near, supervising his life. To Dodington, Dashwood, and all their set, a new vista opened up. George was still young enough to influence, yet he was also likely to succeed to the throne quite soon, and with a potent advantage to start him off. Unlike George I and II, he was English-born. He would shed the foreign taint that had clung to the House of Hanover for so long.

Once again Bolingbroke's Patriot King seemed a possibility. If Prince George could be made to realize his duty, and the power that the Crown still had, he might do what the Duke of Wharton had been the first to demand. He might restore what the opposition insisted was the true Constitution. He might break the grip of the Whig oligarchy, end corruption and placemanship, deliver Parliament from the grandees and manipulators, and govern his people with equal hand through ministers of different parties and no party. In other words he might restore public Liberty, as the Medmenhamites conceived it. That meant, in practice, a sharing out of power among the well-off in general instead of a few dominant families. But some of the benefits would trickle down to the populace, through (for example) peace, instead of the wars that the commercial magnates promoted.

Even apart from such speculation, the middle 1750s were marked by a feeling that the Crown was getting quietly stronger, that its potentialities were growing. Parliamentarians and lawyers debated the meaning of the "royal prerogative." Horace Walpole expressed a fear that if a king ever reigned who knew how to exploit his position, the result might be dangerous. Such a reign, however, was what the Medmenhamites hoped for. Influences began working that were to hoist them into key places in politics, under one of the strangest premierships in English history.

THE SCOTTISH FRIAR

Close to young George was a man whom Dashwood and his friends began to see as their hope. He was an enigmatic Scot, forty-three years old, who had belonged, like them, to the entourage of the late Prince of Wales:

John Stuart, third Earl of Bute (at that time unfortunately pronounced "boot"), who traced his descent to a bastard of King Robert II. The family seat was on the island from which he took his title, and which was then cut off from the mainstream of Scottish life, with a scanty, Gaelic-speaking population. Lord Bute counted as a highlander.

His early career, so far as anybody knew, had been less than remarkable. Coming south in the 1730s, he married a daughter of Lady Mary Wortley Montagu (who disapproved but was reconciled later) and lived for a while at Twickenham. Apart from an obscure term as one of the squad of peers representing Scotland at Westminster, he remained null, and—for a major landowner—poor.

Bute's annexation by Frederick had been a pure accident. In 1747 the prince went to a race meeting at Egham. Rain began to fall, and he took shelter in a tent. Bute was invited into the tent to make a fourth at whist, for no better reason than that he was a gentleman of rank and happened to be nearby. It transpired that he hadn't even come to the races in his own coach; he didn't possess one; he had accepted a lift from a friend. After the meeting the friend and coach were nowhere in sight. The prince invited Bute to Cliveden. He became a more and more frequent guest. He was tall and handsome, with well-shaped legs that he liked to display, and a stagy manner. Soon he rose to stardom in Frederick's amateur theatricals. It was some time before he received a paid post. However, on September 30, 1750, he was appointed lord of the bedchamber.

Dodington and Dashwood met him, of course, during their attendance at the prince's houses. But in those days he made no deep impression . . . except in one quarter. The prince himself never rated his lord of the bedchamber very high. "Bute," he once remarked, "is a fine showy man. He would make an excellent ambassador in a court where there was no business." Augusta's response to Bute was warmer. Much warmer. After she became widowed she was reputed to be his mistress.

They were either lovers or most indiscreet. To judge from a quip that London society was to relish for years, their affair had already progressed past flirtation in her husband's lifetime. Augusta went to a fancy dress ball accompanied by a maid of honor, Elizabeth Chudleigh. Elizabeth, an adroit picker-up of rich men, appeared among the guests wearing a see-through shift, a wreath of roses, and nothing else. She explained that she was meant to be Iphigenia, who was offered up as a human sacrifice, and doubtless disrobed first. Augusta insisted on draping a cloak around her, but remonstrance was worse than futile. Elizabeth said, in several people's hearing, *"Votre altesse royale sait que chacume a son but"*—"Your royal highness is aware that every woman has her aim" or "Bute"; the pun, of course, is lost in English.*

Augusta's liaison, as more and more observers assumed it to be, developed steadily. Bute was often at the widowed princess's house on long private calls. As her son George grew up, he too became involved in the relationship. Slow, rather stupid (he could not read till he was eleven), but with a touching capacity for devotion, he hero-worshipped his mother's tall companion. As the memory of the prince receded, Bute blossomed into a father figure easier to admire than the real father. He possessed the charm, fluency, and ease that the awkward boy felt himself to lack.

So in 1756, when George was set up at Leicester House, he demanded that Lord Bute should be his groom of the stole—chief officer of the household. The king disliked the idea. His grandson was firm, and he gave way, but with a bad grace. He refused to speak to Bute or hand him his key of office in person. A courtier had to slip it into the Scotsman's pocket. The young prince, however, was certain that he needed this adored mentor beside him, to guide and instruct. He could not do without Bute.

Nobody could predict the length of this infatuation, but everybody close to George and Augusta knew it was a fact. Something happened, something now unfathomable. The Scottish favorite, who was already

---

*The sprightly Miss Chudleigh attained her own *but.* She married the Earl of Bristol, secretly, and then married the Duke of Kingston, publicly. The duke gave the earl an enormous bribe to keep quiet, but his duchess was tried for bigamy by the House of Lords and had to leave England. Subsequent lovers maintained her in happy affluence.

visibly molding the next reign, got drawn or steered or pushed into an understanding with the Medmenhamites.

Did he join the Order? According to rumor, yes. He could be the otherwise hard-to-identify "John of London" who appears once in the cellar-book pages. Proof is lacking. If the Order did originate in charades at Cliveden, hazy recollections of Bute's taking part might account for a belief in his actual membership. In the light of the sequel it is safe to speak of a connection, opening a path for backstairs influence and eventual blackmail. It is unwise to do more than guess at the precise nature of the link.

Prince George's education was already a matter of direct concern to the brethren. Dodington had ventured to discuss it with the princess, who complained that while her son was most honest, she "wished he were less childish." Appropriate tutors had been brought in, one of them recommended by Bolingbroke himself. Now the process took a more clearly tendentious turn. Bute was not a party man, and while he taught George respect for 1688 and Whig constitutionalism, he also taught that the constitutional sovereign should be above party. Under his tutelage George struggled with *The Idea of a Patriot King.* Bute also borrowed part of the manuscript of Blackstone's *Commentaries on the Laws of England,* giving his pupil a preview of some rather proroyalist doctrines that that eminent lawyer planned to publish. George was persuaded, with little difficulty, to picture his grandfather as under the thumb of usurping Whig bosses whom it would be his duty to curb when he took over.

Meanwhile Bute continued going to Augusta at Carlton House. He did this in the evenings, usually in a borrowed sedan chair with the curtains drawn. If his object was to preserve incognito and prevent scandal, he could hardly have acted more absurdly. Everybody knew who was in the curtained sedan and took it for granted he had something to hide. Generally, moreover, the chair and its carriers were provided by one of the Carlton House ladies. She was a Miss Vansittart. Three Vansittarts, it will be recalled, belonged to the Medmenham Brotherhood.

POLITICAL PERSUASION

The Seven Years War had broken out. From the British viewpoint it was mainly a colonial struggle with France. In American history it is the French and Indian War. But the royal tie with Hanover meant a Continental commitment. England's ally was Frederick the Great of Prussia, whose aggressions had turned the French against him. King Frederick was also fighting the Austrians, Swedes, and Russians, an alarming coalition that made him expensive to maintain. However, the conflict with France was judged to serve British interests.

The government that declared war was headed by the Duke of Newcastle. The Medmenham brethren, at first, rallied round. One or two were temporarily in office again if not in very important posts— even Dodington. He had recovered from his mishap with the Returning Officer and was treasurer of the navy. Augusta regarded his acceptance of the job as a betrayal. But in 1756 Dodington's wife was dead and his villa finished. His political pursuits kept him going.

When he and Dashwood split off from the wartime Ministry and reverted to opposition, the reason was dramatic and creditable. In April 1756 the French had attacked Minorca, then held by a British garrison. The commander of the expedition was (of all people) the Duc de Richelieu, still flourishing three decades after his Viennese sorceries. In spite of his amusements he was among the best generals the French had. His troops overran most of the island and besieged the garrison in a fortress. Admiral John Byng sailed up with a British squadron and reinforcements, to raise the siege. He judged his force to be too small for the task, and after an indecisive clash with the French fleet, withdrew to Gibraltar. Minorca fell.

Byng had acted correctly to cut losses. Public opinion, however, was inflamed by the defeat. The Government wanted a scapegoat, and it court-martialed the admiral. When Richelieu heard he was horrified. He had gone home in lighthearted triumph to characteristic celebrations, including a concert of honor at which a chorus of society ladies begged him to "sweep their chimneys"; but the news of his opponent's court-martial sobered him instantly. With the aid of Voltaire he composed a true account of the battle showing that Byng was not to blame and sent it to the president of the court.

This enemy backing was hardly helpful to the tormented admiral. But Richelieu's English counterparts at their Thames-side Thélème were also aroused. The trial revealed that the Whig chieftains, whom they had sniped at for so long without deep convictions, actually were hateful. Sudden confrontation with a genuine and tragic issue was a novel experience, quite out of their line.

Sir Francis adapted to it. He led a protest. On February 23, 1757, he raised the question of Byng in the House of Commons. His reception was icy. Together with Horace Walpole (now taking parliamentary membership more seriously) he persisted. So did Dodington, in a speech that Walpole—who loathed him—described as bold and pathetic, at the cost of the office he had so lately regained. Paul Whitehead contributed a pamphlet.

The court cleared Byng of the charge of cowardice, and although it found him guilty of neglect of duty, it entered a unanimous plea for mercy. George II, however, on his ministers' advice, refused a pardon. On March 14 the admiral was shot by a firing squad at Portsmouth, *pour encourager les autres,* in Voltaire's phrase. The governor of Gibraltar—Thomas Fowke, a brother of Martha—was dragged down with him, though not shot.

A month later the Ministry was reshuffled. William Pitt rose to power. His popular leadership turned the tide. Clive won victories in India. Wolfe took Quebec. Hawke shattered a French fleet, assembled for an invasion of England, in Quiberon Bay. Out of office, Dodington was willing to applaud the triumphs of British forces. As to their political masters, he inclined toward the "lions led by donkeys" assessment familiar in the twentieth century. Pitt he regarded as a "ranting buskineer." In a letter to Lord Talbot he wrote:

When indeed I figure to myself Mr. Hawke surrounded by all the terrors a tempestuous sea and approaching darkness can present to the view or press upon the mind: outrunning half his gallant squadron and crowding every sail to rush upon an enemy equal to his whole force, in a bay to which he was an utter stranger, to save the noblest province of Europe—I am not only dazzled, but I am exalted, I am transported with the heroic behaviour of my country-men; but I am not so much transported with those who left that noblest province so expos'd and defenceless that nothing less than that heroic behaviour could have sav'd it.*

After the Quiberon victory, he argued, all British war aims had been achieved. To press on was to incur colossal and criminal expense for the greater glory of Prussia.

So now, apart from all dreaming about Patriot Kings, he and his Franciscan colleagues had a policy: to campaign for peace. And all the time Lord Bute was moving stealthily to and fro, conferring with them at intervals, pulling wires and making contacts.

NEW RECRUITS

Meanwhile the Order had attracted a new member who brought in others, with results that complicated the situation.

By the later 1750s a change had set in. Some of the senior brethren were losing interest and were being replaced by a fresh intake. To this phase, if to any, belongs the reputed membership of Benjamin Franklin. He sounds a surprising person to meet in this setting, but he was more anticlerical, heavier in his drinking, and laxer in his sexual habits and outlook than American hagiography cares to admit. Dodington's pamphleteer James Ralph was a former comrade of his and accompanied him on his first trip to England. Later in the life of Dashwood we encounter Franklin on close and admiring terms with him and staying as his guest at West Wycombe. It was in 1757, however, that Franklin

_____
*Brecht's Mother Courage voices similar thoughts.

made his second visit to England, which lasted five years; the Dashwood connection could have begun then, and the story of his admission to Medmenham has not been refuted.

But the seeds of trouble were sown by a better-attested and very different recruit, in legend the most notorious Medmenhamite of all. John Wilkes was to be the icebreaker of politics, the man who finally succeeded in changing the pattern. It is fitting to find him among the Dashwood Franciscans at the outset of his career, and in a sense they launched him, though the blow was not struck as they intended.

Conspicuous for wit, ugliness, political flair, journalistic verve, disreputability, and scorn for religion, Wilkes was the test case: the man who would make libertinism and liberty go together if anyone could. He had not yet developed when he joined the Brotherhood, which he did in 1758. His sponsor was Thomas Potter.

The background was a shady electoral bargain. Wilkes already belonged to various clubs (the Beefsteaks among them), and through his diversions he met Potter, who introduced him to Richard Grenville, Lord Temple, William Pitt's powerful brother-in-law. Under the Temple aegis Wilkes contested Berwick in the election of 1754. He tried hard in the approved style, bribing a ship's captain, who was bringing some of his opponent's supporters from London, to land them in Norway by mistake. Though defeated, he made his mark, and in the same election Potter became MP for Aylesbury, Wilkes's hometown. Three years later Potter arranged a deal with Pitt for a musical-chairs arrangement enabling Wilkes to take over Aylesbury. He still had to be elected, and the election cost him £7,000. Most of this he borrowed, hanging a load of debt round his neck that stayed with him for a long time.

To the oversexed Potter he was congenial. Furthermore he could be useful in Parliament when the hour struck, and his need for money supplied a hold over him. Accordingly he was introduced to Dashwood. They got on well. Sir Francis, who was colonel of the Buckinghamshire Militia, made Aylesbury's new MP his lieutenant-colonel. In due course Wilkes was enrolled at the Abbey as "John of Aylesbury."

For a while at least he threw himself into it. The cellar-book fragments record his name more often than anybody else's. In 1760 he was present and consuming wine for his "private devotion" on August 28, September 4, and September 5. He composed a comic epistle in Latin verse to his "Father in religion," praying in the chapel of Medmenham, cracking jokes, and presiding over tipsy excursions on the river. One of his letters to Lord Temple mentions coming "from Medmenham Abbey, where the jovial monks of St. Francis had kept me up till four in the morning."* Somewhere along the line he may have taken over part of Whitehead's secretarial duties. That construction could be put on a letter to him from a Mr. Hall, at a Berkeley Square address. Preserved at West Wycombe, it is dated August 31, 1761—a Monday—and apologizes for nonattendance at a meeting that we know from another letter to have been scheduled for the following Monday.

> Mr. Hall presents his compliments to Mr. Wilkes and is still under the scourge of an invincible Cholick which has reduced him to such a state of Contrition that he is obliged to live by rules entirely opposite to those of St. Francis, whose shrine he venerates, but dare not approach under his present Incapacity, he desires ye prayers of ye congregation and hopes their Devotion may be attended with the choicest blessings of their Patron, Health Wealth and never failing vigour. . . .

This "Mr. Hall" is apparently John Hall-Stevenson, whose main entry into the story comes later.

Although he may have helped as a convener, Wilkes formed a low opinion of most of the Friars. To Dashwood himself he conceded "imagination" and "very real mental abilities." Potter of course was

---

*This letter has one incidental point of interest. Dated October 5, 1762, it assumes that Temple knows of the Abbey and its junketings. Since he was not a member, there cannot by then have been much secrecy about the Order's existence. The secrecy was confined to aspects that went beyond simple conviviality.

a valued colleague, especially in the pursuit of women, and they collaborated on scurrilous verses. But Potter's diseases caught up with him. By November 1758 he was on a milk diet, and in June 1759 he died. Wilkes did not care so much for the others. He fraternized, but he never entered the inner circle and perhaps never wanted to, though legend avers that he applied and was voted down. Nevertheless he was observant of all that went on, he had a good memory, and, for political reasons, he finally dropped all pretence of keeping quiet. The result is that his letters and other writings tell us far more about Medmenham than we ever learn from its full initiates.

His description of the house and grounds, as they were in the early 1760s, has been widely quoted. Though written after he turned against the Order, it can almost certainly be relied on. He published it at a time of stress when he would hardly have troubled to invent anything so elaborate. Also, Edward Thompson quotes it at length in his life of Whitehead dedicated to Dashwood and would surely not have done so if it were false.

After mentioning the closed chapter room with its "English Eleusinian Mysteries," and the Rabelaisian motto and images of gods in the refectory, Wilkes ranges outdoors, giving unique glimpses of what the Orders' years of occupation had done to the innocent estate.

> The garden, the grove, the orchard, the neighbouring woods, all spoke the loves and frailties of the younger monks, who seemed at least to have sinned naturally.

Nature again! He quotes French and Latin notices commemorating sexual encounters on various spots. Here as at West Wycombe Sir Francis displayed his tastes:

> At the entrance of a cave was Venus, stooping to pull a thorn out of her foot. The statue turned from you, and just over the two nether hills of snow were these lines of Virgil:

Hie locus est, partes ubi se via findit in ambas:
Hae iter Elysium nobis: at laeva malorum
Exercet poenas, et ad impia Tartara mittit.

The gist of this context (not in Virgil's) is that entry by the wrong route is to be discountenanced. Inside the cave was a "mossy couch" with further Latin lines to encourage the occupants.

Wilkes goes on:

The favourite doctrine of the Abbey was certainly not *penitence;* for in the center of the orchard was a very grotesque figure, *and in his hand a reed stood flaming, tipt with fire,* to use Milton's words, and you might trace out,

PENITENTO

non

PENITENTI

Which has been translated "a penis tense rather than penitence." There is more about the phallic statue:

On the pedestal was a whimsical representation of Trophonius's cave, from whence all creatures were said to come out melancholy. Among the strange, dismal group, you might, however, remark a cock crowing and a Carmelite laughing. The words—*gallum gallinaceum et sacerdotem gratis*—were only legible.

This is an involved misapplication of legend on much the same line as the Virgil text. Trophonius, a minor Greek god supposed to have built the temple at Delphi, had an oracle of his own in another part of Greece. It was in a cave and was so awe inspiring that pilgrims who went in to consult it never smiled again. To this legend the sculptor has applied a Latin saying on a different topic: *Omne animal post coitum triste est, praeter gallum gallinaceum et sacerdotem gratis fornicantem*—Every creature is melancholy after sexual intercourse except a barnyard cock and a priest getting it for nothing. Which gives the "cave" a Freudian meaning. It is interesting that the inscription was so worn. Was this object a ribald antique that Sir Francis had acquired somewhere else and reerected at Medmenham?

Also in the grounds, Wilkes mentions a Temple of Cloacina (i.e., an elegant classic privy). The inscription ran: "This chapel of ease was founded in the year 1760." Again the double entendre—a chapel of ease being, properly, a chapel auxiliary to a church and at some distance away, for parishioners who cannot get to the church. The date 1760 shows that improvements to the Abbey were still going on at a late phase.

It was probably Wilkes who brought in Dr. Benjamin Bates, since the doctor was an Aylesbury neighbor of his. Bates seems to have been a naive character who never quite grasped what it was all about, but he struck up an enduring friendship with Dashwood. A more important Wilkes satellite was the uncouth clergyman-poet Charles Churchill. This formidable man, pushed by his father into the Anglican ministry with no vocation, had been a country curate at South Cadbury in Somerset. There he began to compose the rambling, unequal metrical satires that give him whatever reputation he has. His heart was in literature and the theater. His father's death in 1758 enabled him to live in London, write, and raise his income to more or less the level he needed by teaching at a girls' school and producing a popular satire against actors. Neglecting the ecclesiastical duties he still had, he went about wearing a gold-laced hat, a blue coat, white silk stockings, and silver-buckled shoes.

Churchill was massive, muscular, ungainly, and crude; Hogarth caricatured him as a bear with a tankard. He appeared to be well qualified for the Abbey. Besides having strong and normal lusts (he wrote an entire long poem, "The Times," attacking homosexuality; Wilkes praised it highly), he endorsed—in theory—the Patriot King idea. If he preferred beer to wine, at least he had no alcoholic inhibitions. He joined the Order, or at any rate began attending as a visitor, in 1762.

Though Wilkes was responsible, they were not yet more than acquaintances. The first extant letter from Wilkes to Churchill starts, "My dear Sir"; is dated Tuesday, June 15, 1762; and says, "next Monday we meet at Medmenham." After that summer solstice meeting (which temporarily reduced the ex-curate to a hangover diet of tea, bread, and "cooling fruit") the letters start "My dear Churchill." Clearly the Brotherhood itself brought them closer than they might otherwise have come.

Churchill in his turn attracted another literary member, a former schoolfellow at Westminster named Robert Lloyd. Lloyd had been a bright scholar, but had drifted dismally into teaching and the composition of petty, self-pitying verse. Wilkes described him as "scampering round the foot of Parnassus on his little Welsh pony, which seems never to have tired." He gave up teaching and plunged into journalism without success, amiably insisting as he sank lower that it was better than being an usher. Churchill introduced him to nightlife, paid his debts for him, and brought him along to Medmenham, where he was doubtless recommended by the fact that he had gone on record, if fleetingly, in defense of Byng.

Other new recruits seem to have been joining the Order, or at any rate hovering, about this time. Wilkes's Mr. Hall is not known before, and West Wycombe has a letter dated Thursday, September 3, 1761, from a gentleman who has clearly applied for membership:

My Dear Sir,
This day I received your card, and am to request the Favour of you to present my most humble respects to the whole chapter of Medmenham, and to assure them of the high sense I have of the Honour they intended me which I earnestly long'd for—Nothing therefore but the most unavoidable Business would prevent my waiting upon them next Monday. I hope they will remember me in their prayers and that you will do me the Justice to believe Me Entirely
& Devotedly
J. Luttrell.

The Wilkite newcomers, if not Messrs. Hall and Luttrell, were still fairly young—all under thirty-five. Sir Francis Dashwood was past fifty. A generation gap divided the Brotherhood. Presently Wilkes noticed that the founder himself was not as regular in attendance as he had once been. Since Wilkes's entry, public events had not stood still, and the position of Dashwood and his friends had altered substantially.

10

THE HELL-FIRE MINISTRY

FAVORS FOR THE FRIARS

On October 25, 1760, between 7 and 8 a.m., the king overstrained himself in the lavatory and died. His twenty-two-year-old grandson became
George III. Lord Bute was still, on the face of it, a political cipher. But
in one circle at least they already knew who was going to be on top. As
soon as news of the accession reached Dodington at Eastbury, he sat
down and wrote to Bute asking for a job . . . or could it be a peerage?
He wanted both.

> Whatever favour, therefore, your Lordship shall think me worthy
> to receive, or becoming the Crown to bestow, I shall acknowledge
> with great reverence and respect to the hands it comes from, and the
> most sincere gratitude for your Lordship's favourable and efficient
> good offices.

This, to a man who was technically no more than a palace functionary.
Bubb had inside information.

On the twenty-eighth he left for London. Though no "favors"
came his way during the first weeks, he was not disappointed. George
received him kindly, and he plunged into consultations about organizing Commons support for the impending new government. Just before
Christmas he wrote to Bute again, nerving him up for his task as the

sovereign's servant who would make the Patriot King program feasible, when he was still not supposed to have any power at all:

> Remember, my noble and generous friend, that to recover Monarchy from the inveterate Usurpation of Oligarchy, is a Point too arduous and important, to be atchiev'd, without much Difficulty and some Degree of Danger, tho' None, but what attentive Moderation, & unalterable Firmness, will certainly surmount.

George had learned his lessons and seemed willing to play the role assigned him. His mother and her fine gentleman had taught him to dread and detest the ministers he inherited. Even Pitt, the architect of victory, was in George's eyes "the blackest of hearts." He prepared to reallocate offices on a fresh plan, and his complete dependence on Bute made the Scotsman the only possible person to effect the change— precisely how, they would have to decide as they went along.

The new king started out with at least two assets. At last the House of Hanover had a sovereign who was not foreign. George—as he assured Parliament—"gloried in the name of Briton." Also, if not glamorous, he was young. The effect was spoilt a little by early mishaps and ill-judged actions. Augusta caused some annoyance by demanding the title "Princess Mother," which, in the absence of a precedent, was denied her. At the coronation the Lord Steward, Lord Talbot, rode into the hall on a horse that he had trained so carefully to back *away* from the king that it refused to advance, and backed *toward* him rump forward, amid applause. And when George, pressed by a sense of dynastic duty, looked around for a consort, he picked up yet another German princess and an unprepossessing one, Charlotte of Mecklenburg-Strelitz.

Yet all might have gone well if Bute had been the man for the task. After the long consolidation of Whig vested interests, the task, as Dodington had warned, was a big one requiring a big leader. Precisely because of the backstairs habits that had given him his influence, Bute was unfit to step into the open. He never spoke in the House of Lords, he was little known, he was not much liked. Horace Walpole sneered—not entirely unfairly—that his chief confidants were "Sir Henry Erskine, a military poet, Home, a tragedy-writing parson, and Worseley, a rider of the great horse and architect." He was timid, and at the first mutterings of criticism he took to appearing in public with a bodyguard of "bruisers." Despite Bubb's endeavors it was none too clear where or how he would be able to attract the assistants he needed.

In theory he held several trumps. The scattered politicians who called themselves Tories were glad to endorse him. Not amounting to a credible party in their own right, they approved the project for nonparty government, and their royalist tradition inclined them to favor a leader close to the king. The demise of Jacobitism meant that pro-Stuarts no longer had to be left in the cold, and since many of them were Scots like Bute, they were all the more eager to approach. They turned up at court, some of them expounding the Divine Right of Kings. Among them was a Dashwood—Kitty Dashwood, the "famous old beauty of the Oxfordshire Jacobites." George's consort Charlotte was found for him by another Jacobite, Colonel David Graeme, who had been out in the Forty-Five and was sent by Bute on a Continental bride hunt. When Charlotte became queen, Kitty Dashwood became her duenna.

But all such allies were manifestly suspect, and to get away with employing them, even in the honeymoon of the reign, Bute would have needed extreme skill in handling those who mistrusted them; and he did not possess it. His abstract politics, his lack of outgoingness and broad human contact, his vanity over the wrong things (his own good looks, for example) put people off.

One of George's first public statements was a declaration to the Privy Council. Bute helped him to draft it so as to include the peace policy of his own Medmenhamite backers. The document called the war with France "bloody and expensive." Pitt exploded with fury. He induced them to cut out "bloody" and add "but just and necessary." Though the final text still stressed that England needed peace, the strength of the entrenched regime was apparent. Somehow, Bute had to be propelled forward fairly soon from his advisory position into tangible power. He disliked the prospect; he was afraid of it; but the logic of his strange relationship with his sovereign pushed him on.

Toward the end of 1760 Dodington devised a scheme for getting Bute into the government as secretary of state for the Northern Department. This would involve displacing Lord Holderness. Bute was nervous about the effect of being seen to displace anybody. He put forward a devious proposal for Holderness to go through the motions of quarreling with his colleagues and resign so as to leave a vacancy. Dodington, to his credit, demurred, but on March 25, 1761, Holderness did resign, whereupon Bute slipped in, protesting privately to George about his reluctance.

He still had a long way to go. The Duke of Newcastle, who had no love for him, was prime minister, and Pitt dominated the Cabinet. But his hand was strengthened by an enormous access of wealth. Through his wife he inherited over a million pounds from her father Edward Wortley Montagu. That October Pitt was squeezed out of office. Here too the method was subtle. Spain was preparing to help France. Pitt demanded a preemptive declaration of war on Spain. Bute opposed, Pitt resigned, and then after a short interval war on Spain was duly declared—as indeed a fair assessment of the position had always dictated, to forestall a new buildup and prolongation of the fighting; but Pitt was safely out.

When he went, Dodington expressed pleasure that Bute had got rid of a "most impracticable colleague." Public opinion took it badly. On Lord Mayor's Day the king, Bute, and Pitt traveled to the Guildhall in separate coaches, Bute attended by his prizefighter bodyguard. As his coach climbed Ludgate Hill the crowd mistook it for Pitt's and cheered. Then somebody shouted, "By God, this is not Pitt, this is Bute and be damned to him." A pro-Pitt demonstration made it difficult to reach the Guildhall, and the onlookers received George himself in silence.

Still the king clung to his chosen line, and the favorite had to continue riding the tiger. In January 1762 he screwed up courage to speak in the House of Lords—feebly—while complaining to Dodington in tones of sanctimonious martyrdom. Meanwhile George was exerting pressure on the Duke of Newcastle, threatening to swamp him by a creation of peers. On May 26 he gave way. Bute moved up to head the government openly. Newcastle and Pitt went into opposition.

The new prime minister and first lord of the treasury had to take account promptly of the Medmenhamite network woven round him. Already, in March 1761, Dodington had been awarded a long-coveted peerage as Lord Melcombe. His delight was childish and infectious. Horace Walpole swallowed a deep antipathy to congratulate him. "I came to wish you joy," said Walpole as the fat new lord stumped toward him across a large room. "I imagined so," replied Bubb, "and came to receive it." After all those years he yielded to fashion and wore a short wig instead of a long one. But in 1762 he still had no actual job and was feeling neglected. Soon after becoming prime minister, Bute offered him the plum post of first lord of the admiralty. Faith revived, his cup overflowed. "Joy Joy Joy to my Dearest Lord," he wrote, "this is the greatest happyness I could wish for in this life."

The Friars in fact were moving in, with Sir Francis prominent. Bubb had drawn him closer by getting him a new Commons seat in his controlled borough of Weymouth and Melcombe and had aired the notion of an appointment as secretary of state for war. The post of "Treasurer of the Chamber" was allotted to Sir Francis as an interim measure only. Now his hour struck . . . but he emerged as chancellor of the Exchequer. The choice of a man who had no head for figures and could not give a set speech that required detailed argument quickly became a public joke. Also, commentators asked how a sovereign who made a display of Christian rectitude, as George III did, could bestow the seals of such a high office on this elderly libertine.

It still seems hard to explain except on the hypothesis of a secret "Franciscan" understanding. Dashwood, unable even to pretend that he was suited, tried to pass it off as a joke himself. "I can tell you what will make you wonder, and that very justly," he wrote to Wilkes, "when you licai that His Majesty has been pleased to appoint me his Chancellor of the Exchequer." Wilkes answered in kind, suggesting that Bute had been impressed by Sir Francis's experience in adding up bills for drinks. Someone who wrote congratulating the new chancellor thoughtfully enclosed a short list of recommended reading on finance. The Dashwood style of oratory did not adapt to fiscal matters: Walpole complained that the chancellor "with the familiarity and phrase of a fish-wife, introduced the humours of Wapping behind the veil of the Treasury."

However, he did his best, and his associates rallied around. It was then the custom (as it remained till recent times) that a newly appointed minister had to resign his seat and seek reelection. Sir Francis duly did so; Dodington wrote to the mayor and corporation of his constituency, recommending him as "my best friend," and pumped £1,580 into his election expenses; and he was elected.

Another leading Friar, Lord Sandwich, had a post already in the administration of Ireland, so he did not have to be looked after at once. He was held in reserve for the ambassadorship to Spain when peace should be concluded. Paul Whitehead became a "deputy treasurer of the chamber" at £800 a year. Several more veterans of the old shadow court and the Medmenham circle were reaping rewards. The new reign transformed William Douglas, the scapegoat Earl of March, into a lord of the bedchamber, a knight of the thistle, and, as Bute had once been, a Scottish representative peer. Hogarth was confirmed in the post of royal "Serjeant Painter" that he had held since 1757 and improved his standing (though he was above doing it to a venal extent) with pro-Bute cartoons. David Mallet—one-time friend of Thompson, collaborator on the *Masque of Alfred,* and undersecretary to Frederick—also rallied to Bute, and received a Port of London post that carried a salary and minimal duties.

The prime minister himself was the weak link. For his promised purge of officeholders he employed Henry Fox,* a Whig abler than

---

*Sometimes claimed as another Friar of Medmenham.

himself, whom he made leader of the House of Commons. But when the process aroused the natural enmities, he could not appease them, or resist them except at ruinous cost to his theoretical aims. To get a majority he was driven back to Sir Robert Walpole's methods, and the formation of a new army of bought supporters—a new oligarchy in embryo. His own Scottish background told against him. Fifty-odd years after the Union, anti-Scots prejudice was rampant, presumably because so many Scots had come to England and made good. Also Bute's kindness to Jacobites helped opponents to develop a charge that the Patriot King policy was a cloak for Stuart-type despotism, and that George III was being groomed as a James II. Because of Bute's suspected liaison with George's mother, his premiership was gibed at as the reign of the Boot and the Petticoat.

His retort to propaganda took the inadequate form of counterpropaganda. He hired writers to put his case across to the public. Throughout the Hanoverian age, despite Tory nullity in politics, there had always been a strain of "literary" Toryism or at least right-wing hostility to the dominant Whigs. Dr. Johnson—in sentiment a Jacobite—is the great instance. Goldsmith is another: embedded in *The Vicar of Wakefield* is a long royalist apologia more or less in the spirit of Bolingbroke. Bute tried to harness this body of opinion by subsidizing the literary Tories. "Most of our best authors," he had boasted as early as February 1761, "are devoted to me."

He assigned a pension of £300 a year to Dr. Johnson himself, by way of a hint. Johnson thanked him most courteously but did no more and found in due course that he had to dun the prime minister before the payments came through. Bute was more successful with David Mallet; with the tragedian John Home, whom he had already employed as private secretary, and as one of George's tutors; with James Macpherson, bogus translator of nonexistent Gaelic epics; and above all with Tobias Smollett, the novelist. They all wielded their pens on the government's behalf. Three days after Bute became prime minister, Smollett launched a paper, the *Briton,* dedicated to his cause.

The trouble was that they were all Scotsmen. While Bute had a certain genuine cultural interest, he failed to convince his critics that this had anything to do with his policy. Even the king did not go along with him there. When he lectured George on the need to patronize the arts, George nodded off to sleep. In the words of Walpole once again: "The coins of the King were the worst that had appeared for above a century; and the revenues of the Crown were so soon squandered in purchasing dependents, that architecture, the darling art of Lord Bute, was contracted from the erection of a new palace, to altering a single door-case in the drawing room at St. James's."

CONFLICT AND COUNTERATTACK

As the Bute Ministry was largely a Medmenhamite creation, so its fall was largely a Medmenhamite nemesis. Whereas the principal older Friars had been favored, the principal younger one had been passed over, and his debts would not allow him to be patient.

John Wilkes, "John of Aylesbury," needed a job. Early in the reign he asked for the ambassadorship to Turkey and for a post at the Board of Trade and was turned down. As soon as it was clear that he would still get nothing even when Bute was prime minister, he broke ranks and revolted. He replied to Smollett's *Briton* by starting a paper of his own, the *North Briton*—its title a sarcastic rubbing-in of the "Scottish" difficulty. Wilkes's favorite technique was to undermine the regime by an ironic pretense of praising it. The first number appeared on June 6. It was later in that month that Wilkes made the visit to Medmenham, when he found the Rev. Charles Churchill congenial. He enlisted Churchill as a contributor. Robert Lloyd joined them. Even then, the breach with the Ministry might still have been healed. Wilkes asked for the governorship of Canada, offering to take Churchill and Lloyd with him (Churchill as chaplain, Lloyd as secretary), so that the *North Briton* would be guaranteed to fade out. This deal was rejected, and his offensive resumed.

Wilkes's style was much sharper and livelier than Smollett's. The

North Briton was the first English political journal to pull no punches and name names in full. It assailed the prime minister as a highland chieftain, as a crypto-Jacobite. Wilkes abused Scots in general as a contemptible, poverty-stricken race eager to exploit the English, in whose country they had no better right than any other foreigners. Churchill seconded him. When the king gave Bute the Garter, Churchill advised the new Knight of the Garter to hang himself with it. Besides articles in the *North Briton* he composed an anti-Scottish poem, "The Prophecy of Famine," enlarging on the theme of an impoverished land that drove its ravening sons over the Border to prey on Sassenachs. One line referred to a prospect of "Stuarts without end." Not only was Stuart the prime minister's family name, people had noticed that a list of sixteen military promotions included eleven Stuarts . . . and four of the other officers were Mackenzies. Churchill also insinuated in his satire "The Times" that Andrew Stone, a Bute-appointed tutor to the young prince, had been a homosexual.

Wilkes's campaign was all tactical and quite disingenuous. The birth of his honest and effective radical passion was still far off. As he admitted privately, he had no animus against Bute or against Scotsmen. Churchill, too, rang false if examined closely. In the abstract he favored the Bolingbroke-type program that Bute was meant to be implementing. But however mean its origins, the attack was deadly. Wilkes revealed himself as a master of invective. Churchill was heavier, and by writing verse like Pope's he invited a comparison he could not sustain; but he was copious and hard-hitting. Johnson remarked of him: "To be sure he is a tree that cannot produce good fruit; he only bears crabs. But, sir, a tree that produces a great many crabs is better than a tree which produces only a few."

The "crabs" and *North Briton*s produced a cumulative effect. Grub Street hacks cashed in with lampoons of their own. Mobs marched about waving boots and petticoats, burned the prime minister in effigy and insulted Augusta at the theater. A Scottish takeover of Crown and country, a sellout to France in peace negotiations—these were bogeys that Wilkes successfully raised. Lord Talbot, having been made fun of over the horse fiasco, challenged him to a duel. Wilkes arrived fresh (if that is the word) from an all-night debauch with the Friars, whom he had thus far avoided quarreling with. The duel was anticlimactic and bloodless and did more good to Wilkes's public image than Talbot's.

Bute was wilting. He remained determined, however, to patch up a peace treaty. The preliminaries were signed on November 3, 1762. Wilkes cracked an obvious joke about "the Peace of God which passeth all understanding." As Dodington and the rest had always envisaged, it was a separate peace, leaving Frederick the Great to settle his own problems; and it was neither a total sellout nor a decisive triumph. Some of the British conquests were kept, some were returned to France. When Parliament met on the twenty-fifth, however, Bute was hissed and pelted. Pitt, in black, made an eloquent protest. Bute said he hoped his role as a peacemaker would be recorded on his tomb, provoking someone to comment, "The sooner the better." A Dr. Musgrave, who practiced medicine in Paris, charged that Bute and Augusta were in French pay. Nevertheless the Government won easily. The Commons approved the peace proposals by 319 to 65. In a purely parliamentary sense Bute was doing better than the uproar suggested. But it was a hollow success. Instead of cleansing politics of corruption and empire building, he was creating them himself, through Fox; there was no other way to keep control of the House.

When the treaty was signed on February 10, 1763, and the Pittite protest collapsed, George III's reaction was that he was free to move fully into Phase Two. Augusta exclaimed, "Now my son is King of England!" and the uprooting of the last regime's officeholders was speeded. Bute, however, knew that he was running into deeper danger, even physical danger. He took his bodyguard everywhere and sometimes went out disguised. The bill for the war had yet to be discharged. Somehow, Chancellor Dashwood had to raise the money. A worse crisis loomed ahead.

Income tax had not been thought of. Some indirect levy was the only resource. A linen tax was suggested, but nobody could make Sir Francis understand it sufficiently to explain it to the House. Then a cider tax was suggested, and he undertook to put that in his budget. In March he did so. His speech was a shambles. He laid himself open with idiotic sentences such as, "I am not for an extension of the excise laws but for an enlargement of them," and "All the whole total is anything for peace and quietness' sake." After a merciless debate the cider tax was carried by another well-managed majority, but Sir Francis had no illusions. "What shall I do?" he asked plaintively. "The boys will point at me in the street and cry, 'There goes the worst Chancellor of the Exchequer that ever was.'"

Many squires in the cider counties, whose Tory leanings made them natural props of the regime, rebelled against the "monstrous" tax. Herefordshire and Gloucestershire rumbled with anger. Some of the government's unpopularity rubbed off on King George himself, who might have expected to be left out of the agitation. In the words of a ballad:

> *The King was going to Parliament,*
> *A numerous crowd was round him,*
> *Some huzza'd him as he went,*
> *And others cry'd—confound him!*
> *At length a shout came thundering out!*
> *Which made the air to ring, Sir,*
> *All in one voice cry'd no excise,*
> *No BUTE, no Cyder King, Sir.*

Throughout 1762 Wilkes had never attacked any Medmenhamites directly, unless we count a clash with Hogarth over a pro-Bute cartoon (Hogarth retorted with the now well-known caricatures of Wilkes and Churchill). But the *North Briton* tore into Dashwood over his budget. In the same month Wilkes aimed a shocking blow at the prime minister personally. He published, in the form of an epistle to Bute, an essay

on Ben Jonson's play *The Fall of Mortimer*. This covers the early years
of Edward III, when Roger Mortimer, the lover of the young king's
mother Queen Isabella, wielded all the power and swept his sovereign
aside. Wilkes's sarcastic essay felicitates Bute on the contrast between
the situation then and now, enlarging on this so as to make it clear that
it isn't really a contrast but a parallel. The onslaught was not very consistent with the charge that Bute was fostering a new royal tyranny by
George III himself. But Wilkes did not care, and toward the end he
used the Bolingbroke slogan to hit both of them:

> I beg pardon, my Lord, for having so long detained the *patriot*
> Minister of the *patriot* King, from the great scenes of *sovereign* busi-
> ness, or the rooting out corruption. . . .

Though the king was furious, Wilkes went unpunished. Bute had finally
lost his nerve. For months he had been trying to back out, but whenever
he raised the subject, George would sulk and not speak to him. The
cider demonstrations were too much. Dodington might have braced
him, but Dodington was not there any more. He was dead—killed by
falling downstairs the previous summer, leaving Dashwood as his execu-
tor, with a legacy of £500 to raise a monument to their friendship: of
which more hereafter. Unadvised and panic-stricken, Bute surrendered
where a stronger politician could have hung on. With the excuse that
he had done his job by ending the war, and that continuance in office
would cause trouble for the king, he resigned on April 8, 1763.

The unlucky chancellor followed suit. He let himself be kicked
upstairs. The premier barony of England, Le Despenser, had recently
lapsed. Sir Francis being a nephew of the last holder, the title was revived
for him. On April 19 he entered the Lords as Baron Le Despenser, with
relief and pleasure. He had a new coach made with his baronial motto
Pro Magna Charta painted on the panels in Gothic letters and drove
home to West Wycombe to superintend building operations.

Bute's eclipse had thrown politics into uncertainty. Was he only withdrawing so as to work more insidiously through front men? His successor, Grenville, was his nominee. Some of his associates were holding on and perhaps even creeping up. Lord Sandwich, after a brief spell in the Spanish diplomatic post, was first lord of the admiralty again, working with his old enemy-making vigor.

On April 23, Wilkes issued No. 45 of the *North Briton,* arguing in fiery language that the threat of a corrupt authoritarianism was not past. His further abuse of the peace treaty helped to maintain public resentment against an alleged betrayal. When the Corporation of the City of London presented the king with a loyal address of congratulation, the deputation was hooted on its way to St. James's, and the vicar of a Fleet Street church tolled his bell in mourning. Wilkes was arrested for No. 45 and sent to the Tower. The Government failed to make the arrest stick, and he was released in May to become a popular hero, saluted with processions, fireworks, and (for the first but not the last time) the cry of "Wilkes and Liberty!"

To add to his triumph, he had also been discrediting the Ministry for several months by leaking information on Medmenham. This part of his campaign is obscure, but rude cartoons and kindred digs at the Order can be traced in the press from January 1763. Wilkes supplied details in his own articles and letters; Churchill sniped at the brethren in his poems. A satire called *Secrets of the Convent* told how "Friar Paul" (Whitehead) had got his £800-a-year job through the influence of "St Francis" with "Laird Boot." Such gossip about the Order and its hushed-up activities did serious damage. By this time it was vulnerable. Horace Walpole probably spoke for many when he remarked with distaste how old most of the brethren were; they ought to have reached years of discretion.

They could not rebut, and made no attempt to, but they did counterattack. This was Medmenham's final impact on politics. The weapon with which the Government temporarily floored Wilkes was taken from there. As a member of the Order himself he was vulnerable, one of those proverbial people in glass houses. The moving spirit in his defeat was Lord Sandwich, the most prominent Friar still in office, who disliked him—probably as an upstart. They met socially and chaffed each other, but the chaffing had an edge. During the summer and autumn of 1763 Sandwich was seeking fresh matter to silence Wilkes. He kept Sir Francis informed, but the founder was not very active in the plot. It was a third member of their set, the lately promoted Earl of March, who supplied the fatal evidence.

This was a book, or part of one—the salacious *Essay on Woman* by the deceased Medmenhamite Thomas Potter. Composed in its first form in or before 1755, it had tickled Wilkes's fancy, and he had added some mock-scholarly notes to an improved edition that was known at the Abbey. Opinions differed as to how far he had collaborated on this with Potter, how far he had rehandled it alone; but at some time after Potter's death he had begun getting a dozen or so copies printed, probably to hand out to the superior Friars. The *Essay* was to be found with further scurrilous and antireligious poems. During a search of his house when he was arrested, the officers had seen papers relating to all this.

Such a shady publishing project, even for a limited readership, could surely be exploited to hurt the publisher. The Earl of March's chaplain, the Rev. John Kidgell, picked up some further information. Kidgell was an unpleasant character, a darling of old ladies for his priggish poses and ingratiating sermons, but a neglector of his charge, a sometime interferer with choirboys, a minor pornographer, and a rake of the more sordid kind. Churchill described him as "by Cleland tutor'd," whether in person or via *Fanny Hill* is not clear. At any rate, the chaplain was well qualified for running a dirty book to earth.

During Wilkes's imprisonment Kidgell sought out his printer and offered bribes in return for proof sheets. The process took time. Bit by bit the printer exhorted £233 and disgorged not only proof sheets with corrections by Wilkes but a copy of the printed work as far as it had progressed. Kidgell, trying to cash in on the scandal, subsequently brought out a pamphlet of his own, sketching the contents and denouncing them as "volatile, saline Effluvia of the unchaste Imagination of a prurient Debauchee." When the response was hostile he tried to deny his part in the affair, but he was no longer needed anyhow. March had put the stuff in the Government's hands, and Sandwich had worked it up into a deadly instrument against Wilkes, who was still MP for Aylesbury and could be indicted for conduct unbecoming a member of the House.

No one knows in full what Wilkes planned to publish. Kidgell got hold of a fragment only, and there was certainly manuscript matter that escaped the authorities but never reached print, Sandwich had transcripts made at the Home Office, and versions of the Home Office text still exist. However, even that may not have been wholly authentic. The Government's case was to include a charge that Wilkes was the true author as well as the publisher, and the material handed out to clerks for transcription may have been doctored to incriminate him—perhaps by Kidgell. On top of this doubt, the spread of rumors about the *Essay*, and the public demand for details, produced a crop of fakes. Fourteen of them are still with us to confuse the issue.

A picture of sorts emerges. Like other productions of Thomas Potter, the thing was a parody. The original *Essay on Man* by Pope begins by hailing Henry St. John (i.e., Bolingbroke):

> *Awake, my St. John! leave all meaner things*
> *To low ambition, and the pride of kings.*
> *Let us (since life can little more supply*
> *Than just to look about us and to die)*
> *Expatiate free o'er all this scene of Man;*
> *A mighty maze! but not without a plan.*

The *Essay on Woman* was addressed to Sandwich's ex-mistress Fanny Murray, who may or may not have been a Medmenham nun and was noted for her charms and availability during the 1740s and early 1750s. The excerpts in state archives, and summaries by people who knew, establish two crucial facts. First, that the true text is preserved—so far as it is preserved—in a version that begins:

Awake, my Fanny, leave all meaner things,
This morn shall prove what rapture swiving brings.
Let us (since life can little more supply
Than just a few good fucks, and then we die)
Expatiate free o'er that lov'd scene of Man;
A mighty maze! for mighty pricks to scan.

Second, that there is one and only one original contemporary copy of this, probably printed by Lord Sandwich's order for official use. It is in the Dyce Library at the Victoria and Albert Museum. Copies of it for private circulation were printed during the nineteenth century. One is in the British Museum, one at West Wycombe House. However, they add nothing of independent value.*

While Kidgell, or some other licensed forger, may have tampered in detail, the nature of the fragment that he secured is clear enough. Red ink was used in the final printed version. There was a frontispiece inspired by a phallic statue (probably one of Dashwood's collection) and a comic "author's name"—Pego Borewell, Esq.; "pego" being a slang term for the penis. Then came some prefatory matter, and after that a 94-line portion of the *Essay* with long burlesque notes, some of them facetiously ascribed to Bishop Warburton, who edited Pope's real work, and whose wife Potter seduced. No more of the *Essay* itself was obtained, and perhaps no more was ever printed, but three shorter poems were, and Kidgell got those: parodies of Pope's "Universal Prayer" and "The Dying Christian to his Soul," and of the hymn to the Holy Spirit, "Veni Creator."

If we ask who wrote what, the answer seems to be that the substance of the *Essay* was still Potter's, though a line gibing at Bute, if genuine, shows that Wilkes updated it. The notes are Wilkes's, and so, probably, are the three short poems. Pope is followed closely

*Until recently there was no copy accessible to the general reader. Anybody wishing to look at the *Essay* had to ask special permission. A facsimile of the Dyce copy in Adrian Hamilton's *The Infamous Essay on Woman* (1972) has finally made it public property.

throughout, and the joke depends largely on reading one "Essay" with the other in mind. If Wilkes had ever finished the job he would apparently have printed the *Essay on Man* side by side with the parody. The basic formula is simply to alter Pope's couplets just enough to give them a sexual meaning, and then sustain this logically through each section of the poem. Thus, where Pope begins a section:

> *Say first, of God above, or Man below,*
> *What can we reason, but from what we know? . . .*

Potter begins his corresponding section:

> *Say first, of Woman's latent charms below,*
> *What can we reason, but from what we know?*

He goes on from this to the problem of guessing what you don't see from what you do, and verifying in practice. It is all on the same lines and done quite adroitly, with plenty of vigorous anatomic detail and four-letter words, but the flashes of real wit are rather sparse. Possibly the best couplet in the whole thing is at the beginning of the second main section. Pope has:

> *Presumptuous Man! the reason wouldst thou find,*
> *Why form'd so weak, so little, and so blind?*

Potter changes only one word:

> *Presumptuous Prick! the reason wouldst thou find,*
> *Why form'd so weak, so little, and so blind?*

But he can't (if the phrase may be pardoned) keep it up.

Wilkes's notes are not really very funny either. They are donnish, and full of pseudoreligious witticisms. The line on Bute, if that is his, echoes a current joke about the prime minister's rise to favor with Princess Augusta, and the reason:

Godlike erect, BUTE stands the foremost man.

The vulgar public did better. When it became known that the prime minister gave Augusta advice on the ornamenting of Kew Gardens, the pagoda was dubbed "Bute's Erection." As for Wilkes's shorter effusions at the end, the Universal Prayer is the most interesting. Pope's original is an address to "Dea Opt. Max.":

Father of All! in every age,
In every clime ador'd,
By saint, by savage, and by sage,
Jehovah, Jove, or Lord!...

Wilkes's is an address to the female organ, "Cunno Opt. Min.":

Mother of All! in every age,
In every clime ador'd,
By saint, by savage, and by sage,
If modest, or if whor'd...

This hymn runs to thirteen verses. An abridged form of it may well have been sung in the chapel service at Medmenham.

It is most unlikely that any of the spurious Essays give us authentic matter that escaped Kidgell. Some of them discredit themselves with obviously wrong opening lines. Cleland is credited with a version that begins, "Awake, my Churchill." Another, in the British Museum, is a long printed text purporting to be the complete Essay, which the Government never managed to assemble. Unfortunately this claim has often been accepted. The poem starts:

> *Awake, my Sandwich, leave all meaner joys*
> *To Charles and Bob, those true poetic boys;*
> *Let us, since life can little more supply*
> *Than just to kiss, to procreate and die,*
> *Expatiate free o'er all the female sex,*
> *Born to subdue, and studying to perplex.*

Charles and Bob are Charles Churchill and Robert Lloyd.

The author has grasped the principle of Potter's technique, but he lacks Potter's cleverness and gusto. He is diffuse and feeble and not even frankly dirty except in snatches; he leaves prurient blanks and employs euphemisms like "kiss." One passage is a silly tale of the Garden of Eden (Milton again) in which Eve is driven by Adam's inadequacy to satisfy her needs with the Devil. A description of orgasm is a specimen of the author's embarrassing style:

> *The grasp divine, th' emphatic, thrilling squeeze,*
> *The throbbing, panting breasts and trembling knees,*
> *The tickling motion, the enlivening flow,*
> *The rapturous shiver and dissolving, oh!*

But once more, there is no reason to think that any of this restores lost passages of the genuine Potter—or of Wilkes. As for the other bogus texts, they are proof of nothing but public demand. Reports that Fanny Murray was somehow involved raised hopes of scabrous revelations, and besides fake *Essays,* pamphlets about her "Amours" and her "Monkish Friends of Mednam" were rushed out for a ready market. It was hard on Fanny, who had retired into married respectability years before.

On November 15, 1763, Parliament met. Despite the setback over Wilkes's arrest and release, the Government carried a motion in the Commons condemning No. 45 of the *North Briton.* Wilkes claimed parliamentary privilege without success. In the Lords, where he could not be present, the real trap was sprung. He was accused of libeling a member of that House, Bishop Warburton, on the strength of the notes falsely fathered on him.

Sandwich opened the business by reading out not merely the offending notes, but the *Essay on Woman* fragment itself, all ninety-four lines of it. He paused at intervals to make suitably shocked comments on its indecencies and blasphemies. The drawback was that he was notorious himself for precisely the same things; in fact he was in process of expulsion from the Beefsteaks . . . for blasphemy. Also he probably relished what he was reading. His performance was too much for some of the audience, including Sir Francis, now in the Lords as Baron Le Despenser. The chief Friar remarked in a stage whisper that it was the first time he had heard Satan preaching against sin. Lyttelton, who also had reason to despise Sandwich's conduct, called out to him to stop reading. Bishop Warburton followed with an emotional disavowal of any part in the notes, averring that "the hardiest inhabitants of hell" could not listen to such blasphemies.

Lord Temple, Wilkes's most powerful ally in the Upper House, tried to object to the way the government was proceeding. His protest was crushed, and there was no way even to query whether the text Sandwich had read was genuine, because the only person able to challenge it was in the Commons. A resolution was passed declaring that the *Essay* with its companion pieces was "a most scandalous, obscene, and impious libel." Those who had managed the affair never mentioned Potter and let it be assumed that Wilkes was the author, but they avoided saying so, because if they had, he could have claimed the right to make a defense.

Outside Parliament reactions were ominous. Sandwich was vilified as a traitor to a former comrade. *The Beggar's Opera* was playing at Covent Garden. When the imprisoned highwayman Macheath said, "But that Jemmy Twitcher should peach I own surprises me," the audience laughed and cheered, and Sandwich was nicknamed Jemmy Twitcher ever afterward. Walpole, who did not care for Wilkes, sympathized with him now and noted in his memoirs that the greatest public services are apt to be done by the worst men: "The virtuous are too scrupulous to go to the lengths that are necessary to rouse the people against their tyrants."

Wilkes, however, was doomed—for the moment. Before Christmas he escaped to France. He talked of returning for the meeting of Parliament on January 16, 1764, but was taken ill. On the twentieth the House of Commons expelled him, and in February he was convicted of libel. Moves and countermoves went on through most of that year, but on November 1 a sentence of outlawry was passed against him. He had to resign himself to exile, a state made harder by the loss of Charles Churchill, who died of typhus at Boulogne on November 4, and Robert Lloyd, who died as a Fleet debtor a few weeks later.

THE END OF DAYS

Wilkes, whom some called the "false brother," might be out of the way, but the Hell-Fire Ministry was finished. Its revolution against oligarchy was an exploded dream. The Patriot King would never be accepted as a nonpartisan patron of Liberty. In spite of many suspicions, Bute was not still hovering as a power behind the throne. George had cooled at last and avoided him.

What became of Medmenham? Its twilight is overhung with doubt. A view that used to be held is that Wilkes's exposure of the Abbey was swiftly fatal. Publicity, ridicule, the inroads of sightseers—all these factors must indeed have combined against it. Walpole was among the visitors in 1763, and he found it poorly kept and partly deprived of its splendid furnishings. Yet it was not quite defunct. A faithful remnant did go on assembling there for another two or three years.

There is an undated letter from Paul Whitehead to Sir Francis that proves at least that no feeling of disaster set in. As it begins "My Lord," it cannot be earlier than April 1763, when Dashwood got his peerage, and it may well be considerably later. Like the writers of most of the other surviving letters, Whitehead is excusing himself from attendance. He has gout in both feet and an inflammation of the head.

"Whom God loveth He Chastiseth.". . . Yet methinks I could have wished Heaven had deferred this especial mark of its favour till after the celebration of the Medmenham Rites, as I imagine I should then have been more spiritually qualified for the reception of it. . . . I don't know whether I ought or no, to desire the Prayers of the Chapter for a sick and weak Brother, however if you are convinced that you are not too wicked to prevail, you may try their Efficacy . . .

your repentant Brother,
P. of Twickenham.

Another item of evidence is Churchill's poem "The Candidate," published in June 1764. This contains the passage already quoted (page 141) about "Womanhood in habit of a nun." It continues:

> *A nation's reckoning like an alehouse score,*
> *Which Paul the Aged chalks behind the door . . .*

. . . and proceeds to an image of Dashwood, the muddle-headed chancellor, pouring libations to the "Goddess without eyes" (i.e., Venus—Love being proverbially blind) from a communion cup. The time reference is confused, but Churchill gives the impression that Medmenham is still a live issue.

The cellar-book fragments confirm that brethren were still frequenting the place in 1764. However, the plainest proof as to what happened comes from a source that is also the plainest proof that the Order existed at all, in anything like the form alleged: the correspondence of Dodington's political protegé John Tucker, "John of Melcombe." On August 11 of the same year he writes to Sir Francis, Baron Le Despenser:

My heart and inclinations will be with your Lordship and your friends at Medmenham at the next Chapter, but I am cruelly detained here by the sickness of my mother. . . . If this should reach your Lordship at Medmenham I pray you will present my filial duty

to your Holy Father, and fraternal love and respect to the pious
brotherhood, to whom I wish all possible joy, spirit, and vigour.

The remaining Friars are still active, and one infers, in pretty much the
old way. But on March 22, 1766, he writes:

I was last Sunday at Medmenham, and to my amazement found the
Chapter Room stripped naked.

So between August 1764 and March 1766—probably near the latter limit, in view of the amazement of the uninformed Tucker—
Medmenham quietly expired.

11

AFTERMATH

FINAL WISHES

Sir Francis Dashwood, Baron Le Despenser, was fifty-five when the Wilkes crisis hit him. He was not (as the phrase goes) past it. But the later phases of his Franciscanism fade into mists of rumor. Not only was Medmenham gradually being extinguished, several of the brethren were dead or estranged or far away. However, a stubborn tradition tells of continued meetings in a different venue, the caves under West Wycombe Hill.

When Sir Francis made his road in 1748–52 he took the chalk from a cave already existing. Not content to treat such an unusual spot as a mere quarry, he directed his workmen to carve out rooms and other improvements. The results of this process, and of further subterranean tinkering later, are still there—the scene, possibly, of the last of the Brotherhood's assemblies. Some sort of purpose there must have been, and Dashwood's Italian artist Giuseppe Borgnis dug out a similar cave at Marlow. But the exact motive with either is uncertain.

You approach the Wycombe cave system through a court halfway up the south hillside. Over the entrance is a multiple Gothic arch built of flints. Both court and arch are Franciscan embellishments. The low-vaulted entry tunnel runs straight into the hill for about 200 feet and then swings left. Its extension winds on for nearly a quarter of a mile, passing through several artificial chambers, branching out in places, and then rejoining itself on no evident plan.

All the larger chambers have names, but these are modern and speculative.* The first, on your right soon after the bend in the entry tunnel, is called the Robing Room, on the assumption that the brethren would have put on their costumes here. A few yards beyond, heads are carved on the wall, one wearing a miter. Then the passage splits to run on both sides of a vast round pillar, converging again on the far side of it, and beginning to slope gently downhill. On the left wall are the letters XXIIF. There used to be an inscription XXXIV farther on, but this has been effaced by repairs. The passage divides into a small network of catacombs, and reunites. A branch leading upward on the left does not go far. It may once have led to another exit, and a vague legend speaks of a secret chamber, somewhere about here, where a clergyman carried on an intrigue with that elusive lady Sister Agnes.

Immediately after this the main tunnel runs right, into a circular hall 40 feet across and 60 feet high, with four alcoves that may once have had statues in them. It is known as the Banqueting Hall. A lamp formerly hung from a massive hook in the roof. According to one far-fetched theory it was the Rosicrucian lamp that once lit up Hell-Fire meetings at the George and Vulture. The hall is eerie and dank. With eighteenth-century facilities only, it would have been hard to make it bright or warm enough for revelry.

Beyond this chamber the tunnel slants more sharply downward and branches into a triangular pattern, converging once more at the apex of the triangle. It runs on through a "Buttery" and comes to a strip of water, the "Styx"—a name that can be traced back to early days, unlike the name of the rooms. The Styx is on the same level as the bottom of the valley outside. Visitors used to cross it by boat. Today a bridge spans it. Across is a round vaulted chamber, the "Inner Temple," where the passage ends.

If the atmosphere of these caves suggests anything, it suggests activities of a darker, more mysterious kind than those of Medmenham. The

---

*They may be reconsidered.

place is not cozy enough for drinking parties, banquets, or ordinary womanizing. It would have been difficult to cook without ventilation, difficult to keep food hot if it were brought from outside, and daunting to remove any clothes. There is a story (poorly attested) that Sir Francis once held a dinner in the hall and put out the lamp, whereupon a "hideous figure," glowing luridly and stinking of brimstone, appeared in one of the alcoves . . . needless to say, a dummy; the apparition was a joke—but surely rather a sick joke and out of character. Legend has indulged in further fancies of devil worship or dubious occultism. The modern witch expert Gerald Gardner, who claimed to have the lamp in his museum, also claimed that one of the passage divisions formed a pubic triangle, with further symbolism implied in the Styx. But the plan of the caves gives no convincing support for any purely sexual interpretation.

Whether it supports an occult or pseudoreligious interpretation is another question. The catacombs used to have some odd carvings on the walls, including a figure with horns. More intriguing is the possible clue in Wilkes's allusion to Eleusinian Mysteries. The caves might conceivably have been designed as a better locale than the Abbey for the reenactment of these. Classical authors do assert that the mysteries included a sex rite in an underground chamber, with a priest and priestess playing divine roles. Apuleius, in his *Golden Ass,* sketches his own initiation into the mysteries of the Great Goddess who was worshipped at Eleusis among other places; and this seems to have involved starting out from a temple with a statue of the Goddess in it, putting on special clothes, and going some distance to an inner sanctuary where he "set one foot on Proserpine's threshold"—in Hades, on the other side of the Styx—and "saw the sun shining at midnight and entered the presence of the gods of the underworld and the gods of the upper world." At Wycombe the so-called Banqueting Hall could have done duty as a temple. The pool of water actually was known as the Styx, and the final chamber beyond it could have been the inner sanctuary.

Contemporary references to the caves are few and cryptic, but one at least is interesting. Benjamin Franklin mentions them vaguely in a letter, saying that the "imagery" of West Wycombe is "whimsical and puzzling . . . below the earth as above it." Churchill's poem *The Duellist* hints at the caves as a scene of secret wickedness. In view of the date of Churchill's death, the allusion would imply an overlap with the Abbey. John Hall-Stevenson—a late witness, to be confronted shortly—has a note on "strange events which took place under West Wycombe Hill," attached to a poem with the following lines:

> *Where can I find a cave to muse*
> *Upon his lordship's envied glory,*
> *Which of the Nine dare to refuse*
> *To tell the strange and recent story?*
> *Mounting I saw the egregious lord*
> *O'er all impediments and bars;*
> *I saw him at Jove's council board*
> *And saw him stuck among the stars.*

If Sir Francis decorated his cavern beyond the Styx in an Apuleius-inspired style with gods and heavenly bodies, Hall-Stevenson's verses are a little more comprehensible than they are otherwise. But we simply have insufficient data.

Though the Medmenham meetings petered out in the middle 1760s, the Abbey was not entirely abandoned. Sir Francis used it to entertain occasional guests, including Franciscans. In 1770 he may have attempted a revival or reunion. Early that September we have a letter from Dashwood-King excusing himself, with an obscure allusion to the "Sisterhood." The last cellar-book sheet shows that Francis Duffield was at the Abbey in his Franciscan capacity in July, and John Clarke in September. That, however, does seem to have been the end, as far as the Brotherhood was concerned.

A last scene of interest occurred at Medmenham in 1771. It involved the transvestite French secret agent, the Chevalier d'Éon de

Beaumont. The chevalier has been charged—on as weak authority as various others—with furtive membership of the Order. His diplomatic work for Louis XV did include a spell in England, beginning in 1762, when he was certainly friendly with some of Dashwood's circle during the peace negotiations and was protected by Sandwich against a murder threat. However, he is remembered mainly because of a prolonged and public debate over his real sex. He was baptized as male but named Genevieve as well as Charles, and put in girl's clothes from the age of three to seven. After a male education he was sent on a secret mission to Russia disguised as a woman, so effectively that the empress thought he was one. On his return to France he became a captain of dragoons.

During his time in England, bets on his sex were laid amounting to £120,000. Wilkes was among the speculators. The chevalier came to Medmenham Abbey (according to the press of the day) for an examination to settle the matter. Excitement ran high. On May 24, 1771, a jury of aristocratic matrons met him in the refectory. In a satiric artist's conception of it, the chevalier is on a table wearing a cocked hat, a French decoration, and a towel. The ladies are surveying him at various ranges through magnifying glasses and telescopes and taking notes. After "a most thorough investigation" they gave their verdict as "doubtful."

Some years later the betting led to a second scrutiny and a ruling, "female." D'Éon went to France, then returned to England, where she spent the rest of a long life as a woman without equivocation, giving public displays of fencing. She died in 1810. A postmortem established that she was a man.

By the date of d'Éon's examination at Medmenham, its lingering Thelemic echoes were silent, or nearly so. An inventory was taken in 1774, and in 1777 Duffield sold the property. The last reliable glimpses of the Order as such have a third locale, neither Abbey nor caves. Besides all the rest, Sir Francis was responsible for the Church of St. Lawrence with the gold ball on top, which still overlooks West Wycombe.

He started work on this in 1760, and it was opened on Sunday, July 3, 1763. Unruffled by the recent shocks and exposures, its pious founder attended the ceremony and was greeted with a peal of bells. The organ alone had cost him £6,000. The vicar preached on Charity. There was a double, even a triple joke in all this. It was comical that Saint Francis of Wycombe should follow in the steps of his Assisian prototype by building a church. It was more comical that he should do it with the public image he had acquired. But discerning visitors penetrated the heart of his jest. By any standard of that time, the church was about as unecclesiastical as a church could well be. A lady wrote of it as "striking as a fine *concert* or *ball* room." She went on: "Tis indeed an Egyptian hall, and certainly gives one not the least idea of a place sacred to religious worship."

Charles Churchill took a slap at this church in a poem, as built for show rather than prayer. It was indeed an essay in ostentation, with its eye-catching golden sphere visible miles away. Also the site had a congenial history. Before Christianity a pagan temple had stood there within a system of earthworks. In the Middle Ages a church was started at the foot of the hill, but every night, according to legend, demons and "little crooked men" carried the stones to the top. At length a disembodied voice told the parish priest that his only remedy was to build the church up there. He did, and all was quiet. Sir Francis's church was reconstructed out of the ruins.

It was undoubtedly an odd church, with armchairs and ornate Palmyrene pillars and a font with a design recalling the Rosicrucian lamp. Borgnis and his son worked on the decorations. In a ceiling picture of the Last Supper, Judas was the dominant figure and his eyes followed you about. However, the golden ball on the 80-foot tower was (as it still is) the main focus of interest. It was 7 feet across, made of curved wooden slats covered with gilded lead. A ladder went up to a trapdoor by which you could climb into it. Benches round the inside gave seating space for a small party.

It was a private place—as private, in its way, as the caves below. Sir Francis took Wilkes and Churchill into it during a phase of amity (he never seems to have borne them much of a grudge), and they shared a buttle of punch and sang unecclesiastical songs. Rumors spread afterward about meetings of the remains of the Brotherhood in the same eyrie. They would have been cramped, and their favorite activity would have been very tricky indeed.

Hilltop meetings are authenticated, but meetings in death. On the demise of George Bubb Dodington, and acting on a request in his will, Sir Francis began a mausoleum to go with the church. Here his old companion was the first to be laid. It was a hollow, unroofed hexagon—its shape a reminiscence of the six-sided Abbey of Thélème—with columns and urns and arches and unusual flintwork, still intact today, though somewhat vandalized. Dr. Thomas Thompson was also to have his monument there. Bubb was joined in 1769 by Sir Francis's wife, Baroness Le Despenser.

Her husband's energies, meanwhile, were far from exhausted. He was still improving West Wycombe House, and in September 1771 he opened his gardens to the public to mark the completion of a portico at the west end of the building, called the Temple of Bacchus, with a statue of the god in it. More than that, he staged a pagan dedication. A high priest led a procession of Bacchanals, Fauns, Satyrs, and kindred characters, wearing skins and vine leaves, across the grounds and into the portico. After an invocation and music the procession moved off to a marquee by the lake and sang further paeans and then embarked in a boat decorated with streamers, while cannon fired and the populace applauded.

But mortality still encroached and encroached. . . . Potter, Churchill, and Lloyd were all dead; and in December 1774 Paul Whitehead, the steward of the Order, died. He had been living respectably (except that he refused to attend church) in a cottage at Twickenham. He died, however, while staying in Henrietta Street off Covent Garden. For three days before his death he sat by the fire in his nightshirt burning papers—almost certainly his secretarial records of Medmenham that, if we still had them, would dispel its mysteries. In his will he left his heart to Sir Francis, with fifty pounds for a monument in the mausoleum. The founder and superior performed his final act in that role.

Whitehead's heart was embalmed and enshrined in an urn, with a verse on it about "a heart that knew no guile." On a hot August morning in 1775 the urn was set on a bier in West Wycombe House. The villagers lined the road. A company of Bucks Militia stood to attention, their officers wearing crepe armlets. Behind the soldiers were two music masters and seven choirboys with sheet music pinned to their surplices. A band was ready on the lawn. Presently Sir Francis, Baron Le Despenser, appeared on his terrace. The procession circled the house three times, the boys in file and singing, the band playing. Six grenadiers marched into the hall and carried out the bier with the urn on it.

They all moved slowly down to the gate and up the hill—soldiers, choirboys, a curate; French horns, bassoons, fifes, muffled drums; music specially composed; the six men with the bier; Sir Francis and a column of guests. It took nearly two hours to reach the mausoleum, with the church bells tolling and guns firing salutes from the hilltop. The procession circled the mausoleum as it had circled the house, three times, and then at long last the urn was solemnly borne in. Once it was safe on its pedestal of white marble, the soldiers fired three volleys and marched off "to a merry tune." For several decades afterward, Paul Whitehead's small, black, withered heart, about the size of a walnut, used to be taken out of the urn and shown to visitors, but in 1839 one of them slipped it into his pocket and walked off with it.

Whitehead's funeral was followed a couple of years later by the publication of his collected poems, with Edward Thompson's memoir. The dedication to Sir Francis, implying his endorsement in at least some degree, gives the book a passing interest as his closest approach to an apologia—an offhand, indirect one. Thompson's version of Medmenham is that Dashwood, Stapleton, Whitehead, Wilkes, and other gentlemen rented the Abbey and performed rites ridiculing Catholic religious orders. He tells the story almost entirely by transcribing Wilkes and thus, in the circumstances, confirming him. Then he remarks that Wilkes and Churchill started sinister tales of darker secrets left undivulged. Here is his whole reply:

> Now all that can be drawn from the publication of these ceremonies is, that a set of worthy, jolly fellows, happy disciples of Venus and Bacchus, got occasionally together, to celebrate Woman in wine; and, to give more zest to the festive meeting, they plucked every luxurious idea from the ancients, and enriched their own modern pleasures with the addition of classic luxury.

This, it seems, is more or less what Sir Francis wanted the world to believe.

Otherwise his later years were miscellaneous. He held office again, as joint postmaster-general this time, quite capably and without mishap. He interested himself in the mounting crisis over the Thirteen Colonies, drafting a pro-American peace plan that Benjamin Franklin warmly approved. Franklin came to West Wycombe in 1773, and they collaborated on a revised *Book of Common Prayer.* It was grotesque that Sir Francis should undertake this, and more grotesque that the result, the Franklin Prayer Book, was widely used in American churches. Their proposed version of the Creed is worth noting. The Athanasian and the Nicene have gone, and the Apostles' is shortened to this:

> I believe in God the Father Almighty, Maker of Heaven and Earth;
> And in Jesus Christ his Son, our Lord. I believe in the Holy Ghost;
> the Forgiveness of Sins; and the Life everlasting. Amen.

Saint Francis of Wycombe could cheerfully do away with most of it, but not with the Forgiveness of Sins.

While engaged on the prayer book he was living peacefully with his final mistress, an ex-actress, Mrs. Barry. He was aging but not extinct. In 1774 Mrs. Barry produced a daughter, Rachel Frances Antonina. The end came in 1781. That November Paul Whitehead was seen again, a pale nocturnal ghost haunting the West Wycombe grounds, beckoning and signaling. Several members of the household had glimpses of him, including a sister of Sir Francis's, Lady Austen, who reported the experience to the poet Cowper. Sir Francis himself was already ill, and the ghost's message was obvious. He sent for Dr. Bates of Aylesbury (that former Medmenhamite of the inferior Order), proposing a trip to Italy, but died on December 11 and was buried in his church.

Of the remaining Friars, Lord Sandwich lasted till 1792, and Dr. Bates well into the eighteenth century, reminiscing about his long-ago friends and assuring younger generations that it had all been good clean fun. But the founder's true spiritual heir was someone outside the Order entirely, the unforeseen bastard daughter of his old age. If she had arrived earlier they might have had a happy companionship. Her tardiness was her own loss as well as his, and her life is a strange epilogue to the Franciscan saga.

Rachel Fanny was reared unobtrusively with a governess till her father's death. Then, aged seven, she was packed off to a French convent school with her legacies from her father—boldness, irreverence, opposition mindedness, and £45,000. Her gifts of character were focused by convent education into a more than paternal anti-Christian feud, not controlled by the paternal humor and easygoingness. She returned to England as a young bluestocking full of grievances.

Lacking any title, she drove about in a carriage with "The Hon. Antonina Dashwood" painted on it. At nineteen she was living as a guest with the family of Thomas De Quincey. He may have picked up his scraps of Hell-Fire lore from her—not then, he was too young, but when he renewed the acquaintance later. He was struck by her dark, spellbinding beauty ("a magnificent Witch," he called her, like Lady Geraldine in *Christabel*) and by her crusading zeal against Christianity. She was not only a classicist but a Hebraist, and she had gotten hold of her father's private papers and some of his books on magic. In a copy of Agrippa's *Occult Philosophy* she stuck a bookplate inscribed: "Rachel

Frances Antonina, Baroness Le Despenser." Her claims were expanding, and she was defying not merely one rival but two. The barony had
actually passed to the Medmenhamite Friar Sir Thomas Stapleton, and,
in addition, Sir Francis's sister Lady Austen called herself Baroness Le
Despenser, though with no legal right.

A marriage to a Mr. Lee ended quickly in separation and loss of
money. Rachel Fanny began a campaign to win recognition as Baroness
Le Despenser in truth, and heiress of West Wycombe, on the grounds
of a secret marriage between her parents. When nobody would recognize her as more than Mrs. Lee, she became prey to persecution mania,
fancying that people stole documents from her, putting every scrap of
paper she wrote on in a sealed envelope, and even trying to conduct
conversations by leaving these envelopes around. She accused her female
governess's two sons of kidnapping her and aroused much hostility in
her behavior at the trial, which led to a prompt acquittal.

After a futile attempt to form a society of her own—probably antireligious in a more solemn style than her father's; she was nicknamed
the Infidel—she withdrew to Gloucestershire under family pressure
and plunged into occult studies. Imagining herself a victim of psychic
attack, she moved to a London hotel in 1808. Here she completed a
fairly balanced *Essay on Government*, which was published and sold
well. Wordsworth, unusually for him, read it almost to the end. The
introduction speaks of the divinely ordained law of Nature by which
human beings pursue their own happiness and declares that anything
that really promotes this happiness is permissible—a step toward
serious interpretation of the Rule of Thélème that her father never
took. But according to her, the owner of the hotel was in the pay of
her persecutors. He lodged a pig in the next room, and it kept her
awake at night till she developed a "particular antipathy" toward it.
He hired men to hold up cages outside her window containing parrots
squawking rude words.

For a while Sir John Dashwood-King, who was in possession of
West Wycombe House, allowed her to stay there. Almost every day,

even in winter, she toiled up to her father's hexagonal mausoleum. During lonely wanderings through the village she heard many anecdotes of that "much-beloved but misled" parent. One of her fantasies concerned an obscure Something in the caves. She used to say, "The clue to all my troubles can be found in the heart of the hill." No one ever learned what it was.

In later years Rachel Fanny published, or tried to publish, bizarre pamphlets, including an Invocation to the Jews written in Hebrew. But sickness and madness were gaining on her. She thought she was being poisoned, and she died, not by poison, in 1829. Her father's papers were not among her possessions, but his occult books were, some with pages torn out. She also had a manuscript of the *Kama Sutra,* or rather a rough translation of it, inscribed "Henry Vansittart to the Founder."

THE FRIARS' LEGACY

During the early years of George III, the renegade Franciscan John Wilkes was striding forward instead of fizzling out. He was the only Friar who did. Because he said more about Medmenham than anybody else, its legend, ironically, clung to him rather than to Dashwood. Our image of it has been affected by the image of Wilkes, and the error that posthumously christened it "The Hell-Fire Club" was due as much to the kind of scandal he attracted as to anything that happened during its own lifetime. (In Jerome K. Jerome's *Three Men in a Boat,* when the voyagers passed Medmenham and a bit of Victorian guidebook history is put in, "the notorious Wilkes" is the only member named.) We can see the process underway even before his return from exile.

In 1760–65 a work of fiction was published in four volumes entitled *Chrysal.* Its author was an Irish barrister, Charles Johnstone, who had turned from legal practice to literature because of deafness. He wrote part of it as a guest and gossip collector in the house of Lord Mount Edgcumbe, a naval officer who worked at the admiralty under Sandwich, had some correspondence with Dashwood, and was a close friend of George Selwyn and Horace Walpole. *Chrysal* purports to be the life story of a coin—a golden guinea—told by itself. Since the coin is used in a long series of dealings, it has glimpses of a great many people and events. The title page runs:

> CHRYSAL: or, the Adventures of a Guinea. Wherein are exhibited Views of several striking Scenes, with Curious and interesting Anecdotes, of the most Noted Persons in every Rank of Life, whose Hands it passed through, in America, England, Holland, Germany, and Portugal.

No author's name is given. The book is simply "by an Adept." This may be a play on words. *Adept* could mean an alchemist, who would know the secrets of gold. It could also mean someone initiated into other secrets—those of society, in fact.

Chrysal, the coin, passes from hand to hand observing . . . not strictly "Persons in every Rank of Life," but persons of the sort who would possess gold guineas. This narrows the field and enables Johnstone to sketch the wealthy, modish, and professional classes in various postures. At one point Chrysal is spent on a copy of *Fanny Hill,* already a high-priced under-the-counter item. The coin witnesses London theater management, charity committee work, army and navy service in the Seven Years' War, and many other occasions for satire. Johnstone employs the coin motif to bring in real people who might have had Chrysal in their pockets somewhere along the line. He leaves them nameless and varies the circumstances. One of those, however, who figures in the portion published in 1765, is meant to be Wilkes. His first appearance is at a meeting in a "mock-monastery," which, more or less, is Medmenham. The date is about 1762.

A good deal of spurious Hell-Fire history is a consequence of readers having taken this passage as a factual account. It is not. Conversely, it is not pure fantasy. Johnstone may have gotten information through Mount Edgcumbe from any of the latter's contacts. But his story is important mainly as legend—legend foreshadowing future truth. The Medmenhamite style of behavior is beginning to be pictured, in retrospect, as something like what it actually becomes in later manifestations; something far more would-be satanic than it was in the reality of Medmenham.

One of Chrysal's owners, an asinine nobleman, bets the guinea on a race between two maggots. He loses to a friend who can be identified by clues further on as Sandwich. Next day Chrysal travels with his new master to "a party of pleasure of a most extraordinary character," at the mock monastery.

Two things are clear within a few paragraphs. First, Johnstone is either writing from untrustworthy hearsay or altering such facts as he does know. The Superior, as his "Dashwood" figure is called, has built the house on an island in the middle of a large lake on his estate. So much for literal reportage. Even if Johnstone means the island in West Wycombe park, neither the date nor the details fit. Secondly, while the Superior does provide wine, women, etcetera, on a lavish scale, his main purpose is a half-serious attack on religion, and the ritual includes devil worship. This may not entirely falsify what went on at Medmenham, but it certainly shifts the bias. Also there is no hint of the political tinge, though some of the members engage individually in politics.

The society is described as being on two levels. Above is the Superior with a "higher order" of twelve. So far, so (probably) good. But he pretends to be Jesus Christ, and each of the others plays an apostle. There is a lower reserve order of twelve more. When an apostle dies or resigns, the gap is filled from this reserve. Plenary rites for the whole body are held in a chapel decorated with "emblems and devices too gross to require explanation to the meanest capacity" and obscene pictures of Christ and his companions.

The "Sandwich" character has served his novitiate in the lower order and is now applying to fill a vacancy in the higher. It turns out that he is not going to be elected unopposed. An unnamed but identifiable "Wilkes" presents himself as a rival.

They put on white robes and kneel in the chapel before the Superior and his apostles, who wear biblical costume. Each candidate has to make a profession of faith parodying the Creed. The Superior then prays to *the Being whom they serve,* meaning Satan, to guide the election; "Sandwich" gets the most votes and is admitted. They sit down to supper, which is provided in the chapel. "Wilkes" is disgruntled and has a revenge ready. Inside a chest he has hidden a baboon dressed up as the Devil. A cord leads from the chest to his chair, so that he can open the lid at any moment. While "Sandwich" is amusing the company with a speech inviting Satan to join them, "Wilkes" pulls the cord and the disguised baboon hurtles out of confinement. This prompt response causes a panic. Most of the brethren bolt, but "Sandwich" falls on the floor and the baboon squats on top of him, scaring him into begging for mercy on the plea that he isn't as wicked as he makes out.

Order is restored. The sham devil is recognized for what it is. "Wilkes" tries to pretend that it got through the window from points unknown. However, some servants who helped with the trick give him away. "Sandwich," who has a long-standing grudge against him, insists on his expulsion, and this is agreed. But the servants' gossip in the neighborhood causes so much superstitious alarm that the Superior thinks it best to disband the society and build a church.

Johnstone's version of the recurrent baboon yarn has been solemnly repeated as if it really happened. Yet he could have adapted it from an earlier source, Ned Ward's story of the prank that broke up the Atheistical Club. In any case it is inconsistent with other and likelier versions. If the baboon was a present from the Vansittarts, and a mascot of the Brotherhood, it would have been well known and would have caused no panic. Nor is there any reason to swallow the story till someone explains how a large, dressed-up monkey can be kept quiet inside a box for hours and yet be in a state to emerge full of energy when you raise the lid.

The further difficulties need not be dwelt on. Sandwich belonged to the inner circle long before Wilkes arrived, and the Order was not dissolved because of local gossip. The main interest lies in the nature of the practical joke, and its context of comic devil worship and people guying biblical characters. This all suggests that rumor and imagination were retroactively turning the Order into a group more like the real Hell-Fire Club of Wharton. After this it was natural that the two should be bracketed together and known by the same name, and *Chrysal* gave impetus to the change.

Johnstone follows up with sketches of the Superior and two other mock monks. He gives "Dashwood" high marks for wit and charm, but insinuates an early warpage through his Jacobite upbringing, which was to blame for his Italian tour with the papist tutor. The farce of the cats at night is told at some length. *Chrysal* has no more scenes at his mock monastery, but in a later section the guinea comes to a poet who is more or less Churchill. Through him, "Wilkes" turns up again and owns the guinea himself during several adventures, based on the events of 1763 and the *Essay on Woman* episode.

These later chapters are dull. But it is worth stressing that "Wilkes" does turn up again. Through the whole meandering length of *Chrysal,* he is the sole major character who fully reenters the story after once dropping out of it. When Johnstone writes, he is already a living legend, and he attracts, and molds, other legends.

This is undoubtedly an added factor in the altered picture of Medmenham and the Hell-Fire misnomer following from it, which occurs (in the *Morning Post*) in 1776 if not earlier and is now, of course, a fixture. Though Wilkes was never a man to go in for organized diabolism, his fame as a blasphemer in the eyes of the virtuous was bound to give that flavor to any reputed secret society he was a member of. The same focusing on Wilkes could explain why the politics are obscured. These, in the real Order, were bound up with Bute and his government: since Wilkes was not part of it, a Wilkes-centered tradition might well leave out the larger political aspect.

The only relic of politics that *Chrysal* embalms is, precisely, the bit that Wilkes carried on, and Johnstone introduces it through him and not through the mock monastery. This is the semantic aftereffect of Bolingbroke's opposition schemes that made *patriotism* a dirty word. In *Chrysal,* "Wilkes" says: "You don't know perhaps that I have turned patriot, and attacked the ministry." Further on, Johnstone remarks on the decline of patriotism from a public-spirited sentiment into a catchword of demagogic opposition, a device for stirring up trouble for your own ends. That feeling in the 1760s and even later underlies Dr. Johnson's often-quoted saying that patriotism is the last refuge of a scoundrel. It had become, for the moment, a Hell-Fire word used by seditious and shocking people—by the later Bolingbroke (damned in Johnson's eyes by his religious views), and Dodington, Dashwood, Wilkes himself.

Wilkes's later career added several twists to the history of the Rule of Thélème in practice. He returned from exile in 1768 and plunged back into political life. His impact was startling. He broke the political mold at last. For a while, the arch-rake's career made "Do what you will" look like a truly emancipating lifestyle. What he did was to get imprudently elected MP for Middlesex. George III, who called him "that devil Wilkes," was determined to keep him out of Parliament. Consequently he was jailed, fined, declared ineligible—and reelected four times by the Middlesex voters. The 1763 slogan, "Wilkes and Liberty!" was revived as the battle cry of a near revolution. Though the Government managed to defer its surrender till surrender had ceased to be dangerous, politics were never the same again. Real issues, real party distinctions, were henceforth firmly on the map. Meanwhile Wilkes, like Sir Francis, had taken up the cause of the American colonists, but with much more energy. He became their chief English adviser. Their debt to him is recognized in a number of U.S. place names.

With Wilkes, liberty and libertinism again seemed to go together, and in his own ebullient spirit they did. But the alliance went no further. Franklin was in England during the Middlesex uproar, and he judged that the hero's morals or nonmorals were self-defeating. The public might be restless but was also respectable. King George would have been routed at once, very likely deposed, if he had had a bad character and Wilkes a good one. As it was, the short-term success of Liberty could only be limited.

In 1780 the roles were reversed, with even deadlier effect, by the Gordon riots. An easing of the laws against Catholics enabled the mad Lord George Gordon to stir up the London mob in what began as an anti-papist pogrom and turned into a free-for-all of looting, burning, and anarchy. Here were the anti-Catholicism and the casting-off of restraint that Medmenham had built into an Order for political gentlemen, blossoming outside gentlemanly confines as a mass frenzy. By this time Wilkes was a City alderman. He could hardly dodge the issue. Confronting the flames and violence, he decided that they had nothing to do with Liberty. The rioting was largely a delayed outcome of his own Middlesex campaigns, his own rousing of the people to a sense of their power; but now he took the lead in suppressing it, thereby forfeiting his mass support and destroying the movement that had gathered round him. Leadership passed to others. Once again, it seemed, a Thelemic principle was confirmed. Unbridled freedom could work only inside a select club. When the random myriads began doing as they willed, or as they pleased, they required curbing. Universal, benign, liberating Nature was not to be trusted.

IMITATION AND INSPIRATION

Sir Francis's Order was not sterile. Sterility would have been out of character. Directly or indirectly, it inspired other ventures. One of them introduces a great and unexpected figure.

A late entry in George Bubb Dodington's diary (December 23, 1760) records a dinner party with a "Mr. Sterne" among the guests. This was *the* Mr. Sterne, Laurence, author of *Tristram Shandy*. Vicar of Sutton-on-the-Forest in Yorkshire, and well into his forties before he took to writing, Sterne struck a new vein of irreverent farce and Rabelais-indebted satire that made him an instant bestseller. Most of *Tristram Shandy* was published during 1759–61, and Sterne flourished in London society as the chief literary lion of the hour. Somebody—perhaps

Bubb himself, more likely Wilkes—gave him some inside information on Medmenham. In part 5, chapter 36 of his novel, written during the autumn of 1761, he quotes or slightly misquotes the motto of the Cave of Trophonius in the carving, *Omne animal post coitum est triste*.

Back in Yorkshire lived an old Cambridge crony of his, John Hall-Stevenson, who called Sterne his "cousin" and appears in *Tristram* as Eugenius. Eugenius is a discreet, sensible fellow; this is a private joke. The real-life Hall-Stevenson was an unbalanced anti-Catholic witch hunter, collector of dirty books, and hypochondriac. Whenever an east wind blew he retired to bed in the belief that he was dying. Stevenson had inherited Skeleton Castle, a short distance inland from Saltburn in the North Riding and rechristened it Crazy Castle. He was in touch with Wilkes as well as Sterne—they planned, after the novelist's death, to write a biography together, though nothing came of this—and also with Paul Whitehead. In June 1762 he visited Medmenham, afterward speaking of it derisively as the "shrine of St. Francis" that didn't produce any miracles. But he was two-faced on the subject. He founded a northern fraternity of his own on what he conceived as Medmenhamite lines.

Sterne, who had found much to interest him in the Crazy Castle library, warmly endorsed the scheme; Hanoverian England had some remarkable clergymen. They got Dashwood to join in as an adviser, or, as they put it with a typical turn of phrase, Privy Councillor. Crazy Castle was an authentic medieval pile, not a pastiche like the Abbey. It had a moat, dismal and stagnant, with no drawbridge—you had to cross by ferry. It had crumbling stone terraces and battlements. Hall-Stevenson commissioned a picture of it with ravens flying round the tower and an owl sitting on an urn. All very Gothic. In this promising setting his society was launched as "The Demoniacs."

It soon showed symptoms of a decadence that makes the successor groups of Medmenham (so far as we can trace them in fact and fiction) a great deal less interesting. They revert to mere disreputability or worse, or get stuck in a groove. The Demoniacs had a ritual including parody baptism and assumed names. But most of the names were no more than pointless aliases. Hall-Stevenson was Antony. The Rev. Robert Lascelles was Pantagruel—this at least made sense, but they reduced it to Panty. Other members called themselves Paddy Andrew and Don Pringello. Few of the Yorkshire neighbors who joined came anywhere near the caliber of Sterne, or indeed of Hall-Stevenson. The society declined into a convivial group assembling to drink, gamble, and swap dirty stories. As to the last, Hall-Stevenson (who fancied himself in the role of a new Rabelais) composed some, improved others, and published a versified collection as *Crazy Tales*. One of the tales is attributed to Sterne, who is said to have tried out bits of *Tristram Shandy* on the Demoniacs. But he got bored and ceased to attend. The club faded into limbo.

After Hall-Stevenson's death, more verses of his were published, including a nasty doggerel entitled *The Confessions of Sir F— of Medmenham and of The Lady Mary, his Wife*. It vaguely accuses Dashwood of incest with female relatives and hints at abortion and a Medmenhamite liaison with a temporary "wife" of lesbian tastes called Mary—possibly his half sister Mary Walcott. The thing is too muddled to be evidence of anything but its author's unpleasantness.

We meet Sterne again in the dedication of *The Fruit-Shop*, that strange piece of unfunny donnish erotica hinting at politics behind the Medmenham facade. The unnamed author cries Armstrong's "Oeconomy of Love" and Churchill's satire on homosexuals, "The Times." Most of his book is a melange of double entendre and anti-Christianity. Toward the end, however, he gives a twelve-page account of a "sect of philogynists"—womanizers—holding frankly sexual meetings preceded by ritual. The sect is depicted as an underground movement that has been going on for centuries and, one gathers, is still in being. The impression is strong that this is fake history in the Masonic or Rosicrucian style, meant to supply a pedigree for a secret society in the author's own London. He describes the ritual: a short talk from the leader; wine and fruit, music and dancing; a travesty hymn beginning "Veni spiritus amoris" (we have a link here with the *Essay on Woman* fragment); and then the real business of the evening.

The whole book is so full of pseudodata that a reader has no way of telling whether the "sect" actually existed. If it did, it may be a link between the English societies and an alleged movement of Hell-Fire inspiration in France. The French groups are obscure, and so is their connection with England. However, the French writer Ducis mentions the *Essay on Woman* as "revealing the philosophy of a society of monks founded on the code of the Abbey Thélème," and a free-love club known as Les Aphrodites is described by Andrea de Nerciat. Through these there may in turn be a tenuous succession to a greater and grimmer phenomenon a few years later, foreshadowed also by the ideological tinge of the *Chrysal* story.

That phenomenon, however, was still in the making. Before it dawned, there was a sharp revival of the Dublin Hell-Fire Club after decades of nullity. The revival was denounced in the *Freeman's Journal* for March 12, 1771, which declared in tones of outrage that the Club already had branches in various parts of Ireland, and that most of its members were young men of fortune who ought presumably to know better. Its official title was "The Holy Fathers" in imitation of the pseudo-Franciscans, but the new name failed to stick. Its regular toasts were "The Devil" and "Damn us all."

This reborn body lasted for about thirty years. Its most famous member was a latecomer, Thomas "Buck" Whaley. Born in 1766, he was the son of "Burn-Chapel" Whaley, a rich Protestant pyromaniac whose idea of fun was setting fire to papist places of worship. Burn-Chapel Whaley is said to have once been president of the old Dublin Hell-Fire Club, and to have caused the deaths of several members when he poured brandy over a servant and set light to him, starting a blaze that got out of control. This accident indeed has been blamed for the Club's midcentury decline. Burn-Chapel's son Thomas, the Buck, tried living in Paris with £10,000 a year, but his near-compulsive gambling got him into difficulties. Back in Dublin he recouped by several freak bets: for instance, that he would ride to Jerusalem and back in a year (he did); that he would jump from a window into the first open carriage that passed and kiss the occupant (he did). He sat in the Irish Parliament, not creditably.

As a Hell-Fire ringleader he returned to the old meeting area on Montpelier Hill and went in for satanic and homosexual parties. One lurid tale is that he set up a man-trap there, caught a farmer's daughter in it, and had her killed and smoked "like a side of pork" and carved up for sharing among his fellow members. Whaley repented, however, and moved to the Isle of Man, where he built a house still called Whaley's Folly. His desertion and premature death in 1800 deprived the Club of its liveliest spirit and may have finished it off.

In England the last Whartonian flickerings were at the universities. Another Oxford Hell-Fire Club is alleged to have been suppressed about 1780. Nothing is known of it. Byron seems to have picked up notions at Cambridge: in 1809, soon after leaving Trinity, he held a meeting at Newstead Abbey commemorating the supposed devil worshippers of Medmenham and drank burgundy from a human skull. Then Oxford comes in again with a tale like the Cambridge legend of the Appalling Club, but feebler. The late date assigned to this tallies with Oxford's role as home of lost causes.

Actually, Oxford's third Hell-Fire Club may never have existed. It may be merely part of the mythology of an even later body, the Phoenix Club of Brasenose. This did flourish in the Victorian era. Its members held ceremonies in fancy dress. Their permanent vice chairman was Satan. A place was reserved for him at the meetings, and his health was drunk. The Phoenix claimed to have risen from the ashes of a Hell-Fire Club that met twice weekly at the same college in 1828 and came to a spectacular end. One night the chairman, while uttering "horrid blasphemies," burst a blood vessel and dropped dead. At that very moment the Devil appeared to a don passing in the lane outside. Not being in the secret, the don was alarmed, and his alarm increased when he saw what appeared to be the defunct chairman being dragged out through the window by some invisible agency.

In spite of a few names and details being given, there is no solid reason to believe in this 1828 club. The only proved fact is a scandal about an illicit party where a girl died. The legend is probably an aftergrowth that the undergraduates of the Phoenix annexed or even invented.

PART THREE
Nightmare

12

THE GOTHIC PLUNGE

GOD AND NATURE, GOOD AND EVIL

London had its Gordon Riots before Paris had its Bastille Day. The conviction that erring mortals could *not* be safely allowed to do-what-they-would took longer to triumph in France than it did in England. Rousseau's disciples were still hymning Nature, and the goodness of the human heart, through most of the second half of that century. But (and this is important) even they were preaching their faith as a militant, controversial dogma with a radical message, in a milieu where it was no longer part of a gentleman's common-sense equipment. The atmosphere had altered since Leibniz, Pope, Bolingbroke. The sunshine of alleged Reason had clouded over. The natural rightness of "unspoilt" Man might still be a fact, but it had at the very least to be reinterpreted.

This change was reflected in minor as well as major things—in, for instance, the reversion to puerile diabolism and low-caliber naughtiness by the last Hell-Fire groups, and perhaps to really sinister conduct by individual members such as Buck Whaley. Even within a chosen clique, let alone a city mob, the Rule of Thélème could no longer flourish as the expansive anything-goes principle of Medmenham. "Do what you will" seemed to have meaning now only as being deliberately bad—lining up on the side of evil in a world that was no longer easygoing even for the comfortable, a world where conflicting values were real again. Conversely, there was a new public earnestness for which the relaxed opposition stance of Medmenham was out of date. Wilkes was not the only apostle of Liberty who no longer found it interesting or relevant to belong to a merely libertine organization.

People were thinking and acting differently. Cosmic optimism had begun to crumble when Sir Francis's Order was still at its zenith, and it is here that the third phase of Thélème opens. A precise date—almost a precise moment—struck a traumatic blow at the mind of Europe. On November 1, 1755, at about 9 a.m., a colossal ten-minute earthquake assaulted Lisbon. The Portuguese capital was then a rich and brash commercial metropolis with close English ties. As November 1 was All Saints' Day, most of the virtuous were gathered inside the churches and therefore suffered heavier casualties. For a week the city was on fire, and later in November came further quakes. About fifteen thousand were killed, many thousands more were injured and homeless.

An age persuaded that God (if remote) was good, that Nature wore a wise smile, that all was for the best in this best of possible worlds, had to come to terms with a huge, meaningless horror. In its various ways, it tried. The surviving Lisbon clergy preached sermons about divine judgment on an acquisitive society . . . but then, so many of the victims were poor, so many were children. Protestants, including Wesley, spoke of divine vengeance against popery. A French Jansenist observed, erroneously, that the earthquake had destroyed all seven houses of the Jesuits; Wesley observed, correctly, that it had spared the solitary Protestant chapel. In England a public fast was proclaimed and masquerades were banned to avert God's further seismic wrath. In Germany the six-year-old Goethe heard pious grown-ups discussing the disaster and felt his first doubts of God. In France Madame Pompadour gave up rouge.

If the Christians were unconvincing, the philosophers of Enlightenment did no better, at least on the positive side. Voltaire struck a new note with a poem in direct retort to Pope's *Essay on Man*. Philosophers, he urged, might theorize about everything being for the best, but they lived far from trouble. They should go to Lisbon and take a look. We simply do not know, said Voltaire. God is silent, and Nature, let us at last be honest, has no message. We must suffer and submit.

Rousseau wrote a reply making out that the earthquake was good because it had taught civilized Man a lesson. The citizens of Lisbon, instead of obeying the Rousseauan version of Nature, had elected to live in high houses and were reaping the consequences. Kant too made a stand for optimism, arguing that we never see the complete picture as God does. But Voltaire struck again in 1759 with his satiric novel *Candide,* and this time decisively. Henceforth no one could take the all-is-for-the-best line without sounding like Voltaire's comic character Pangloss; parody killed reality, and the case was abandoned.

Other events were helping to change the mood. The Seven Years' War did its share. Besides the normal atrocities, it included the political murder of Admiral Byng (Voltaire's famous remark on this, that the English shoot an admiral sometimes *pour encourager les autres,* is made in *Candide*). Within two weeks of that came the Damiens case in Paris. Robert-François Damiens, an ex-soldier, stabbed Louis XV. The king was not seriously hurt. Damiens was captured. His punishment took place in a public square. After various minor tortures, such as having his hand burnt, he was laid out flat with teams of horses harnessed to each of his limbs. The horses were lashed forward and pulled him to pieces. He was tough; the executioners had to cut through his flesh to make him come apart more easily. Even so it took hours to get both his arms and his legs off, and he was still not quite dead, though witnesses disagreed as to how long the head and trunk kept twitching before they stopped.

This performance was watched by a large and fashionable audience of both sexes. One lady cried out how sorry she felt for the poor horses. Medmenham was represented by George Selwyn, that connoisseur of cruelty, who made a special trip for the occasion. (One hardly knows how to relate that fact to the manifestly civilized quality of an age when he could travel freely to Paris in time of war.) As he pushed forward through the crowd, a French nobleman asked if he was an executioner. Selwyn replied, "No, monsieur, I have not that honour; I am only an amateur." One of Damiens's guards promptly shouted to the onlookers to make way for this "English amateur," and Selwyn enjoyed the dismemberment from a ringside seat.

If Selwyn had no scruples, others in England, including some of his fellow Franciscans, were developing them. Issues of real public good and evil were just beginning to be acknowledged again. Sides were beginning to be taken, though not in any clear pattern. As we saw, Sir Francis Dashwood himself was active in the fight to save Byng; so were Dodington and Whitehead. On the other hand, David Mallet, generally their friend though not a Franciscan, was among the anti-Byng propagandists.

By the late 1760s, after Medmenham, lines were being drawn much more sharply. A genuine political reform movement was sprouting from Wilkes's election battles. A quiet progress in humanitarianism was checking the savagery of the law. Statistics for London and Middlesex show that while juries went on convicting prisoners for the many capital crimes, the percentage actually hanged fell decade by decade from 68 percent in the 1750s to 29 percent in the 1790s. Meanwhile a new reading public, large enough to support commercial book production on a big scale, was breaking the grip of literary patronage; and new clubs such as Brooks's, formed by men under thirty, were breaking a similar grip of social seniority. Brooks's was the headquarters of Charles James Fox, Henry's son, who transformed Whiggism.

Not only an observant hoverer on the fringes of the Medmenham story and a seconder of Dashwood in his pro-Byng efforts, but also a man ahead of his time as the new trends took shape, was Horace Walpole. In the prelude of the third phase of Thélème, he moves— briefly and without meaning to—from the outskirts to the center.

RISE OF THE GOTHIC CASTLE

While Dashwood's Abbey rose and fell, Walpole's Castle of Indolence, Strawberry Hill, had gone on. That too, however, passed through a crisis of allegiance. As a result it was Walpole who did most to revive the Rabelais-descended motif, but indirectly, gradually, and with a somber change of spirit. His imagination created a revamped framework in which Thelemic freedom assumed nightmare forms such as Medmenham had never dreamed of. Yet he had no idea what he was doing.

Walpole was more than commonly sensitive to the darkening of the sky after 1755. He noted in his memoirs that the past century or so, the Age of Reason as he called the whole period, had been mainly good; but the war, and Byng, and Damiens, were exposing the thinness of the veneer. Prodded into an active role as an MP, he recalled more often than hitherto that he was now a son of the great prime minister, whom, in a retrospective glow, he idolized. He dreaded what he thought was the neoroyalism of George III; he followed the Bute crisis anxiously; and in spite of attacks on him in the *North Briton,* he came to sympathize with Wilkes.

In April 1764 he applied his talents for wire-pulling to the grievances of a cousin, Henry Seymour Conway, whom he regarded as a test case in the struggle against the Crown's encroachments. Conway had been dismissed from an official post and an army command because he spoke up for Wilkes and voted in the Commons against the king's wishes. Walpole sprang into frenetic action on Conway's behalf. The Strawberry Hill dilettante was replaced by a crusader, determined to prove a worthy son, at last, of Sir Robert. He had chosen poor ground to fight on. Conway was no Dreyfus, and Walpole's attempts to unite an opposition movement around his case led chiefly to boredom and to very little appreciation from Conway himself, even when restored to favor.

But the effect on Walpole was profound. As he sat at Strawberry Hill dashing off pro-Conway letters and literature, the wonderful house began to trouble him. It was escapist. It stood for what he now saw as the less admirable side of his character, tempting him from his duty as his father's real heir. Strawberry Hill's gentlemanly liberty was a different thing from the public kind that he was battling for. The mansion that indulged his whims was becoming a burden on his conscience.

Early in June 1764, just as he was putting the final touches to a pamphlet for the Conway campaign, weeks of tension caught up with him and he had a dream—one of the most influential in the history of literature. His Gothic house had grown into a vast, ancient, eerie pile. He looked up a staircase and saw an immense hand in a gauntlet of mail. Waking, he began to write, at first hardly knowing what or why. A rare fury of literary energy drove him forward. On August 6 he stopped and drew breath. His novel *The Castle of Otranto* was finished.

The Castle of Otranto is an outlandish book for such a person to have written. It is not, as is sometimes said, a mere confection by a dabbler in medieval antiquities. It can only be explained by an upsurge of subconscious factors, on which the cool rationality of Strawberry Hill had been clamping down: promptings of conscience and romantic family loyalty and a suppressed hunger for mystery and the supernatural (Walpole's collection, after all, included that scrying stone of Dee's). The title of the story is apt. It is "about" the Castle, a dark dream projection of Strawberry Hill housing characters symbolizing Walpole's conflicts.

At the outset, Manfred is in possession, an unattractive, self-seeking prince. A prophecy declares that the Castle and Lordship of Otranto will "pass from the present family whenever the real owner shall be grown too large to inhabit it." Manfred's son Conrad, betrothed to Isabella, is found in the Castle courtyard just before his wedding, crushed under a gigantic helmet a hundred times too big for a mortal wearer. A young peasant named Theodore points out that this helmet is like the one on a black marble statue of Alfonso the Good, one of the former princes. Soon further portents appear, all in the same style—a gigantic armored leg, a gigantic sword, a gigantic hand. The tremendous shade of Alfonso is plainly present and hostile to Manfred. After various adventures, in which Theodore is the sympathetic figure, the Castle walls collapse. Alfonso rises complete and colossal from the ruins, announcing that

Theodore is his long-lost heir, and ascends to Heaven. The usurping Manfred abdicates. Theodore takes over and marries Isabella.

The dream symbols underlying this tale are obvious. Manfred is Horace Walpole as lord of Strawberry Hill, a dark, traitorous aspect of his psyche. Alfonso is Sir Robert, whose vast and increasingly insistent shade is shattering Manfred's Gothic mini-Utopia. Theodore is the new political Horace who has belatedly recollected his birth and task in life and will come into his own as the Castle perishes. The end, however, is prophetic. Even when he is Lord of Otranto Theodore remains a cipher. He marries Isabella without ardor, as a companion in the melancholy that possesses his soul. Deep down Walpole must have foreseen that his political action would be only a gesture righting the balance, not the start of a fresh career.

It petered out, in fact, after 1765. But he still took stands from time to time, denouncing slavery and the conquest of India, and making shrewd predictions of war in the air, and even in outer space, as soon as the first Montgolfier balloons took off. *The Castle of Otranto,* similarly, is a book of the future—that is, the future from the standpoint of the date when it was written. It foreshadows the Surrealists with its out-of-place, out-of-proportion images. It gives the earliest hint of the Byronic hero—black haired, pale skinned, forbidding, haunted, mysterious. And it establishes the Castle (where the frivolous Yorkshire Demoniacs did not) in a new role very far from Thomsonian Indolence, as a shut-in scene of preternormal terror and guilt, a potential Thélème for wills unrestrained in evil. Walpole's qualms over Strawberry Hill, by making the enclosed domain irresponsible and dangerous instead of agreeably free, carried him beyond Thomson. Thus he created the Gothic novel.

The Castle of Otranto alone might not have made much stir, and Walpole never followed it up. But his hints were seized and enlarged on by an author who made them her special study, Ann Radcliffe. Born (intriguingly) on July 9, 1764, when Walpole himself was in the full flood of invention, she spent the years from 1789 to 1797 pouring out novels in the same vein, only more so. Best known is *The Mysteries of*

Udolpho. Ann Radcliffe's castles are places given over to dark passions and dreadful sights. They are bathed in uncanny moonlight, tormented by winds. Supernatural horrors—or horrors that appear so—terrify the occupants. Dark, lawless, enigmatic men prowl about, scheming. Innocent virgins, cut off from the outer world, undergo ordeals—more than once at the hands of clerics; the anti-Catholicism of the Hell-Fire club tradition is here too.

It was all best-selling stuff. The road from Otranto through Udolpho led to *Frankenstein, Melmoth the Wanderer,* and a swarm of lesser romances of terror, diabolism, black magic, and female suffering. Byron himself first tried to *be* the Radcliffe-type hero-villain, then perfected him in poetry, and handed him on to later authors still: to Emily Bronte, for instance.

Long before that, however, Gothic romance had come under the scrutiny of a Frenchman who absorbed it into a system of his own. This genius also admired Rabelais and Richardson. To explore his own Thelemic vision he imitated those whom we have seen (as it were) building castles in Hell; but thanks partly to the Gothic romancers, partly also to the Wharton legend transmitted by way of Richardson's Lovelace, his castles were infinitely more hellish.

13

THE DIVINE MARQUIS

THE DARK SIDE OF REASON

Among Walpole's correspondents in the Otranto decade was the Marquise du Deffand. Once the presiding spirit of a Paris salon, she was now seventy and blind, but still alert. A letter she sent to him in 1768 described a sexual scandal involving a French nobleman. It was uncannily apt that Walpole should have been the first known Englishman to hear about the activities of a portentous figure whom his own work was to supply with a technique of horror.

Donatien Alphonse François, Marquis de Sade, was born in 1740. His Provençal family was ancient and distinguished. His genealogical tree included the Laura who inspired Petrarch's love poetry. After service in the Seven Years' War, Donatien Alphonse François married Renée de Montreuil but deserted her for long periods to live with her younger sister Anne. Renée—who loved him and bore him children—was patient and forgiving. Madame de Montreuil was not; and the influence wielded by his implacable mother-in-law was a major and ignominious cause of the Marquis's being sent to prison for spells totaling twenty-seven years. Sexual infamy was the basis of the reasons alleged but would not have condemned him in itself. Other French aristocrats of his time went further.

The plain priapic energy of an earlier generation, the Duc de Richelieu's, was souring into passions of a nastier kind. Having lost status at home and prestige abroad, the nobles were tempted to sexual barbarities, explicit or disguised, as the only means of recapturing a sense of power. There was more to the Damiens atrocity than a perverted notion of justice, and even when a seigneur indulged impulses more blatant, the atmosphere of the time usually allowed him to get away with it. The notorious Duc de Charolais, who found women exciting only when he was shedding their blood, was far more luridly orgiastic in practice than Sade ever was. Sade suffered partly because of the tragicomedy of the feud with his mother-in-law, but more because of his ideas and the way he expressed them.

Endowed with tastes that were abnormal and unendearing, but not specially interesting in themselves, he made his name immortal by the unique feat of building a cosmic philosophy around them. He not only reaffirmed "Do what you will," but was ready to reinterpret the whole universe on nightmare lines rather than admit that any other being could have a right to criticize him or curtail his peculiar freedom.

It is uncertain when he began the process. During the 1760s, though maintaining (on and off) a normal family life in Provence, he may have got his nickname of the "Divine Marquis" in Paris society from a likeness to the Divine Aretino, an uninhibited Renaissance wit. When Madame du Deffand wrote to Walpole, Sade had already acquired a modest reputation for "horrors." The actual case that caught her attention occurred at Easter 1768. Sade picked up an unemployed seamstress named Rose Keller in Paris and took her to a country house. She asserted afterward that he had offered her a domestic job; he insisted that he had made the main object clear. At any rate, when she was safely in the house, he told her to take her clothes off and threatened her if she did not comply. He tied her on a sofa face down, whipped her, then put ointment on her wounds and gave her some food. She escaped and went to the police, saying she had been cut with a knife as well as flogged, a charge that remained unproved. Sade escaped by paying her 2,400 francs.

In 1772 came a second scandal in Marseilles, which was hardly more spectacular, but much more revealing. Sade and his valet hired four girls from a brothel, took them to a private suite, and fed them sweets doctored with Spanish fly. Various permutative exercises ensued. They included the flagellation of the marquis himself, who (this is one of the characteristic touches) got up every so often, went over to the mantelpiece, notched it to record the number of lashes he had received, and then went back for more. Unfortunately the aphrodisiac made one of the prostitutes ill. Sade was sentenced to death for sodomy and attempted poisoning. He slipped away to Italy with his wife's sister, and the sentence was allowed to pass into suspension; when he returned to France he was imprisoned for a time but escaped with absurd ease, to his mother-in-law's annoyance.

His third documented practical effort was begun at his Provençal home, La Coste, in the winter of 1774–75. This was his nearest approach to a real life Thélème of his own. With the connivance of his much-enduring marquise he set up a complex multiple harem. He took on a carefully chosen chambermaid and other young female staff, several handsome menservants, and an equally delightful male secretary and female cook. But the charmed enclosure of post-Rabelaisian fantasy failed, in this case, to enclose. Society pressed in. The harem grew unruly and gradually disintegrated. The servants gave notice. The secretary's parents told him to come home, and he did. The chambermaid left in an advanced state of pregnancy, blaming the master, and the cook's father appeared on the doorstep with a gun.

In 1777 Madame de Monteuil won at last. Through her wire-pulling at court, Sade was jailed in earnest—first at Vincennes, then in the Bastille. Prison was not totally restrictive for a man of his rank. He could live fairly comfortably and indulge his imagination. On October 22, 1785, in the Bastille, he started his first book. It was a survey in a fictionalized setting of all the sex deviations he could think of, to the number of 600—a clinical work far ahead of its time, packed with cruelty and ugliness, and strikingly titled *The 120 Days of Sodom*. Supplies of paper being limited, Sade wrote in a microscopic hand on both sides of a hundred-odd small sheets. With all his economies he completed only about a third of the book, summing up the rest in notes until such time as he could handle it properly. He glued all the sheets together to make a 40-foot strip and rolled it up. In 1787 he got another stock of paper but did not return to *The 120 Days*. Instead he wrote some new stories, of which the most important was a short novel, *Justine*.

Meanwhile the Revolution was brewing. The Bastille housed only a few prisoners, but Sade was one of them almost to the last . . . not quite to the last. He played a little-known part in precipitating the events of July 14. During June he had been tossing notes out of the windows describing the ill treatment of his fellow inmates. On July 2 improvising a megaphone from a tube and funnel, he called out that the prisoners were about to have their throats cut and urged the people to rescue them. Fearing an attack, the governor had him moved out to the insane asylum at Charenton. He left many possessions behind. The attack came, with results still annually celebrated. When the turmoil had died down, the marquise loyally went in and retrieved some of her husband's manuscripts, but many were lost. One of the storming party had walked off with the *Sodom* roll of paper. It would be interesting to know whether he read it and, if so, what he made of it. Long afterward it was traced in a private collection, but Sade himself never saw it again, and much of his copious later writing was an attempt to present the same subjects in more dramatic forms.

A few months after his transfer, the Revolution set him free. Now somewhat adrift (his wife had withdrawn into a Carmelite convent) he professed support for the new order and served on various committees but never got properly in step. Suspect as an aristocrat who hung on to his chateau—which was wrecked and looted in 1792—he was too extreme for the politicians in some ways and not extreme enough in others. He opposed capital punishment, even saving his mother-in-law from the guillotine; the Terror did not please him at all, because the killing was being done from a bad motive, politics instead of pleasure. During 1793 he was jailed again, as a moderate. This imprisonment was briefer, but after another spell of freedom he was accused in 1801 (probably unjustly) of propagandizing against Bonaparte, and committed as insane (probably wrongly) to the Charenton asylum. The head of the asylum treated him kindly and gave him work as an unofficial assistant. He organized dances and amateur theatricals for the inmates. But he never got out and died there in 1814.

Sade has been half hidden till lately by a conspiracy of silence and censorship. Below the surface, however, his effect on Western civilization has always been recognized by some. He has been praised as the only man who dared to think the Age of Reason through to its logical end, completing the work that the Lisbon earthquake began. He has been picked out, if hardly praised, by Camus, for instance, as the first clear prefigurer of the world we now live in. No amount of respect for his genius, however, can make him a nice person. He was not even the masterful ogre whom the word *sadism* might evoke. As his history shows, he lacked boldness and enterprise. People scared him, and he had a silly, erratic temper and was easily trapped. Even his appearance, preserved in a police description, is disconcerting. The Divine Marquis was somewhat undersized and pudgy, with blue eyes and very fair hair, whitening in his fifties. With advancing years, he grew fatter. There is no authentic portrait.

As for his attitude to life, its ruling themes may be summed up as follows.

Pleasure—your own—is the sole object worth pursuing. This should be done in a scientific spirit, with no restraints whatsoever.

The only authentic pleasure is sexual. Other kinds are feeble and limited and should never be allowed to compete.

Perversion, so-called, is a higher pleasure than normal intercourse, which has distracting associations of love and parenthood.

Furthermore, the essence of the pleasure in sex is egotistic and manipulative. Hence it reaches its height where there is the most selfishness, the most cruelty, the most tyranny over the partner, or rather victim.

And the pursuit of pleasure along these lines need not imply a narrow, monomaniac life, because the converse is true if you dare to make it so. Since the secret of the supreme thrill is (in conventional language) evil, an ever-widening repertoire of evil can be built into your sex practices and be made the basis of ever-more-fiery, ever-more-exotic thrills. This is the royal road to an anti-moral superhumanity, which the null virtuous can never hope to rival or to stand up against.

It was Sade's achievement to work at these obsessions of his till he had created an upside-down religion: a religion with a sacred book— his novel *Juliette,* the monstrous companion to *Justine*—which has a ghastly compulsive interest and is by no means easy to refute.

VICE AS VIRTUE

Sade's outlook being what it was, he believed at heart in Liberty without either Equality or Fraternity and equated it with libertinism in plain terms. The characters in his books who express his notions of freedom are actually called "libertines." This raises the question of what he meant by Liberty; hardly what Rabelais meant, or the dissident Whigs, or John Wilkes. It would be a mistake, though, to get completely involved in abstractions and treat him as a pure novelist of ideas. He would have built his Thélème if he could. It was the failure of active life that made him an author.

The recurring Sade conception or daydream is in fact the same that we have in a number of guises—Thélème itself, the Hell-Fire clubs, *The Castle of Indolence,* Medmenham: the select emancipated community, the group of libertines outrageously asserting and enjoying their freedom. It is a proof of the strength of this idea that even Sade, whose tastes might seem to lead to an isolated position, seldom thought of the libertine as entirely alone, even in the sense of being alone with his victim. However hateful Sadian Man made himself, he would have companions. Sade's single major attempt in person, at La Coste, involved a whole team. When he turned from reality to fiction, he pictured his most typical libertines acting together. To observe and be observed without shame, to compare notes, to concoct horrors in partnership—for him these were all part of the liberating experience.

But prison made his imagination more inhuman and vengeful than it might otherwise have been. When he took up literature, the groups of libertines in his chief works were sinister as no Hell-Fire club was, and he drew on grim literary models to provide settings for them. He liked Rabelais, and even called a character the Marquise de Thélème, but Rabelais's cheerful exuberance failed to rub off on him. He studied Fielding's *Jonathan Wild* with its apologia for crime, and Richardson's *Clarissa* with its motifs of tormented maidenhood and male persecution by Lovelace-Wharton. It is not certain that he read *Fanny Hill,* that saga of voyeurism and group sex, but he did read *Thérèse Philosophe.* Finally—and with a good deal of critical acuteness—he read Gothic romances in the Walpole-Radcliffe stream. These could be related to the chateau life of his earlier years, and to the Bastille itself, and they helped him to conceive citadels of terror and torture, secret fastnesses cut off from the prying world. There—almost outside the everyday map and calendar—a few rich, relentless, experimentally minded characters could be portrayed gathering in privacy, to live as he would have wished to live.

Having absorbed all these useful influences, Sade still never managed to write as if it were his true vocation. Most of his characters are contrived figures voicing ideas or points of view, and, especially in *Juliette,* they tend to voice them at off-putting length. He describes their orgies in increasingly minute detail, passing through a *Fanny Hill* stage of circumlocution (used in *Justine* for stylistic reasons) to eventual clinical exactitude, with the French equivalents of four-letter words. Yet the result is hardly ever seductive or stimulating. He was long under a ban as unprintable, yet without being aphrodisiac—without being pornographic, even in quite the normal sense. His specialized language and interests often make his world strangely unreal. Flaubert once remarked that "there is not an animal, not a tree" in Sade's novels. This is a comment on Flaubert, too, because in the later parts of *Juliette* there are trees in abundance, as well as animals, so

Flaubert presumably didn't read it right through. But he had a point.

Before looking at Sade's fantasies closeup, can we get any further with the ideas behind them—the ideas that turn the moral world inside out to rationalize his own desires?

The marquis was well read. He gathered masses of miscellaneous knowledge from travel books and hoarded it as ammunition against the ethics favored in his own country. He relished Machiavelli. He knew some of the books that Curll published, such as Mcibomius's *Treatise of Flogging*. He glanced at occultism but preferred the would-be scientific materialism of Julien de La Mettrie, author of a work with the honest title *L'Homme Machine*. In the outcome he accepted the Age of Reason's stress on "Nature" as our guide . . . but he inverted it.

This was the step of ruthless logic that everybody else had recoiled from. Until the 1750s the prevailing optimism had said: "Live according to Nature, it's the only rational thing to do. Nature is well planned and benign. Obeying her promptings means being good. Live like that, please yourself in a nice sensible way, and you can't be bad." Enlightened rakes like the Hell-Fire brethren, and the author of *Thérèse Philosophe*, had made the last part of this advice look dubious but had never seriously shaken the main argument.

Then the earthquake and *Candide* threw optimism into confusion. Sade, and Sade alone, pointed out that the only way the Age of Reason could put its philosophy together again was by embracing the consequences. "Live according to Nature, yes. Nothing has happened to change the fact that this is the only rational thing to do. We realize now, of course, that Nature isn't well planned or benign. She is at best neutral, at worst appalling. But live according to Nature still. Be appalling! And if you can beat her at her own game, so much the better."

Sade appeals adroitly to the promptings of Nature in sex itself. He pushes the argument of the amiable Dr. Armstrong the rest of the way. Nature dictates sexual enjoyment, but she does *not* dictate "normal" sexual mores, and outside western Europe hardly anyone pretends that she does. You can think of no lust or perversion that isn't approved somewhere. Anybody not blinded by Christian or post-Christian prejudice must admit that Nature wouldn't allow men to enjoy (for example) sodomy if such conduct offended her.

To live by Nature is to gratify yourself. That's the whole of it. The ideal libertine would destroy a Lisbon to enhance his own orgasm. There are no moral absolutes to forbid him. Right and wrong are a matter of local custom. They can be set aside, and they should be. "The most perfect being we could conceive would be the one who alienated himself most from our conventions and found them most contemptible."

The sole motive for so-called virtue is that it may give you pleasure. And yes, fair enough, it may. But if so-called vice gives you greater pleasure, then the natural and proper course is to scrap virtue. Which will usually be the result if you face facts, because virtue is weaker. Virtue means not doing things. Virtue means timidity, obedience. Virtue means conforming to custom. Vice, on the other hand, is (or should be) bold and adventurous and enlarging. Really, the only solid justification for virtue's existence is that it provides something rather special for vice to triumph over.

Sade has no use for petty misbehavior. He favors a proud rivalry with Nature at her most dreadful, intoxication with power and crime, gleeful infliction of the maximum suffering. This, by the way, is the right foundation for political ambition: it leads to such opportunities . . .

The strong individual, when he despoils the weak—when, that is to say, he actively enters into the enjoyment of those rights which Nature has conferred upon him, and exercises them to the full— reaps pleasure in proportion to the extent to which he realises his potentialities. The more atrocious the harm he inflicts upon the helpless, the greater will be the quiverings of voluptuous delight which he will feel. . . . Such a man glories in the tears which his hand wrings from the unfortunate whom he persecutes; and the more he persecutes, the happier such a despot will feel—for it is thus that he makes the greatest use of those gifts Nature has bestowed on him.

The parallel with the Inner Party in *Nineteen Eighty-Four* is close, but not as close as it looks. Orwell's tyrants are puritans. Note, by contrast, those "quiverings of voluptuous delight." All joys are to be carried to the highest pitch by linking them with sex. The Sadian despot may torture and masturbate at the same time, so that the conditioned reflex will make torture more fun. The marquis's foreshadowing of Pavlov is often marked. To the criticism that sex and cruelty don't "naturally" go together, his reply is simply that they do. A great deal of sexual satisfaction comes from possessing, affecting, stirring up the partner—therefore, the more effect, the more satisfaction you will have—and cruelty produces the strongest effects of all (death, for instance). Love? Merely an entanglement best forgotten. The physical thrill should be the whole thing.

A Sadian libertine is held to be a true apostle of Liberty precisely because he is hideous in society's eyes. He alone has the courage to go all the way in defying it. In that spirit he will practice, say, perversions even if he has no taste for them. A male heterosexual who learns to enjoy sodomizing his own kind is far better than a homosexual who finds it easy. But he shouldn't stop there. He should go on to the sick and disgusting. He should try, for example, copulating with turkeys. The true libertine doesn't even feel as most people feel. He excites his own senses with detached skill and stifles all scruples and sense of guilt, because these would amount to an admission that others have the right to judge him.

One word more. The English language compels the use of *he* and *his* for convenience. But Sade concedes the same high privileges to women, and the arch-libertine of his masterpiece is female, not male.

From this, finally, emerges Sade's restatement of the Rule of Thélème. It occurs more than once, with italics for emphasis, in *Juliette*.

Nature's single precept is *to enjoy oneself, at the expense of no matter whom.*

Or more fully:

All the defects in humans belong to Nature; accordingly, man can have no better laws than those of Nature; no man has the right to repress in him what Nature puts there. Nature has elaborated no statutes, instituted no code; her single law is writ deep in every man's heart: it is to satisfy himself, to deny his passions nothing, and this regardless of the cost to others.

If that is what Nature teaches, then her "law" has nothing to do with order, at least as religion and morality understand it. Nor is there any purpose or design above her. Sade is a fierce atheist, deploying a battery of anti-God arguments that are ably reasoned but none too consistent. At one moment God is said to be meaningless, as inconceivable as colors are to the blind. At another we can conceive him enough to be certain that he doesn't exist. Then again, God is an oppressor interfering with freedom, to be hated with an elaborate fury that seems overdone if one is so sure he isn't there. The Christian God in particular is unworthy of the slightest respect, and his Church is an economic racket that keeps human beings in servile misery.

But, for Sade, this raises difficulties. One of his characters does believe in God, for the very logical Sadian reason that God can make life more horrible. You can hope to get your victim damned in the next world as well as tortured in this. Also Sade flirts with diabolism when he ought to dismiss it as pointless superstition. He sneers at Milton—that unexorcisable specter haunting the eighteenth century—yet has his own echoes of Satan. He sneers at ritual and then brings in a Black Mass or two himself. To be fair, however, such touches are interesting chiefly as further links between Sade and the Hell-Fire tradition. It would be wrong to stress them to a point where they might seem to reduce his originality.

SADE'S NOVELS

Sade planned his first large work, *The 120 Days of Sodom,* as documentary fiction. It was to portray every sexual possibility, except "normal" intercourse, in a context where matters could be seen in the proper light. Even in its unfinished form, on the 40-foot roll of paper salvaged from the Bastille, it is a pioneer study full of detailed knowledge, going far beyond anything before it.

The story is set in the time of Louis XIV, toward the close of his reign, when profiteers had made fortunes out of the king's wars and could enjoy themselves opulently amid public distress. Four middle-aged men of this type get together to set up a series of orgies that shall eclipse all others, lasting a hundred and twenty days. They are the Duc de Blangis; his brother, a bishop; the President de Curval, a judge; and "le celébre Durcet." All four have varied tastes. Having formed themselves into an *ad hoc* family by marrying each other's daughters (except that the bishop, being celibate, forms an incestuous partnership with an illegitimate daughter of his own), they start assembling a team. Well-paid procurers are sent out who, by various illicit methods, collect 150 boys and girls of good family. The candidates are brought to the organizers, who pick eight of the best-looking of each sex and put the rest to death.

These recruits make up the number to twenty-four. To them are added eight giant menservants—all sodomites, all superbly equipped, exact measurements being given—plus ten miscellaneous staff and four elderly retired prostitutes. One of the prostitutes is a lesbian. Another is thin, hideous, and lacking an eye and several teeth. Ugliness is part of the Sadian scheme. While beauty is pleasant, you must get over the limitation of needing it.

After a few trial spins we come to the main story, which is a prison fantasy charged with hate for mankind. All the main characters are psychopathic, and some are diseased. The four leaders stand for the Establishment—aristocracy, religion, justice, finance—and are therefore "respectable," but respectability is sick, secretly despising the society it maintains. Judge de Curval wishes he could blot out the sun, or use it to burn the Earth and destroy humanity. He and his friends, with their carefully selected party, form a hidden community in a Gothic setting—a super-Bastille to keep the world out, not to keep prisoners in.

Durcet makes the arrangements. He acquires a castle in the Black Forest, vast and gloomy and impregnably fortified, with access barred by woods and mountains. It is built round a court like the Castle of Otranto, and amply provided with food, drink, and instruments of torture. The program is to be an alternation of debauches and lectures. Each of the four repellent ex-prostitutes will describe 150 sexual practices. When all is ready, proceedings begin on November 1, which is All Saints' Day (a gibe at virtue) and also the date of the Lisbon earthquake (a gibe at God).

The program is carried out, though Sade's paper shortage reduces the later parts to a bare summary. Every day has a timetable, with a good deal of semiritual nudity and fancy dress. The prostitute of the day begins her lecture at 6 p.m. Time is allotted for questions and discussion. Supper follows at ten, and the main amusements come after that. The practices, which are coolly described, grow more bizarre, more complicated, with an anal and excremental bias. Many combine mental cruelty with physical. One form of Sadian entertainment is to involve people who do have scruples and force them to commit acts that revolt them, more or less at gunpoint. Brother-sister and father-daughter rapes, for instance, are dwelt on with pleasure. The composition of the team at the castle allows some of these refinements to be performed as well as described. Mortality is high, but it doesn't matter. On the 120th day most of the survivors are massacred anyhow. Forty-six people entered the castle; sixteen come out.

At the *Sodom* stage Sade's ideas were not highly developed. He got into his stride with *Justine*. This, unlike its stolen precursor, was published in his lifetime. He dashed off the first version of it in the Bastille during the summer of 1787. After his release he expanded this, adding long passages of discussion and anatomical detail. The result was given to the public in 1791 as *Justine; or, the Misfortunes of Virtue* and is said to have been a favorite book of Danton's. Events in France during the Terror inspired Sade to blow it up again into a third version, more intellectual and even longer, and to combine this with a vast sequel about Justine's sister Juliette. It is the final omnibus *New Justine* including *Juliette,* published in 1797, that earned the description of the novel by a French critic (Maurice Blanchot) as the most scandalous book in the whole of literature. *Justine* alone, as of 1787 or 1791, is still only a step along the road.

It came out with no author's name, and Sade tried to disown it—one of the unheroic touches that made him less impressive in practice than in theory. Theory, however, was the important thing. Up to a point Justine is Richardson's Clarissa over again, persecuted female virtue incarnate. Only . . . she isn't a martyr; she brings it on herself by the blind naïveté of her innocence. Her misfortunes are not caused by any single villain; they are caused by the Nature of Things and more especially human society. Justine is a Christian in the style made fashionable by Rousseau, swayed by "goodness of heart" and virtuous "feelings"; and she becomes a Christian Quixote, because she never faces the fact that Nature is against her, that persecutors are the rule and not the exception, and that the more brutally self-seeking their behavior, the stronger, better off, and more unassailable they are likely to be.

The flavor of a Sade novel is hard to convey in any summary. He has a strange flat relentlessness that is boring yet insidious. He has odd ironies and ambiguities: he makes use of moral language and words such as "horror" that imply disapproval, with his tongue in his cheek. Also he has passages of black comedy. It seems impossible to retell his longer stories at all faithfully without making them sound funnier than they are, because a retelling loses the duller parts and keeps the accumulation of grotesque shocks.

Justine and Juliette are linked from the outset. Daughters of a prosperous father whose business crashes, they are thrown on the world and separated while still of school age. Juliette is amoral and does extremely well for herself. In the original novel her career is disposed of in a few pages, after which we are told that while she was traveling one day with the rich man who was currently keeping her, she met a young woman under guard as a criminal and asked to hear her story. This of course turns out to be the long-lost sister, and the adventures of poor virtuous Justine make up the body of the novel. She describes a long series of encounters with people who have swindled her, ill-treated her, raped her in various ways, and got her into all sorts of undeserved plights, meanwhile lecturing her, interminably and improbably, on Nature and atheism and kindred topics.

This tale begins* with her departure from school. She goes for her first interview with an employer. This leads to nothing but a verbose and squalid attempt to deflower her. Still intact, she finds a domestic post with a moneylender, who tells her to rob a neighbor for him, and when she indignantly declines, accuses her of stealing a diamond and has her jailed. A fellow prisoner, Madame Dubois, sets fire to the jail. Ten inmates die, but Madame Dubois escapes with Justine, who is first grateful and then horrified, because her rescuer leads her to a gang of bandits. They propose to take turns amusing themselves with the charming new recruit and then, if she has offered any objection, stab her to death.

Justine manages a second escape, this time alone and through a wood. She has not gone far when she sees a young gentleman disporting himself homosexually with a servant. They accuse her of spying, tie her to a tree facing the trunk, hoist her skirt and produce hunting knives. The young man, however, the Marquis de Bressac, relents and takes Justine to his house as a maid. De Bressac lives with his mother and soon tries to involve Justine in a plot to murder her for her money. Although Justine will have nothing to do with it, he fancies her, and then, with two of his boyfriends, prepares to "punish" her. His imagination is limited: he repeats the tree exercise, but with a combined homosexual play that it excites him for, and that his victim is too innocent to follow.

*It is not exactly the same in the successive versions. I follow the English translation by Alan Hull Walton.

He seized me brutally by the arm and dragged me to his satellites. "Here," he said to them, "is the woman who wished to poison my mother. . . . I should perhaps have placed her in the hands of the law; but then she would have lost her life, and it is my wish that she should retain it so that she shall have a much longer time in which to suffer. Strip her quickly of her clothes, and tie her with her belly against this tree, so that I may chastise her in the manner she deserves."

. . . Making me embrace the tree as closely as possible, they tied a handkerchief around my mouth and bound me to it by my shoulders and legs, leaving the remainder of my body free, so that nothing should come between my flesh and the blows it was to receive. The Marquis, agitated to an astonishing extent, seized one of the lashes. But before he struck me the inhuman devil closely observed my face. You might have said that he feasted his eyes on my tears. . . . Then he moved behind me to a distance of about three feet, and I suddenly felt myself struck with all possible force, from the middle of my back down to my very calves. My butcher then stopped for a minute and brutally touched all the parts he had mangled. I do not know what he whispered to one of his satellites, but within a second my head was covered with a handkerchief, which no longer left me the slightest possibility of observing any of their movements. There was, in fact, a considerable amount of motion behind me before the resumption of the further bloody scenes to which I was destined. . . .

"*Yes!* Good—*that's it!*" exclaimed the Marquis, before he lashed me again. And hardly had these incomprehensible words been pronounced than the blows rained down with even greater violence. There was another pause. Once more the hands moved over the lacerated portions of my body, to be followed by further whispering. Then one of the young men said aloud: "Am I *not better thus?*" These words were equally mysterious to me, but the Marquis only replied: "*Get nearer, get nearer!*" A third attack followed, still more brutal than those that had gone before, and during which Bressac

exclaimed repeatedly, mingling his words with terrifying oaths: *"Go
on then, go on, both of you—can't you see that I wish to make her die
on the spot, and beneath my very hand!"*

But he doesn't really. He lets her go. The death of his mother has made
him rich—all the "evil" characters prosper—and the crime is firmly
pinned on Justine, who has to lie low. An apparently kind surgeon
named Rodin attends to her wounds and lets her stay in his house.
Besides his practice he runs a small mixed private school. Justine presently realizes that this is a cover. It enables him to get attractive adolescents into his house and molest them, which he does under the pretext
of punishment for trifling or imaginary faults. He also has orgies with
his servants and with his own daughter Rosalie. As with many Sade
characters, sexual excitement is a lunatic frenzy for him, yet ultimately
under control.

> He cursed, shouted, and blasphemed as he whipped. . . . A thousand
> kisses, each more warm than the rest, gave expression to his ardour.
> . . . Then the bomb exploded, and the pain-intoxicated libertine
> dared to taste the sweetest of pleasures in the bosom of incest and
> infamy. At length he felt the need of restoring himself after his exer-
> tions. The women were sent away, and Rodin went in to seat himself
> at dinner.

The cool anticlimax end is typical Sade.

Justine remains in this household for some time, giving Rosalie
religious instruction. Then she learns that Rodin and a colleague have
plans to dissect her alive in the interests of science. However, they do
not pursue this project far, merely cutting a toe off each of her feet, pulling out a couple of teeth, and branding her. After that she is dismissed.

Hobbling along in the neighborhood of Auxerre, Justine comes to
a monastery in a forest, Sainte-Marie-des-Bois, where she hears there is
a popular shrine. She goes to the door asking to be let in to pray and

is surprised to meet several naked girls. Predictably, the monastery is a haven of secret vice. In fact it is a reduced version of Durcet's castle in *The 120 Days,* with four monks taking the place of the four profiteers and maintaining a constantly renewed harem with a strict timetable and a rota. Justine is trapped.

The community aspect is strongly marked. The monks operate together, by various methods. It is at a party of this kind that Justine loses her long-preserved virginity, though still not at once. Father Raphael, the Superior, leads off while Antonin and Clement hold her down. Clement and Jerome follow him. None of these three employs the usual mode of access. That is left to Antonin, who deflowers Justine at last with "furious cries," "murderous excursions" over every part of her body, and "bitings like the bloody caresses of a tiger."

Teamwork applies to both sexes, though always for the benefit of the monks, not their women.

> This species of group activity took place very frequently. It was nearly always customary, when a monk was enjoying himself with one of the sisters, for the other three to surround him, exciting his senses in every part, so that voluptuous ecstasy might diffuse itself throughout his entire being.

As in more commonplace pornography, the characters' sexual prowess is carried far beyond probability. Besides the unending round of debauch, the monks make use of their women to fake apparitions of the Virgin and to celebrate Black Masses; the pious Justine has to take her turn as a living altar.

After a long time the monastery is reorganized. Father Raphael is promoted to be General of his Order, and the new Superior disbands the harem. Justine wanders on. An old woman begs alms from her, then robs her and leaves her destitute. While wondering what to do she sees a man assaulted and left by the wayside. She binds up his wounds, and he takes her to his home with every sign of appreciation for what she has done for him. He turns out to be a coiner. The machinery is powered by his discarded mistresses, and Justine is to join them.

> Showing me a wide and extremely deep cistern neighbouring on the gate, where two chained and naked women continually moved a wheel which drew water to feed a reservoir—"Do you see this pit?" he continued. "These are your companions, and this will be your work. On condition that you work twelve hours a day turning this wheel, you will be given six ounces of black bread and a plate of beans once every twenty-four hours. Moreover, you will be well and regularly beaten each time you attempt to rest. As for liberty, you can renounce all thought of that, for never will you see the sky again. As soon as you are dead you will be thrown into this hole, which you can see beside the well—on top of thirty or forty other bodies which are there already—and your work will be taken over by someone else!"

Justine asks him, what about gratitude? He replies:

> "And what, I beg you, do you mean by this feeling of gratitude—this feeling by which you imagine you hold me captive? Such wretched creatures as yourself should reason better than this! What did you do when you helped me? You had the choice of continuing on your way, or of coming over to assist me. You chose the latter, inspired by some profound emotion springing from deep within your heart. ... That in itself is a kind of pleasure, so how in the devil's name can you claim that I should be obliged to reward you for pleasures which you grant to yourself?"

Justine is eventually released when the coining gang is broken up, though her master has got away to Venice and prosperous retirement. She has a few further adventures that culminate in her trying to save a child from a fire and being accused of starting the fire herself, robbing the house, and murdering the child. This is why she is under guard when she meets her sister.

Juliette and her lover are deeply moved. The lover exerts his influence to get the case reexamined, and Justine is cleared. Her tribulations are over, money will be provided. . . . A thunderstorm breaks out and she is struck by lightning, which enters by her right breast and leaves by her mouth, converting her into a repulsive corpse.

The end of this novel, in the versions of 1787 and 1791, is a sudden access of suspect morality in the manner of *Fanny Hill*. Juliette is sobered by her sister's fate. She repents and withdraws (like the Marquise de Sade) to a Carmelite convent. But when Sade returned to the sisters a few years later, and dealt with the amoral one in detail, the outcome was very different.

THE LIMITS OF SADISM

Juliette; or, the Prosperities of Vice, the sequel incorporated in the 1797 *Justine* after separate publication a year earlier, is the Bible of "Sadism" in its true sense. It is a work of disillusion, written after the Terror and reaction, and after Sade's own maltreatment at the hands of a Revolution he tried to assist. Its tone is anarchic. Characters denounce law in general, civilization, society itself, and suggest that Man might be better off in a savage state concerning himself solely with food and sex. But as society does exist, they make the best of it. They "enjoy themselves at the expense of no matter whom" and pursue wealth and power ruthlessly to that end.

To live up to her role, Juliette has to be an adventuress as well as a libertine. By embodying his ideas in a heroine rather than a hero, Sade gives the novel a curious flavor of Women's Lib, if with no marked understanding of women. He also anticipates Ian Fleming's talent for making a mad story seem half credible by embedding it in precise, ingenious detail and a world the reader can recognize. His black comedy of horrific invention is not at all unlike Fleming's. Thus Juliette arranges for Grillo, an Italian duke, to catch his wife with a lover. . . .

Furious Grillo, drawn dagger in hand, hurls himself upon the adulterous pair. Aiding his arm, I see to it the blow falls upon his faithless spouse: the blade sinks deep into her flank, the Duke would now vent his rage upon the lover, but nimble Dolni rolls away, springs to his feet, scampers from the room, Grillo hot in his pursuit. They race down a long corridor. . . . At its farther end two trap doors open, one dropping the young man into an underground passage, where he is safe, the other tumbling Grillo into the works of a frightful machine fitted with a thousand sharp blades for carving to ribbons whatever is placed inside it.

"Great God, what is this? what have I done?" cries the Duke, "oh, hideous snare!"

One of Juliette's helpers tosses the wife into the same pit, and then they lower a grating over it and look down at the prisoners.

Grillo starts impulsively toward his wife, but his movement releases a spring, the machine starts to whirr, its many blades to turn, their edges slash at the two victims who in less than ten minutes are threshed shapeless, of them nought but bloody and splintered bone remains. I need not describe our ecstasy.

Besides the authenticity of imagined detail, several of the events in *Juliette* are based on real ones, and several of the characters have originals. Some are actual persons without disguise—Pope Pius VI, Cardinal Albani (the same who recommended the designer of Dodington's villa), the king and queen of Naples. The pope, who is luridly libeled, was still living and reigning when *Juliette* was written, and so were the Neapolitan royalties: they are the ones who entertained Emma Hamilton and Nelson. The long discussions that make the book unwieldy refer to myriads of facts, or alleged facts, in support of the ideas put forward. Lastly, the language is very plain indeed and leaves nothing vague. Where *Justine* often minces words, *Juliette* is nearly always direct.

The story she tells begins as her sister's does, at a convent school. But it diverges. Juliette is initiated by the abbess into atheism, lesbianism, and other nonconventual matters. When an orgy with some priests nearly causes the death of a novice, the abbess calms Juliette's misgivings with an eloquent discourse on all-wise Nature. After leaving the convent Juliette enters a brothel where she learns not only physical techniques but methods of stealing from her clients.

At length she becomes the mistress of an unsavory intellectual named Noirceuil, one of whose specialities is to insist on his wife watching and assisting his multiple antics with partners of both sexes. Noirceuil introduces Juliette to a powerful politician, Saint-Fond. Saint-Fond employs her as his procuress and also gives her a secret service job—specifically, poisoning enemies of the state at 30,000 francs per victim. She lays the foundations of a fortune. One of Saint-Fond's projects in statesmanship (based, it is said, on an actual Jacobin proposal) is to starve two-thirds of the population to death, but he never puts this into effect.

Juliette spends some time in Angers running a gaming house. She marries the wealthy and respectable Comte de Lorsange; produces a daughter; kills her husband; and, greatly enriched, goes to Italy, leaving the baby with a guardian. In Turin an attractive cardsharp teaches her his trade, and she keeps him with her as she grows richer still and mixes in high society. She helps to arrange orgies for the pope (in a screened-off section of St. Peter's) and for King Ferdinand of Naples. After many more adventures, still young, she returns to France in triumph.

This, in outline, is the plot. All the interest, however, lies in particular passages rather than the whole. It has been suggested that in the sexual scenes, which are many, Sade is trying to reconstitute his lost *120 Days of Sodom*. Certainly he returns to his daydream of an anti-moral community, a Thélème of the totally unfettered will. Early in her career Juliette teams up with a Madame de Clairwil, who has gone further along the path than herself. Clairwil belongs to a Paris club called the Sodality of the Friends of Crime and gets Juliette admitted to it. This Sodality is one of Sade's vaguely authentic touches. It may be founded on the real club of the Aphrodites, which in turn may have had links with the English groups. But as always in *Juliette*, everything is inflated to monstrous proportions.

One fact that Juliette learns about the Sodality has become, with the passage of time, extremely interesting. It is a mixed body with full equality for women, and in practice the women have tended to take it over. (This is probably the first step in literature toward a later romantic inversion, as in Swinburne, where the woman becomes the more active partner in debauches and cruelties.) The Sodality has forty-five statutes that are quoted. No. 6 confines membership to the well-off—dues are fixed at 10,000 francs a year. No. 7 makes an exception of No. 6, allowing reduced rates for a small quota of authors and artists, in keeping with a policy of patronizing the arts: we are still in touch with the Dilettanti tradition. No. 31 limits total membership to four hundred, with a rough balance between the sexes. Other statutes prescribe secrecy, abstention from politics, and absolute internal freedom except where it would interfere with libertinage. On this last ground, gambling is forbidden on the club's premises—it would be too much of a distraction. So is the expression of any sentiment savoring of love, for the same reason.

The Sodality has a luxurious clubhouse where, in effect, anything goes. While the members must observe certain restraints and courtesies toward each other, no such rules apply to the two seraglios attached to the building. One contains three hundred males aged seven to twenty-five, the other three hundred females aged five to twenty-one. These are at the members' disposal unconditionally, with an expert staff in attendance.

> There are twelve torture chambers per seraglio, where everything is at hand for dealing with victims in the most awful, the most unspeakable manner. . . .
>
> There are in addition twelve dungeons per seraglio, for the use of those who enjoy subjecting victims to the slow death of incarceration. . . .
>
> In each seraglio are four executioners, four jailers, eight whippers,

four flayers, four midwives, and four surgeons all at the orders of Members who, in the heat of passion, might have the need of the ministry of such personages; it being understood of course that the midwives and surgeons are present not by any means to render humanitarian aid, but to assist in tortures.

Further on in the story comes a full-fledged Gothic castle outglooming any imagined by Walpole or Ann Radcliffe. It is in the Apennines, a Radcliffe-type location, but its owner is a gigantic Russian named Minski, who invites Juliette and her fellow traveler to visit him.

> After three hours of nearly perpendicular ascent we came to the edge of a lake; on an isle in its centre was to be seen the donjon of the castle where our guide had his abode. . . . We had been some six hours coming this far and during that time we had espied not a single house, not a single individual. A black bark, like a Venetian gondola, was moored to the shore. . . . We stepped into the boat, the giant ferried us to the island. His castle lay two furlongs back from the water; we arrived before an iron gate set in the thick outer wall; spanning a moat twenty feet wide was a drawbridge that was raised once we had crossed over it; here was a second wall, again we went through an iron gate, and found ourselves in a belt of trees so close-spaced that we had indeed to force a passage between them, and beyond this enormous hedge was the castle's third enclosure, a wall ten feet thick and without any gate at all. The giant stoops and lifts a great stone slab no one else would have been able to budge; thus does he uncover a stairway; we precede him down the steps, he replaces the stone; at the farther end of that underground passage we ascend another stairway, guarded by another such stone as I have just spoken of, and emerge from dank darkness into a low-ceilinged hall. It was decorated, littered with skeletons; there were benches fashioned of human bones and wherever one trod it was upon skulls; we fancied we heard moans coming from remote cellars.

Minski tells his life story. He is forty-five. He has traveled through most of the world studying the vices of every nation and committing every crime in safety himself under the protection of immense wealth. He now dwells in this Italian fastness, with a lavish establishment of both sexes but no equal. His only companions not subject to him are guests who come and go, chosen for their probable willingness to join in the fun.

> "Much philosophy is needed to understand me, yes, I realise it, I am a monster, something vomited forth by Nature to aid her in the destruction whereof she obtains the stuff she requires for creation. . . . I am happy in my little domain; in it I dispose of all a sovereign's privileges, in it I enjoy all the pleasures of despotism, I dread no man, and I live content."

The most original feature of his happy existence is a diet of human flesh, which he eats in the belief that it is aphrodisiac. His orgasms, which he describes and demonstrates, are copious, violent, and frequent beyond normal capacity.

Minski's dining room furniture is made of live girls "cunningly arranged." Their vaginas are used as candle holders. When hot dishes are placed on the living table, resting on bare breasts and buttocks, there is "a pleasant convulsive stir" like "the rippling of waves." After the meal, Minski, at Juliette's prompting, rapes a child of seven. He then strangles her. Juliette queries the second part of this performance and inspires a quintessentially Sadian exchange.

> "Do you then never taste this pleasure without it costing some individual his life?"
>
> "It often costs the lives of several," the ogre replied. "If I had no human beings to kill I do believe I would have to give up fucking. For it is death's sighs answering my lubricity's that fetches forth my ejaculation, and were it not for the death my discharge occasions I don't know how I'd be able to discharge at all.

"But come with me into the next room," the Russian continued, "ices, coffee, and liqueurs are awaiting us."

Minski indeed is not indifferent to refinement, and his bedroom is decorated with splendid frescoes. He has also equipped it with a wall-to-wall torture apparatus. In a mirrored alcove are sixteen black marble columns to which his victims are tied. By means of a control panel by his bed he can inflict sixteen varieties of pain on them—stabbing, burning, flogging, and so forth—till, if he pleases, the alcove is drenched in blood.

The catch in this kind of thing is that it has its limits, even for the superhuman libertines of a Sade novel. Juliette and her confederate Clairwil have attacks of ennui. Their crimes have made them rich, they live sumptuously in tasteful surroundings, yet at times their appetites become jaded. Restlessly they crave ghastlier thrills. Sade's philosophy, in the end, defeats itself. If Nature endorses anything and everything, then you can't be really outrageous; you can't defy Nature, except perhaps by outdoing her. You can outrage Respectability as the rakes did in England, but to Sadian intellectuals that is a trifle. They yearn for a living mystique of outrage, and their own arguments seem to make it impossible. "When," sighs Clairwil, "shall I be able to do an authentic evil?" Again, "Could I set the planet ablaze, even so would I curse the Nature that had provided only one world for my desires to feast upon." Sade puts the best-reasoned statement of this problem in the mouth of his hypocritical pope.

So, to what ultimate horror does it all lead? Juliette explores. She breaks with the code of the Sodality of the Friends of Crime to the extent of taking a mild interest in politics. She lectures the king of Naples on statecraft and listens patiently to a long account from Clairwil's brother of a conspiracy in Sweden. Besides a natural fondness for Machiavelli, Sade shows himself attracted by the "secret society" theory of history. The Swedish plotters belong to an anti-Catholic, anti-royalist Lodge supposed to have been founded by the fugitive Templars when their Order was suppressed in the fourteenth century. The Masons are linked with it as its agents and dupes. Sade's reason for believing in a secret organization like this is of course the delicious vision of its attaining power and wielding it like the Inner Party in *Nineteen Eighty-Four*. A Swedish conspirator explains that the Lodge aims to overthrow kings in general in the name of Liberty, but with covert motives:

> Once upon the throne of the kings, there shall never have been a tyranny to equal ours, no despot shall ever have put a thicker blindfold over the eyes of the people; plunged into essential ignorance, it shall be at our mercy, blood will flow in rivers, our Masonic brethren themselves shall become the mere valets of our cruelties, and in us alone shall the supreme power be concentrated; all freedom shall go by the board, that of the press, that of worship, that simply of thought shall be severely forbidden and ruthlessly repressed; one must beware of enlightening the people or of lifting away its irons when your aim is to rule it.

Juliette, however, has no such conspiracy to join. Her experiments take other forms. They include scenes of incest, necrophilia, coprophilia (which fascinates Sade), and bestiality. She runs a hyperbrothel. She dabbles in magic and sacrilege, without much enjoying either. She works hard at conditioning her own reflexes so as to link crime with sexual pleasure. Her early training in theft is helpful, and she learns to get a thrill out of stealing for its own sake.

The experienced Clairwil is her mentor. Once, as a venture of her own, Juliette makes a show of befriending the family of a peasant and then sets fire to his cottage, burning several of the inmates to death. This throws her into a frenzy of delight, and she thinks she has done rather well. Clairwil is unimpressed. The crime was too small and imprudently conducted. Juliette should have chosen a house close to other houses so that the fire would have spread. Also she should have concealed her emotions, which might have betrayed her, and taken care to fix a charge of incendiarism on the peasant.

Suitably guided, Juliette discovers the joys of treachery. While in

Italy, she and Clairwil take one of their partners in lesbianism—who has been with them for some time and is fond of them—on an excursion to Vesuvius. Beside the crater they suddenly strip the woman, bind and gag her, stick pins in her buttocks, pluck out her pubic hairs, and then toss her down the volcano, masturbating each other after letting go, to enhance the excitement.

Occasionally in the course of a very long story, Juliette has scruples. Whenever she does so the result is disastrous, and under Clairwil's tuition she learns to stifle such impulses of restraint and remorse as she has. And that is how, after two thousand pages of ghastliness, she still manages to create a climax of sorts . . . literary as well as physical. She goes back to France and recovers Marianne, the daughter she bore to her deceased husband. She also rejoins her old partner Noirceuil. When he lusts after Marianne, aged seven, Juliette allows him to do his will. After various brutalities he throws the child in a fire. Juliette beats her daughter with a poker to stop her from crawling out, and, before Marianne is even quite dead, goes off to spend the night with the adequately stimulated Noirceuil.

When Juliette has told all, an epilogue relates the death of her virtuous sister Justine by a lightning bolt, more or less as in the previous versions. But this time nobody shows any compassion for her, and nobody repents. Juliette's male friends put the corpse to unpleasant uses and then leave it by the roadside.

SADISM AND SOCIETY

In other writings, and in his brief spell as an activist for the French Revolution, Sade tried (so to speak) to extrapolate the Castle. That is, he considered whether his extreme Do-what-you-will, with the anarchic reasonings behind it, could be carried outside little groups of libertines and applied to society. The sole result was a muddle, sometimes acute, sometimes grotesque: in Aldous Huxley's words, *a reductio ad absurdum* of revolution.

Like his admired Machiavelli, Sade professes to discuss society as it is, without any ethical preconceptions. His critique is left wing rather than right wing, but always in his own style. It has very little do do with his actual conduct in the Revolution, which was opportunistic and failed to recommend him to anybody. The main statement of his theories (not the only one) is a pamphlet he brought out in 1795 entitled *One More Effort*. Embedded in another novel, this voices an idea hinted at in *Juliette,* that it is wrong to have general laws at all because human beings vary so much. Legislating is like trying to dress an army in uniforms all the same size. In practice, Sade maintains, this process is always rigged in favor of the lawmakers themselves and the property-owning class they belong to. Everybody else is cut down into conformity with that class's interests.

But he doesn't want to restructure the system in the name of morality. The intensely moral Robespierre was the worst of tyrants. The answer is not to make supposedly better laws, but to prune—to have as few laws as possible. Which is fewer than you might think, because, by and large, there is no reason to forbid anything. Sade defends every sort of crime as justified sometimes, and therefore not to be put under a blanket ban: libel, theft, murder, and of course sexual misconduct. He favors total permissiveness for men and women equally.

As in his novels, he reels off lists of foreign nations with different ethics from the French. Killing is the easiest subject to document. Murderers are honored in Mindanao. The inhabitants of Borneo believe that people they kill will serve them in the next world. "Even devout Spaniards make a promise to St. James of Galicia to kill a dozen Americans a day." This leads to the unexpected conclusion that capital punishment should be abolished. Since murder may be justified, murder should not be prescribed as a penalty for it. Killing by the state in the name of justice is killing for a wrong reason, without lust.

Having reduced society to anarchy, what does Sade offer on the constructive side?

He wants—in theory—the emancipation of women, the reform

of education. He wants a classless commonwealth without private property—again in theory: this doesn't apply to him or his estates. He allows that there has to be a collective mystique of some kind, and patriotism is or can be a Good Thing. Religion? The church has to go, as an anti-rational fraud that upholds privilege and curtails freedom; but instead of insisting on an atheist state, Sade makes the weird suggestion that France should revive classical paganism, the religion that made Rome successful.

Sade was never skillful as a propagandist for his own age. He admitted, too late, that it was a tactical blunder to put so many of his own thoughts in the mouths of characters whom readers would recoil from as evil. That error backhandedly turned *Justine* into a prop for religion. The Revolution showed no sign of following a Sadian course. In his eyes its excesses were not only senseless but ineffectual. They failed to alter society, and they had no coherent purpose. He declined to approve them. So he himself, who believed at heart that the revolutionaries were not going far enough, was jailed for his apparent belief that they were going too far.

When the third version of *Justine* was published, with its disillusioned companion *Juliette,* France had passed under the control of the five-man body called the Directory. Sade presented copies to all five directors. How he hoped to influence them, or whether he did, it is impossible to say. He retained a glimmer of loyalty. However deep his despair for France, he never joined the emigrés or looked abroad for salvation. But he admired England and praised English honesty, an unusual tribute from a Frenchman. He also predicted that the United States—then no more than the Thirteen Colonies plus a sparsely settled hinterland—would grow to the size of the Roman Empire and "make the entire earth tremble."

Yet his flashes of insight never added up to public sagacity, and his philosophy never added up to a program. As his image of Nature grew more dreadful it robbed even Sadism of practical point. It is all very well to say, "Enjoy yourself at the expense of no matter whom." But there are limits to sheer physical capacity, and, it must be reiterated, how can you go on getting kicks out of being outrageous if nothing *is* outrageous? The perfected Sadist has to live on a mental level that very few could attain, in a Sadian commonwealth or anywhere else. Outside these novels such a person is rare even in fiction.* He asserts freedom by the only nonconformity that is still open: trying coolly to beat horrific Nature at her own game.

He has passed beyond ordinary enjoyment into a conscious, experimental stoicism of sex and violence, where even frenzy is self-induced and under control. He has no feelings as most human beings have them; no love, of course; no inclination to value anything for its own sake, or prefer A or B except as it gives him greater pleasure. Since even beauty must never throw him out of gear, or be a thing his lusts really need, he cultivates the repulsive and learns to acquire perverted tastes ("the greatest pleasures," says a character in *Juliette*, "are born from conquered repugnances"). He is entangled with nobody, has an exterminatory contempt for everyone except his co-Sadists, and is ready to betray even them.

We are in a quite different atmosphere from Thélème or Medmenham. However, despite the Marquis's revolutionary posturing, we are still in a closed circle—a Castle in Hell. Libertinism equals liberty for a tiny minority only. Besides being a most unusual person, the true Sadist must have a great deal of money and a special immunity. Juliette and her friends use up an astounding number of victims. Minski not only rapes and tortures his, he eats them as well. To keep this mode of life going (or anything remotely like it) one would need a large and discreet staff, expensive equipment, spacious accommodation, extreme privacy, and the resources to hush up scandal and keep the law at a distance. Juliette says it herself.

He who has succeeded in ridding his heart of every idea and trace of God or religion, *he whose gold or influence removes him beyond*

*Some of the diabolists in C. S. Lewis's *That Hideous Strength* might just qualify.

the reach of the law [italics added], he who has toughened his conscience and brought it firmly into line with his attitudes and cleared it utterly and for ever of guilty remorse; he, I say, and be certain thereof, he may do whatever he pleases and whenever, and never know an instant's fear.

Minski, during his wanderings before settling down, was condemned to death four times, but as he remarks, "wealth is a guarantee against anything." Conversely, however, poverty or even a moderate income rule out true Sadism: you can't afford it . . . in any sense. That is why the Sodality of the Friends of Crime admits only well-off applicants, apart from the few authors and artists whom it accepts at reduced fees and takes under its wing.

Sade himself, in his later years, had no further chance to put his theories into practice. He wrote many stories and a number of plays but remained immured at Charenton. His last wish was for a non-religious funeral. On his death in 1814, however, the authorities gave him a Christian burial. Two phrenologists examined his skull and reported that its bumps indicated "motherly tenderness and great love for children."

14

END OR BEGINNING?

LIBERTINISM IN LITERATURE

As a would-be revolutionary the Marquis de Sade led nowhere, at least in his own lifetime. He failed to affect politics, he attracted no disciples, he founded neither a community nor a movement. The last posthumous twitch of his public career was an anonymous reissue of *One More Effort* during the upheavals of 1848, within a few months of the *Communist Manifesto,* but with less effect. As an influence through his novels, however, Sade was a major figure, and he remains so. During the nineteenth century the influence was sometimes acknowledged, more often kept underground. The later mutations of the Thelemic idea and outlook can be followed on from Sade, with no major break, to the present day.

Justine and *Juliette* came out during one of the few periods prior to the late 1960s when they could be published and sold without restriction. The ground was fertile not only because of the brief wave of decensorship after the Revolution, but because of a continuing taste for the cruel and corrupt in fiction. Gothic romance had not remained a monopoly of Mrs. Radcliffe. Imitators were taking it further. Sade himself, in an interesting essay, argued that the real atrocities of the Terror had made most fiction seem tame; the Gothic novelists were flying to extremes in the effort to shock a public that could no longer be shocked by normal methods. Hints from his own *Justine* probably insinuated themselves into the greatest Gothic best seller of all, Matthew Gregory Lewis's *The Monk,* published in 1796.

In *The Monk,* however, it is worth noticing what persists and what doesn't, and the reasons. "Monk" Lewis was the twenty-year-old son of a rich Jamaica planter; a pleasant, popular young man, quite unembittered, quite unscandalous. His book takes the moral norms for granted. In some respects Lewis foreshadows his American namesake, the author of *Elmer Gantry.* His hero-villain is a Spanish ecclesiastic, Ambrosio. Ambrosio has an adoring public and keeps up a show of holiness out of pride and self-interest rather than virtue. He succumbs to various temptations and receives his deserts, rather more in fact, at the end. Lewis exploits several Gothic and Sadian motifs—sex, cruelty, black magic, anti-Catholicism, sheer physical horror, and foulness—with the same recurrence of enclosed places and secret cells. But the object is simply to make a lurid tale. No questionings of the human condition ever intrude. By making garish use of the supernatural, while avoiding Sade's physical detail, Lewis plants his novel in a fantasy world where it has nothing to do with real issues.

Much the same is true of later Gothic tales such as Maturin's *Melmoth the Wanderer* (from which Oscar Wilde took his pseudonym in exile). They carried on various themes and an atmosphere, without frankly challenging accepted ethics or even, as a rule, accepted decencies. Lewis himself caved in to protests and brought out an expurgated *Monk,* though the record of what he altered and what he left alone makes peculiar reading. In *Melmoth* we seem once to be hovering on the brink when an innocent maiden watches a Hindu festival through a telescope, and her male companion offers to explain *and demonstrate* phallic worship . . . but the maiden isn't that innocent, and she changes the subject.

In Romantic literature, the serious cult of the anti-moral will was developed by Byron rather than the Gothic brigade. The relationship between Byron and Sade cannot be determined, but they converged with potent effect—Byron as the open influence, Sade as the undercover one. This is no afterthought of critics. It was recognized at the time, in France at least—guardedly in 1824 by the academician P. S. Auger, explicitly in 1843 by the mighty Sainte-Beuve. Byron, as an aristocratic flirter with Hell-Fire, refocused the impulse of revolt by way of satanism. First among major English authors (though anticipated by Schiller in *The Robbers*), he warped the Miltonic scene so far from Christianity as to place God's enemies in an avowedly sympathetic light. Also he studied the somberly fascinating Fatal Men in Ann Radcliffe's novels, tried to copy them in real life, and improved on them in poetry. With a dash of Satan the Gothic adventurer became the "Byronic hero" in proud and lawless rebellion against mankind, who appears not only in Byron's own works but as Heathcliff and kindred figures in later fiction composed under his spell.

From the Gothic-Sade-Byron complex it is easy to trace further variations on the original themes—easy, but, for the present purpose, not very useful. Sometimes we find vulgar sensation seeking, as in the novels of Eugene Sue, and that Protestant classic *Maria Monk*, which has been described as "a poor man's *Justine*." Sometimes we meet with the anti-moral spirit in wayward half-comic guises, as in De Quincey's essay *On Murder Considered as One of the Fine Arts*. De Quincey opens with an allusion to a "Society for the Promotion of Vice," by which he means Medmenham, and an alleged "Society for the Suppression of Virtue" in Brighton, from which he goes on to sketch a "Society for the Encouragement of Murder," which reads rather like a parody of *Juliette*.

Sometimes the same preoccupations strike far deeper notes, as in Baudelaire, who adopted Sade's view of Nature: "We must keep coming back to Sade, that is to say to the natural man, to explain evil." Sometimes we confront a satanism that tends to be weaker and uglier than Byron's, as in fin-de-siècle French decadents, with English counterparts charmingly teased in Max Beerbohm's *Enoch Soames;* and the Neo-Sadist Lautreamont, author of *Maldoror,* who underlies the Symbolist poets and is claimed as an ancestor of the Surrealists too.

But here again, most of the literature veers away from the philosophic issue of Liberty that Sade himself placed at the center. The Thelemic "Do what you will" is forgotten, or implied rather than stated. There is a gradual decline into mere corruption as such. (Which admirers of Milton's Satan had no excuse for not foreseeing. Even in *Paradise Lost,* the splendid rebel angel of the earlier books degenerates into the lying serpent of the last four.) So far as the Sadian philosophy trickles down through these channels, it comes out into daylight chiefly as a factor in Fascism and Nazism—certainly present if hard to document, though one thinks of creatively morbid "men of action" such as Gabriele D'Annunzio. The continuity of Sade's libertarian ideas, of the left wing as we might call it, can be traced as well but is less diffuse and somewhat aloof. It is in England; it is literary there too for most of the way. It emerges at last, however, in a new form that is more than literary.

LADIES OF PAIN

We must tread with care. Concepts can easily be stretched to bring in people who do not belong here. Shelley is an obvious candidate: not only because of his constant hymning of Liberty, but because of his friendship with Byron, his Gothic juvenilia, his insistence that Satan is the hero of *Paradise Lost,* and his choice of a story of cruelty and incest for his single theatrical venture *The Cenci.* At one stage he liked going to Medmenham to write. But whatever one may think of his conduct in practice, he was no anti-moralist in principle, and the tone of his work is remote from Sade and even from Byron at his most characteristic.

The same applies to William Blake. He too was an apostle of Liberty, he too discussed Milton and asserted that true poets are "of the Devil's party." Also, which is more to the point, he denounced moral rules in favor of inspired impulse. But Blake is too intensely himself, and too great, to be fitted into a common scheme with Rabelais and Dashwood and Sade. Although the phrase "Do what you will" occurs in a poem of his, it is not meant as an injunction.

The important person here is neither Shelley nor Blake, but an

English poet who derived in part from the former, wrote the first study of the latter, and also discovered Sade as neither of the others did: Algernon Charles Swinburne.

Swinburne set himself up as the mid-Victorian bard of Revolt and Freedom, more or less in the Romantic succession, but he approached his ideals by a somewhat devious route. His instantly famous *Poems and Ballads* (1866) stood closer to eighteenth-century Hell-Fire than to any current mystique of revolution. His verse, at that stage, asserted freedom by being shocking; and as with Sade, the main motifs were evolved out of the author's own sexual quirks.

Swinburne's obsession was algolagnia, the association of pleasure with pain, but not exactly in Sade's spirit. He wanted (in theory at least) to feel the pain himself. His youthful fantasies were about martyrdom. Over a long stretch of ostensibly mature life he was working with care on a secret pseudoepic, *The Flogging-Block*. This dwells on his memories of corporal punishment at school and has never been published except in brief excerpts. He frequented "special establishments" for flagellation, of the sort described in that Victorian porn classic *My Secret Life*. The flogging was not aphrodisiac with normal intercourse as the end, it was a substitute. His poetry tends to circle round a dream of delight as "the powerless victim of the furious rage of a beautiful woman." The maltreated heroine of the Clarissa-Justine tradition has turned the tables.

Thus far the impression is masochistic rather than sadistic . . . sadistic, that is, in the narrow sense with a small *s*. But Sadism in a broader sense came in after all, partly because of a compensatory desire to make virile noises and appear masculine, partly also by way of the Fatal Woman herself. Swinburne's poetry rings the changes on her as tyrannous queen and destroying goddess, as *belle dame sans merci* and mythified tart; and she inflicts and relishes horrors that he doesn't want to inflict himself, but revels in by proxy through his hothouse imagination. His woman is the Empress Faustine, the Venus of Tannhauser, Mary Queen of Scots, and the synthetic harlot goddess Dolores, Our Lady of Pain. In her various guises she is frequently fatal to her lovers, and not only her lovers. When she kisses, she may kill, and she habitually bites.

Swinburne liked Byron, yet could not identify with the virile Byronic hero. For one thing he was too small and slight. When he discovered Sade (also a small man) he hailed the marquis as greater than Byron. The introduction occurred in 1862 through Richard Monckton Milnes, afterward Lord Houghton. Milnes was a Liberal, traveler, and society figure, the model for Mr. Vavasour in Disraeli's *Tancred*. He described Turkish harems from inside knowledge. Other literary activities included helping his friend Tennyson to the laureateship and collecting strange books, notably occult and obscene ones. The works of Sade fell into the latter category. They were outlawed, difficult to get, and, in England, unmentionable.

Milnes took an interest in the twenty-four-year-old Swinburne. The poet already adored Sade without having read him, and Milnes, after some hesitation, opened up the private shelves of his library. Swinburne started with *Justine* and found it a letdown, lacking in sexual imagination, and unintentionally comic. *Juliette* gave him a better understanding of what Sade was about and restored the spell. He remained cautious, however. In his book on Blake, begun during the same period, we renew acquaintance with one or two old friends—with Rabelais, whom Swinburne enjoys, and with Aucassin, whose preference for Hell he cites with approval—but the entry of Sade himself is anonymous. What Swinburne does is to say he is going to illustrate some remarks with a "lay sermon by a modern pagan philosopher." Then he gives not a straight extract, but a précis of several bits of *Justine* and *Juliette* about the malignity of Nature. The general drift is that Nature supplies us with a blank check for evildoing by her own example. But it is amusing to see how he rewords and reflavors the text to make Nature more like a living person than she is in Sade; more like his own Fatal Woman, enlarged to cosmic proportions.

She takes the pain of the whole world to sharpen the sense of vital pleasure in her limitless veins: she stabs and poisons, crushes and corrodes, yet cannot live and sin fast enough for the cruelty of her great desire. Behold, the ages of men are dead at her feet; the blood of the world is on her hands; and her desire is continually toward evil, that she may see the end of things which she hath made. . . .

She is weary of the ancient life: her eyes are sick of seeing and her ears are heavy with hearing; with the lust of creation she is burnt up, and rent in twain with travail until she bring forth change; she would fain create afresh, and cannot, except it be by destroying: in all her energies she is athirst for mortal food, and with all her forces she labours in desire of death.

Swinburne's play *Atalanta in Calydon* dilates on such Sadian themes as the doom of virtue, the voluptuousness of pain, and the duty of holy insurrection against the hateful phantasm of God, who is called the "supreme evil." In *Laus Veneris,* his Tannhauser poem, the image of Venus leads on to images of murder:

> *Ah, not as they, but as the souls that were*
> *Slain in the old time, having found her fair;*
> *Who, sleeping with her lips upon their eyes,*
> *Heard sudden serpents hiss across her hair.*
>
> *Their blood runs round the roots of time like rain;*
> *She casts them forth and gathers them again;*
> *With nerve and bone she weaves and multiplies*
> *Exceeding pleasure out of extreme pain. . . .*
>
> *Yea, all she slayeth.*

The Empress Faustine gloats over the fights in the Roman Circus, for which, of course, she shares the responsibility:

> *She loved the games men played with death,*
> *Where death must win;*

As though the slain man's blood and breath
Revived Faustine.

And so on through a gallery of characters, to the climax of Swinburne's public Sadism in the funny yet compelling "Dolores." Its best-known phrase is the contrast between the "lilies and languors of virtue" and the "raptures and roses of vice," which is the Divine Marquis to the life. But there is plenty more. The litany of the prostitute is a learned blasphemy travestying the Litany of the Blessed Virgin:

O garment not golden but gilded,
O garden where all men may dwell,
O tower not of ivory, but builded
By hands that reach heaven from hell;
O mystical rose of the mire,
O house not of gold but of gain,
O house of unquenchable fire,
  Our Lady of Pain!

Swinburne voices Sade's doctrine that we should forget about love and similar socially OK feelings, and stick to plain sensual excitement, which is more potent and less ensnaring. By a paradox, the pain Dolores inflicts is harmless:

Could you hurt me, sweet lips, though
  I hurt you?
Men touch them, and change in a trice
The lilies and languors of virtue
For the raptures and roses of vice;
Those lie where thy foot on the floor is,
These crown and caress thee and chain,
O splendid and sterile Dolores,
  Our Lady of Pain. . . .

Ah beautiful passionate body
That never has ached with a heart!
On thy mouth though the kisses are bloody,
Though they sting till it shudder and smart,
More kind than the love we adore is,
They hurt not the heart or the brain,
O bitter and tender Dolores,
      Our Lady of Pain.

In due course comes the intoxicating Black Mass of *Justine* and *Juliette*:

I have passed from the outermost portal
To the shrine where a sin is a prayer;
What care though the service be mortal?
O our Lady of Torture, what care?
All thine the last wine that I pour is,
The last in the chalice we drain,
O fierce and luxurious Dolores,
      Our Lady of Pain.

There is a covert allusion to Sade in person as author of *Justine*—"good shall die first, said thy prophet"—followed by speculation about his end:

Did he lie? did he laugh? does he know it,
Now he lies out of reach, out of breath,
Thy prophet, thy preacher, thy poet,
Sin's child by incestuous death?
Did he find out in fire at his waking,
Or discern as his eyelids lost light,
When the bands of the body were breaking
      And all came in sight?

Dolores grows into a symbol, the presiding genius of pagan antiquity,

when lust and cruelty were free—with special reference to the glories
of Nero:

> *There the gladiator, pale for thy pleasure,*
> *Drew bitter and perilous breath;*
> *There torments laid hold on the treasure*
> *Of limbs too delicious for death;*
> *When thy gardens were lit with live torches;*
> *When the world was a steed for thy rein;*
> *When the nations lay prone in thy porches,*
> >   *Our Lady of Pain.*

> *When, with flame all around him aspirant,*
> *Stood flushed, as a harp-player stands,*
> *The implacable beautiful tyrant,*
> *Rose-crowned, having death in his hands;*
> *And a sound as the sound of loud water*
> *Smote fear through the flight of the fires,*
> *And mixed with the lightning of slaughter*
> >   *A thunder of lyres.*

Thence to Sade's condemnation of Christianity:

> *What ailed us, O gods, to desert you*
> *For creeds that refuse and restrain?*
> *Come down and redeem us from virtue,*
> >   *Our Lady of Pain.*

So the masochist arrives, via the tyrannous Fatal Woman herself, at
Sadian visions and conclusions.

The animus against Christ reappears, with more power and dignity, in Swinburne's "Hymn to Proserpine"—his poem with the famous
shock line about the pale Galilean whose breath has turned the world

gray. This is a sad poem, and in Swinburne's earlier career, when his ardors cooled, his poems usually were sad. So was he. His friends worried about him and wondered "what could be done *with* and *for* Algernon." In 1867 Dante Gabriel Rossetti and Richard Burton tried to set up a therapeutic liaison for him. Their choice of a seductress was excellent. They picked on the American circus performer Adah Menken, a fiery, much-married lady a little older than Algernon and a lot bulkier. She wrote verses herself and had caused a stir with her act as Mazeppa, bound to a horse's back and wearing flesh-colored tights. Adah and the poet were photographed together, and he was glad to allow gossip to spread, but the affair went no further. According to rumor Rossetti gave her £10 and said she could keep it if she actually got Algernon into bed with her. After some weeks she handed back the £10 and left England.*

Another attempt to do something with, or for, Algernon took the shape of guiding his zeal for Liberty into political rather than moral channels. He was already attracted to the cause of the Risorgimento. Arrangements were made for him to meet its prophet, Mazzini. This time the treatment took. He produced *Song of Italy, Ode on the Proclamation of the French Republic,* and *Songs before Sunrise.* In these, as with Sade and to some extent under his continued prompting, libertinism did seem to have led to liberty. But as with Sade and as with Wilkes, if for different reasons, the alliance was unreal. Swinburne could only handle Liberty, the Nations, and kindred conceptions by personifying them . . . and he turned them into terrible goddesses like his other terrible goddesses. When he lost that vision, he flagged. The more political he got, the more empty, verbose, and mechanized his poems became. His stock of imagery ran out. He was no more successful than Sade had been—in fact, less so—in projecting the Rule of Thélème beyond the castle or club or "special establishment," into the struggle for human freedom at large.

---

*The story has been dismissed on the ground that she was making plenty of money and there could have been no question of a £10 professional fee. But surely it was a bet?

He acquired a reputation in France, and it is interesting to see for what. He became one of the prime sources for the French legend of *le vice anglais,* sadism with a small *s,* sex-through-cruelty. This twist of his fame confirmed his linkage with the Hell-Fire tradition. A second Englishman who fascinated the French in the same way was George Selwyn, that lover of executions who attended meetings at Medmenham and pushed through to watch the dismemberment of Damiens. In a novel much read by decadents, *La Faustin,* Edmond de Goncourt blended the two into an English gentleman-sadist, "The Honourable George Selwyn," who looks and sounds like Swinburne and remains a prototype of *le vice anglais* as the French have understood it. Later and lesser works of French fiction introduce wicked English poets called Algernon Filde and Algernon Isburne.

It must be confessed that Swinburne asked for it. When he took a villa at Etretat he named it Dolmance Cottage after a Sade character, and called his garden path the Avenue de Sade. Here he entertained Maupassant, and Maupassant's description of him to Goncourt underlies the perverted Englishman in Goncourt's novel. In the end it was Hell-Fire that won out.

CROWLEY'S INTERPRETATION

In 1875, when Swinburne was on a last poetic plateau before his decline, the wife of a Warwickshire brewer and lay preacher produced a son. This son was to inherit Swinburne's mantle to the slight extent that anyone did. He was also to invest the Rule of Thélème with a new meaning, thereby breaking out of a cul-de-sac into country that is still largely unexplored. Despite his links with Swinburne in outlook and style, the inspiration did not come from the senior poet. It came from magic—partly from the magic of Dee and Kelley, resurgent after three centuries.

Swinburne himself had perhaps flirted with magic, but in the world of the decadents and eccentrics a great deal more than flirtation went on. J. K. Huysmans blew what he claimed to be the gaff on Parisian diabolism in a novel, *Là-Bas*. Joséphin Péladan, a lesser French author who exploited *vice anglais* and cited Swinburne as evidence, was cofounder in 1888 of the "Kabbalistic Order of the Rose-Cross." This was devoted to white magic and the reconciliation of occultism with Christianity, though, in practice, one of Péladan's colleagues died mysteriously at thirty, and another went mad.

Such concerns were very much in the air. At about the same time as the French venture, a new Rosicrucian body was founded in England, the Order of the Golden Dawn. During its erratic career it enrolled several members of talent, including Arthur Machen (inventor of the Angels of Mons) and Algernon Blackwood, and one genius, W. B. Yeats. The Golden Dawn revived the magic of that earlier figure in the Thelemic story, John Dee. The head of the Order, S. L. MacGregor Mathers, made a study of Dee's unpublished papers and derived a system from them.

Mathers himself did not stress the anti-moral element in Dee's magic, or the angelic command "Do even as you list." It is doubtful whether anyone has, except possibly Rasputin, if the story of *his* study of Dee's papers is true. The Golden Dawn, like its French contemporary, was meant to be "white." Its members adopted mottoes that generally suggested spiritual uplift. Nevertheless, Yeats chose the motto *Demon Est Deus Inversus*—"the Devil is the Converse of God"—and is said to have held branch meetings at the Killakee Dower House, the ancient haunt of the Dublin Hell-Fire Club. Alongside him in the London group (much to his vexation) there briefly appeared the young poet born in 1875: Aleister Crowley.

Crowley, the "Great Beast" and alleged black magician, was by far the most remarkable of the Golden Dawnists *as* a magician. He claimed the Dee succession by saying he was a reincarnation of Edward Kelley, and made elaborate and alarming experiments in Dee-Kelley magic. Since his death in 1947 he has come under so much scrutiny that there is no need to review his whole life. What matters here is his Neo-Thelemic maxim, "Do what thou wilt shall be the whole of the Law" and the meaning he attached to this.

From his father and mother he inherited money that he frittered away, managing, however, to accomplish plenty in the process. He was a divided, versatile person, able to do several things well (mountaineering, for instance, as well as the pursuits that made him notorious), but rarely wholehearted in any single role. Even his pictures suggest three or four different men. On top of his genuine oscillations he was a poseur and humorist, and his quarrelsome scorn for nearly everybody he knew set up resentments that confused his reputation still further. Crowley was perverted in a deeper sense than the vulgarly sexual; he was often preposterous; and he was brilliant—just how brilliant, it is only now becoming possible to appreciate.

Besides poetry that is like Swinburne's, he wrote fiction that is sometimes like Sade's. His sexual impulses were normal, strong to the verge of morbidity, and quite indiscriminate; he had hypnotic powers that he used freely for seduction. But he could also throw himself into Swinburnian abasement toward Fatal Women, several of whom appear in his poems. *Jezebel,* for example . . .

> *Now let me die, at last desired,*
> *At last beloved of thee my queen.*
> *Now let me die, with blood attired,*
> *Thy servant naked and obscene;*
> *To thy white skull, thy palms, thy feet,*
> *Clinging, dead, infamous, complete.*
>
> *Now let me die, to mix my soul*
> *With thy red soul, to join our hands,*
> *To weld us in one perfect whole,*
> *To link us with desirous bands.*
> *Now let me die, to mate in hell*
> *With thee, O harlot Jezebel.*

Later on he insisted on the importance of a "Scarlet Woman" as a magical partner and cast several of his mistresses in that role, though in the end none was satisfactory.

His Golden Dawn membership did not last long. However, it gave him a clue that led to his grand discovery. Besides working on Dee, Mathers translated a French book purporting to preserve secrets of Jewish occultism, *The Sacred Magic of Abra-Melin the Mage.* This book indicates that the Great Work—that is, the mysterious operation that raises a successful magician above normal humanity—consists in achieving "the knowledge and conversation of one's Holy Guardian Angel." Each of us is linked with a higher being, and wisdom, power, and fulfillment are to be found by breaking the barrier that divides him from us.

Crowley tried this by methods described in *Abra-Melin,* and by others of his own devising. While he was visiting Egypt in 1904 with his wife (Rose Kelly, sister of Gerald Kelly, later president of the Royal Academy), she drew his attention to a stele in a museum in Cairo, depicting the god Horus. Aleister invoked Horus, and with the god's aid, after sundry experiences, his angel at last came through. This being's name was Aiwass. He dictated a long text, which Crowley took down in breathless haste and entitled *Liber Legis,* the Book of the Law.

The style of this outpouring is Swinburne derivative, Wilde derivative, Nietzsche derivative . . . and yet Crowley's claims for it as a revelation are not entirely absurd. For him it was the Bible of a new era. Mankind had passed through the epochs of the Mother Goddess and the Father God and would now move into the epoch of Horus, the Divine Child. There is a parallel here with Powys's view of Rabelais as a wise-childish prophet for the Aquarian Age. The watchword of Crowley's new era was in fact *Thelema,* meaning "will" in Greek and recalling Rabelais directly. The key maxim, stated in *Liber Legis,* was "Do what thou wilt shall be the whole of the Law." For the rest of his life—after a futile attempt to evade destiny—Crowley repeated this formula in season and out of season, using it as a greeting and starting his letters with it. The *Daily Telegraph* leader-writer quoted on p. xviii had Crowley in mind.*

What did the "Law of Thelema" mean for him? His conduct often seemed to imply that it meant "Do as you like" and was no advance on Sade. He mistreated Rose and drove her insane. He adopted megalomaniac titles such as The Great Beast, Therion, an allusion to the Apocalypse, chapters xiii and xvii. He founded odd magical societies of his own and a publication, the *Equinox,* which was a personal platform disguised as a magazine. He experimented with drugs, and with forms of sex magic taught by a dubious German "Order of Oriental Templars," which included deliberate sodomy quite in Sade's manner.

All the same, there was more to Crowley's Law than this. In 1920 he acquired a villa at Cefalu in Sicily and called it the Abbey of Thelema. A community gathered around him, including people of some distinction, such as the novelist Mary Butts. Here he expounded the Law. "Do what thou wilt," he explained, did NOT mean, "Do as you like." After four centuries he broke free from the tangle over "Nature" and natural promptings, by coming down heavily on the meaning of *will.* He interpreted it as something like "vocation." Everyone has a calling in life, a proper path of self-fulfilment and spiritual deliverance. Most human beings are embroiled in day-to-day pursuits and do not consciously know what their true wills are. The prime essential is to find out. And in a sense you do know all along, if you can only silence the clamor of the conscious mind and let the knowledge rise to the surface. This process has nothing to do with such crudities as psychological testing. It is a revelation from a buried True Self.

When Crowley started out on his magical career he would have stated this in the Abra-Melin jargon: "Your Guardian Angel knows what you're really for—contact him and he'll tell you." By the time

---

*Horus was one of the two deities whose images are known to have stood in Medmenham Abbey. Wilkes mentions him in the same paragraph as the inscription *Fay ce que voudras.* Did some forgotten bit of reading about Medmenham cause the god to evoke the slogan in Crowley's subconscious?

he launched his Sicilian Thélème he had reached a position akin to Jung's. The Guardian Angel was real, but he was a second and higher self in a more intimate sense than the old magicians supposed. He was an aspect of the Unconscious. That was why sex could lead to revelation. It unleashed the libido and stirred the depths. A Crowley disciple vowed to "perform the Great Work, which is to obtain the knowledge of the nature and powers of my own being." This did not mark any shift of ground; it was simply the Abra-Melin formula about the Guardian Angel, rephrased.

If you find your true will, Crowley insisted, everything else will fall into place and no other laws will be needed. Your life will come right instinctively, and you will be free to progress without limit. In practice he added a second clause—"Love is the law, love under will"—which is a partial reversion to St. Augustine, but this was never given the same weight.

Crowley certainly helped some of his disciples. Others revolted and deserted or killed themselves. Cefalu closed down in an atmosphere of scandal, to some extent deserved, but not altogether. Superficially this is the same tale over again: the closed circle, the special community, the failure to make the Rule of Thélème relevant outside it. Yet Crowley did get further. For one thing, he gave the Rule a new meaning and a claim to be taken seriously in the light of psychology. For another, he maintained that it *was* for all, and although his attempts to prove this were purely abstract, he never came ideologically unstuck like Sade. His notion of the new age is elitist but credible. Those who follow his lead and find their vocations will attain freedom and need no further ethics. But beyond that, they will be wiser, better integrated, and more effective than others; they will attain a gradual ascendancy; they will work a sort of alchemic change through society, reordering it in terms of their own salvation. Crowley's commonwealth as foreseen by himself is too like Plato's Republic to be attractive, but it does deserve attention, and the idea underlying it could perhaps be put in more acceptable terms.

As for Crowley himself, the prophet, his own true will was simply to proclaim the Law. Aiwass, his Guardian Angel or alter ego, had made that clear. The last decades of his life seemed a poor advertisement for his doctrine. He fizzled out, dying poor and neglected at a boarding house in Hastings in 1947. Today he is harder to dismiss.

MODERN WILL*

To revert at last to Charles Manson's homicidal Family, it stands out in its own right and cannot be reduced to a repeat performance of eighteenth-century Hell-Fire or even a ghastly exaggeration of it. Yet the tradition that comes down from Rabelais can give the Family a context and relate it to other phenomena, both ancient and modern. It was a perverted product of the quest for alternative lifestyles among those juniors who were vaguely lumped together as hippies. One advantage of knowing the Thelemic record is that it sheds light on this quest. Emphasis on drugs and drug culture tended to confuse the issues, and that aspect of it has come to look worse in retrospect with the souring of the drug scene. Even here, however, the sometime LSD Messiah Timothy Leary noticed a fact that was more significant than he realized. In its expansion during the late 1960s, the movement was thought of as American; yet it had a substratum of English inspiration, stretching back through the more publicized influences—the Beatles, Aldous Huxley's mescalin visions—to older and subtler ones. Leary, in *The Politics of Ecstasy,* referred to the English approvingly as a nation of "heads" (in his own sense of the word) for many generations.

The ghost of Crowley was present in Californian cults, but the ghosts of Wharton and Dashwood were present too, though unrecognized. Like Hanoverian England, America seemed complacent under a

---

*This concluding section, when it was written, considered various things that were very recent and in some cases continuing. They could be discussed as contemporary, more or less. They are still relevant, but no longer contemporary. Without making major changes, I have tried to set them at an appropriate distance and have added a little about developments since.

solid Establishment. There could be protests on particular issues, but there was no jumping-off point for dissent of a more comprehensive kind. So dissent could only be anarchic, one might almost say rakish, with more than a dash of outrage and shock. The Rule of Thélème revived in a quasi-Crowleyan guise as Doing Your Thing. Libertinism, to resurrect the old-fashioned term, was again seen as Liberty. America produced junior centers and communes, as the London of Anne and George I produced clubs—foci and meeting places where the like-minded could gather—as well as a subversive "underground" press to spread the word, with far-off echoes of the *True Briton,* and the *Craftsman,* and, in a different way, Edmund Curll.

Within the pattern there was an appreciable amount of fresh thinking, goodwill, and offbeat sanity. But America also produced its counterpart of the uglier freedom that once disturbed London and Dublin. The eloquently named Hells Angels were the Mohocks reborn, and more. Motorcycle gangs were not new, but years of conflict with quieter citizens built up into secession from society and a tribal mystique. There was urban terrorism in the Mohock style. There was also ritualized repulsiveness such as Sade might have relished—initiations where neophytes were baptized with urine and excreta; the wearing of filthy clothes till they dropped off; the flaunting of Nazi insignia; group rape and homosexual displays in public.

Hell-Fire clubs reappeared under new names, and sometimes with an explicit commitment to what society regarded as evil. In 1966 the Church of Satan was founded in San Francisco. Its president Anton Lavey, or LaVey as he spelled it, held satanic baptisms, weddings, and funerals and published a Satanic Bible. His Church was a crude adaptation of earlier occult orders. It taught that "Man must learn to properly indulge himself by whatever means he finds necessary" and that the Seven Deadly Sins are life-enhancing virtues. The sect had a moment of notoriety through the death of the film star Jayne Mansfield, who was an active member. One of her pronouncements was that chastity is a "really sickening perversion." Her satanic activities worried her lawyer and boyfriend Sam Brody, who was afraid they might mar her public image. LaVey put a curse on Brody, and Jayne died with him in a car crash, being almost decapitated. LaVey asserted—with doubtful veracity—that he played the part of the Devil in the film *Rosemary's Baby*, directed by Roman Polanski, whose wife Sharon Tate was the most famous of Manson's victims. One of the younger Satanists, Susan Atkins, joined the Manson Family and took part in Sharon Tate's murder, though she later repented. LaVey died in 1997. His organization went on, beset by disputes.

With the Church of Satan, and still more with the Family, the old syndrome recurred: the confinement of doing-what-you-will to a clique, whether rich or dropout. LaVey vetoed the formation of branches, and the Family was largely a web spun out of Manson's all too magnetic self, embodying an autocratic daydream like some of Sade's. Manson's talk of an outgoing movement made no more sense than it did with the Divine Marquis. To say this is not to condemn the wider cult of alternative living, which was truly liberating for many, but the satanic factor never had much to do with this. The beneficiaries were among those who experimented with genuine communes, do-it-yourself social services, radical publishing. In such settings, Doing Your Thing was more than a mere nose-thumbing gesture. It was bound up with much that was creative, and even, in a more or less ordinary sense, moral.

The principal sequel was unexpected. That period saw the emergent notion of the Age of Aquarius. Enthusiasts claimed, on astrological grounds, that the world was moving into a fundamentally different phase, a time of "increasing harmony, understanding, and spiritual growth." Hippiedom faded out, but the Aquarian motif, inheriting its exploratory character without its rebellion, bore fruit in the New Age. This was a medley of unconventional mysticism, oriental religions, neo-witchcraft, ecology, astrology, mythology, alternative medicine, Goddess worship, and supposed spiritual transformation. The New Age was a multiple dissent from various orthodoxies, and in some degree it continued the tradition of living and thinking differently, but it was not revolutionary and its manifestations tended to be personal rather than social. While it sometimes expressed the Thelemic spirit after a fashion, it was too heterogeneous to count as a movement. The story, for the moment, ends here.

What emerges? First, that outright anti-morality is something of a dead end. As a way of life it does not liberate or fulfill outside a privileged circle, the select company of Thélème who are in a position to practice it. Whether in sunny Rabelaisian or decadent satanic forms, that is its logic. The Castle in Hell remains a castle; it has no way of expanding into a housing development.

Second, however, it is still worth asking how far the Rule of Thélème might be given the profounder meaning that Crowley professed to give it when he said, "Do what thou wilt shall be the whole of the Law." To reject his magic as absurd and repellent is not to dispose of the serious question that he raised. In those depths of the psyche that Freud and Jung believed they had glimpsed, perhaps each individual's True Will or vocation is embedded. Perhaps there *is* meaning in the ideal of finding it and living by it, "doing what you will" in the sense of doing what you are *for* in a truer liberty, under the guidance of a right orientation, which rules in general can subserve. But to pursue such a vision any further would mean saying goodbye to the Hell-Fire brethren and all their kind and moving into fresh territory.

A NOTE ON SEX

The last section may call for an added word on the loosely related, overdone topic of modern sexual permissiveness in action and print: "doing what you will" in that sphere alone and shedding a naysaying morality. One thinks of the onset of release, followed by sexploitation, in films and books (the first complete English *Juliette* was published in the United States in 1968); of sundry medicine man prophets hymning the orgasm; of media heroes such as Hugh Hefner, expounder of the Playboy Ethic. This type of emancipation undoubtedly does go outside select circles. But does it have an effect beyond itself? It is perhaps a libertinism that makes for liberty?

With all due respect to Mr. Kenneth Tynan, I remain unpersuaded. The individual may show up well in individual cases. Just as Dashwood defended Byng, and Wilkes fought three elections, so Mr. Hefner has befriended victims of illiberal laws. Socially, however, unbridled sex merely seems to encourage a certain relaxation, a certain nonfanaticism. It links up with Thélème at Rabelais's level rather than Sade's or Swinburne's. Relaxation and nonfanaticism may be good, but they are negative. The sex revolution, so far as it exists as more than a commercial invention, is no likelier than any other neo-Rabelaisian conduct to promote revolutions—or even reforms—in nonsexual areas.

BIBLIOGRAPHY

This bibliography is the one appended to the first edition of this book. While it does not go beyond 1972, my impression is that few later publications are likely to have enough specific relevance to make a case for inclusion. Donald Thomas's biography *The Marquis de Sade* (1992) gives immensely more information than has gone into chapter 13, but I question whether it affects my restricted outline of Sade's ideas. One modern topic, the Church of Satan, is the subject of an article by Jack Boulware in the magazine *Gnosis,* published in San Francisco, issue no. 50, Winter 1999. Another book about the principle Hell-Fire figure is *Dashwood: The Man and the Myth* by Eric Towers (1986).

Most of these items may be left to speak for themselves. However, a few supplementary comments are in order.

Our knowledge of John Dee is still largely provisional. Recent research suggests that he was more important in the history of thought than appears on the surface. Even if Kelley faked the angelic messages, he may have taken hints from ideas of Dee himself, which have yet to be properly reconstructed.

Previous accounts of the "Monks of Medmenham" have been weakened by the inadequate use of strangely obvious bits of evidence, such as the cellar-book fragments and letters at West Wycombe. Betty Kemp's denial that the Order existed is certainly mistaken. Both McCormick and Mannix (who is entertaining but inexact) go wrong over the *Essay on Woman*. On this, Adrian Hamilton's work supersedes all others. For the broader eighteenth-century context, I have found John Carswell invaluable.

Almon, John, ed. *The New Foundling Hospital for Wit*. London: J. Debrett, 1771, 1789.

Athenaeum. 1859, 11.78. (Article on Martha Fowke.)

Bakhtin, Mikhail. *Tvorchestvo Fransua Rabele*. Moscow: Khudozhestvennia Literature, 1965. Translated by Helene Iswolsky as *Rabelais and his World*. Bloomington: Indiana University Press, 1965.

Beauvoir, Simone de. *The Marquis de Sade*. London: Calder, 1962.

Bolingbroke, Viscount. *Letters on the Spirit of Patriotism and the Idea of a Patriot King*. Edited by A. Hassall. Oxford: Clarendon Press, 1917.

Briggs, Asa, ed. *How They Lived*. Vol. 3, 1700–1815. Oxford: Basil Blackwell, 1969.

Brown, Huntington. *The Tale of Gargantua and King Arthur*. Cambridge, Mass.: Harvard University Press, 1932.

Cammell, Charles Richard. *Aleister Crowley*. London: Richards Press, 1951.

Carswell, John. *The Old Cause*. London: Cresset Press, 1954.

Cavendish, Richard. *The Black Arts*. London: Routledge & K. Paul, 1967.

———, ed. *Man, Myth and Magic*. New York: Marshall Cavendish, 1970. (Most of the relevant articles are in the supplement "Frontiers of Belief.")

Churchill, Charles. *Poems*. Edited by James Laver. 2 vols. London: Eyre and Spottiswoode, 1933.

Cole, Hubert. *First Gentleman of the Bedchamber: The Life of Louis-François-Armand, Marechal Duc de Richelieu*. New York: Viking, 1965.

Crowley, Aleister. *The Confessions of Aleister Crowley*. London: Cape, 1969.

Day, James Wentworth. *A Ghost Hunter's Game Book*. London: F. Muller, 1958.

Deacon, Richard. *See* McCormick, Donald.

Dobson, H. Austin. *William Hogarth*. London: William Heinemann, 1907.

Dodington, George Bubb. *Political Journal*. Edited by John Carswell and Lewis Arnold Dralle. Oxford: Clarendon Press, 1965.

French, Peter J. *John Dee*. London: Routledge & K. Paul, 1972.

Fuller, Ronald. *Hell-Fire Francis*. London: Chatto & Windus, 1939.

Gear, Norman. *The Divine Demon: A Portrait of the Marquis de Sade.* London: F. Muller, 1963.

Gorer, Geoffrey. *The Revolutionary Ideas of the Marquis de Sade.* London: Wishart, 1934 (revised 1953).

Haining, Peter, ed. *The Necromancers.* London: Hodder and Stoughton, 1971.

Hamilton, Adrian. *The Infamous Essay on Woman.* London: Deutsch, 1972.

Hodgart, Matthew, ed. *Horace Walpole: Memoirs and Portraits.* New York: Macmillan, 1963.

Howe, Ellie. *The Magicians of the Golden Dawn.* London: Routledge and K. Paul, 1972.

Joelson, Annette. *Heirs to the Throne.* London: Heinemann, 1966.

Johnstone, Charles. *Chrysal: or, The Adventures of a Guinea.* 4 vols. London, 1760–65.

Kemp, Betty. *Sir Francis Dashwood: An Eighteenth-Century Independent.* London: Macmillan, 1967.

Kendrick, T. D. *The Lisbon Earthquake.* London: Methuen, 1956.

Ketton-Cremer, Robert Wyndham. *Horace Walpole.* London: Duckworth, 1940.

Lely, Gilbert. *The Marquis de Sade.* Translated by Alec Brown. London: Elek Books, 1961.

Lovat, Fraser, J. A. *John Stuart, Earl of Bute.* Cambridge: University Press, 1912.

Lucas, Frank Laurence. *The Art of Living.* London: Cassell, 1959.

Madden, R. R. *History of Irish Periodical Literature.* 2 vols. London: T. C. Newby, 1867.

Mannix, Daniel P. *The Hell-Fire Club.* London: Four Square, 1961.

McCormick, Donald. *The Hell-Fire Club.* London: Jarrolds, 1958.

———. [Richard Deacon, pseud.] *John Dee.* London: Muller, 1968.

Melville, Lewis. *The Life and Writings of Philip Duke of Wharton.* London: John Lane, 1913.

Nicolson, Harold. *The Age of Reason.* London: Constable, 1960.

Notes and Queries. Various items in 1854, 1860, 1866, 1868, 1881, 1892.

Plumb, J. H. *The First Four Georges.* London: Batsford, 1956.

Pope-Hennessey, James. *Monckton Milnes: The Flight of Youth.* New York: Farrar, Straus & Cudahy, 1951.

Postgate, Raymond. *That Devil Wilkes.* London: Dobson, 1956.

Powys, John Cowper. *Rabelais.* London: Bodley Head, 1948.

Praz, Mario. *The Romantic Agony.* London: Oxford University Press, 1960.

R. B. *The Hell-Fire Club: kept by a Society of Blasphemers.* London: J. Roberts and A. Dodd, 1721.

Robinson, John Robert. *Philip Duke of Wharton.* London: S. Low, Marston, 1896.

Spectator. Various issues in 1712 and 1714.

Spurgeon, Caroline. Preface to *The Castle of Otranto,* by Horace Walpole. London: Chatto & Windus, 1907.

Straus, Ralph. *The Unspeakable Curll.* London: Chapman and Hall, 1927.

Symonds, John. *The Great Beast: The Life and Magic of Aleister Crowley.* London: Macdonald, 1971.

Taylor, G. R. Stirling. *Robert Walpole and his Age.* London: J. Cape, 1931.

Thompson, Edward. *See* Whitehead, Paul.

Walton, Alan Hull. Introduction to *Justine* in English translation. London: N. Spearman, 1964.

Ward, Ned. *The Secret History of Clubs.* London: J. Dutten, 1709.

Whitehead, Paul. *The Poems and Miscellaneous Compositions of Paul Whitehead: With Explanatory Notes of His Writings, and His Life.* London: G. Kearsley, 1777.

Wilkes, John. *The Correspondence of John Wilkes and Charles Churchill.* Edited by Edward H. Weatherly. New York: Columbia University Press, 1954.

Willcocks, M. P. *The Laughing Philosopher: Being a Life of Francois Rabelais.* London: Allen and Unwin, 1950.

Wraxall, N. Williams. *Historical Memoirs of My Own Time.* 2 vols. London: T. Cadell and W. Davies, 1815.

INDEX

Abbey of Thelema, 263, 264
Abra-Melin (magic), 262, 263, 264
admittance to "Order of St. Francis," 138
adultery, 96
Age of Reason, 35–36, 220
Agrippa. *See* Cornelius Agrippa
Aiwass, a spirit invoked in Egypt,
     262, 265
alchemy, 22, 27, 29
algolagnia (pleasure with pain), 252
anti-monastery, 13–15
anti-morality as a way of life, xvii
aphrodisiacs, 80, 218, 240, 252
Aphrodites, Les, 205
Appalling Club, 64–66
Aquarian Age, 3, 262, 267–68
Armstrong, Dr. John, 75–81, 89, 91,
     92, 97, 115, 117
Arthur, King, 10–11
Art of Love, The (Ovid), 139
Art of Preserving Health, The
     (Armstrong), 75
atheism, 38, 132, 226, 237
Aubrey, John, 26
Aucassin, xv–xvi, xix, 16, 17–18, 120
Aucassin and Nicolette, xv–xvi
Augusta of Saxe-Gotha, Princess
     (wife of Prince Frederick), 101,

     102, 126, 147, 149–50, 152, 163,
     171, 179
Augustine, St., 15
Austen, Lady (sister of Francis
     Dashwood), 194, 195
Autumn (Thomson), 98

baboon dressed as chaplain or devil,
     140, 199
Bacchus, dedication of temple to,
     West Wycombe, 191
Bacchus's Tomb, 108
Backsliding Teacher, The (Curll), 74
ball, gilded, on West Wycombe
     Church tower, 189–90
Bastille, destruction of, 219
Bates, Dr. Benjamin, 136, 159, 194
BBC and Christianity, 49
Beaumont d'Éon (transvestite, also
     known as Genevieve), 188–89
Beefsteak Club, 46, 108, 109, 131,
     155, 181
Beggar's Opera, The (Gay), 38, 39,
     181
Belle Dame sans Merci, La, 252
bestiality, 70, 242
Bible, the, xvi
Bishop's wife, seduction of, 133

blackballing, 101

black baptisms, 140

black cat of Killakee Dower House, 62, 63

black magic, 61, 63

Black Masses, 63, 67, 140, 233, 256

Blake, William, 251

blasphemy, 47, 48, 52, 61, 181, 206

bloodletting, 135, 217

"bloody," (in regard to war with France) and Pitt's objection to, 164

Boarding School Rapes (Curll), 74

Bolingbroke, Viscount Henry, 36–37, 59, 81, 99, 102, 125, 147

Bonaventure, St., 12

Borgnis, Giuseppe, 107, 123, 135, 185, 190

boxers, 132

Brahe, Tycho, 26

Breast of Venus (meat dish), 48

Briton (pro-Bute newspaper), 169

Brody, Sam, 267

brothels, 42

Brotherhood of Friars (bogus). *See* Order of Friars

Bubb, George. *See* Dodington, George

Budé, Guillaume, 3

"Burn-Chapel" Whaley (father of Thomas), 205–6

Bute, Earl of. *See* Stuart, John, third Earl of Bute

"Bute's Erection" (Kew Gardens), 179

Byng, Admiral John, 152–53, 160, 210–11, 212

Byron, George Gordon, 6th Baron B. of Rochdale, 249–50, 253

Calvin, John, 5, 19

"Candidate, The" (Churchill), 183

Candide (Voltaire), 210, 223

capital punishment, and Sade, 219, 244

caricaturists, 96, 159, 172

Carymary, Carymara (expletives), 8, 21

Cases of Impotency and Divorce (Curll), 71

Case of Seduction (Curll), 73

Case of Sodomy (Curll), 69

Castle of Indolence, The (Thomson), 115–20

Castle of Otranto, The (H. Walpole), 213–15

caves, meetings in, at West Wycombe Hill, 185–88

Cecil, William (Lord Burghley), 26

Champion (newspaper), 104

Charitable Surgeon, The (Curll), 69–70

Charity in the Cellar (Hogarth), 67

Charles Edward, Prince (Young Pretender), 65, 111–12

Charlotte of Mecklenburg-Strelitz, 163, 164

Christianity

  as a source of laughter, 36

  of the Walpole era, 48

Chrysal (Johnstone), 196–201

Chudleigh, Elizabeth, 150

Churchill, Rev. Charles, 110, 136, 141, 159–60, 169–70, 174, 175, 179, 180, 182, 183, 190, 191, 193

Church of Satan, 266–67

cider tax, 172–73

circumcision, 72

Clarissa Harlowe (Richardson), xi, 60, 82–83, 105, 222

Cleland, John, 83–90

Cliveden House, Cookham, 102, 103, 114, 123, 149

Cloacina, Temple of, 159

clubs, growth of, and listed, 44–46

coffee houses, 45

Commentaries on the Laws of England
(Blackstone), 151
communion chalice, misuse of, 135
Conway, Henry Seymour (cousin of
H. Walpole), 212
coprophilia, 242
copulation, in graveyards, 134
Cornelius Agrippa, 23–25, 26, 92, 194
Craftsman (newspaper), 59, 98–99, 266
Crazy Castle, 203
Crazy Tales (poetic anthology), 204
Creed of the "Order of St. Francis,"
138, 193
Crowley, Aleister (magician), 260–68
crucifixes, inverted, 140
crucifixions, mock, 62
crystal-gazing, 27–28
Curll, Edmund, 68–75, 108, 133, 266
list of books published by, 73–75

Daily Telegraph, The, xviii–xix
Damiens, Robert-François, 210–11,
212, 217, 259
"Dancing Masters," 39
Dante, 5, 258
Dashwood, Sir Francis (later Baron
Le Despenser), 67, 105–12,
121–29, 130–34, 137–39, 142–43,
144–45, 146, 152–53, 154–59,
161, 166–67, 171–73, 175, 181,
182–84, 185, 187, 188–94
Dashwood, Kitty, 164
Dashwood, Rachel Frances Antonina
(daughter of Francis) (the
Infidel), 193–196
Dashwood-King, Sir John (half-
brother of Francis), 132, 134,
142, 188
D'Aubrey, Sir John, 132, 134, 136
de Charolais, Duc, 217

Dee, John (magician), 25–29, 64, 128,
259, 260
Defoe, Daniel, 72
Demoniac Society, 203–4
demons and little crooked men
(legend of), 190
de Monteuil, Renée (wife of Marquis
de Sade), 216, 218, 219
d'Éon. *See* Beaumont d'Éon
de Quincey, Thomas, 67, 194, 250
de Richelieu, Duc. *See* Richelieu, Duc de
de Sade, Marquis. *See* Sade, Marquis de
Despenser, Baron Le. *See* Dashwood,
Sir Francis
Devil, pacts with, 64, 205
Devil's cause asserted, 52
Devil Tavern, 41, 46
devil worship, 61, 140, 198, 200
Dilettanti, Society of, 108–12, 115,
117, 120, 131
disciples of Venus and Bacchus,
138–39, 193
dismembering, 210–11
Divan Club, 111, 123, 131, 142
"Divine Marquis." *See* Sade, Marquis de
Divine Right of Kings, 164
divine vengeance, 209
Dodington, George (known as Bubb,
formerly George Bubb and later
Lord Melcombe), 59, 94–105,
112, 113–15, 122–23, 125–27,
130, 134, 144–45, 146, 148,
151–54, 162–67, 173, 191
"Dolores" (Swinburne), 252–57
007 the first (in 16th century), 25, 26
Douglas, William, Earl of March (later
Duke of Queensberry), 135, 167
"Do what thou wilt shall be the
whole of the Law" (stated by
Crowley). *See Liber Legis*

"Do what you will" (St. Augustine) (adopted as Rule of Théleme), xix, 15, 18, 34, 46, 84, 117, 118, 120, 129, 201, 208, 217, 225–26, 251, 258, 259, 260, 262, 263, 264, 267, 268, 269. *See also* Do Your Thing

Do Your Thing, 266, 267. *See also* "Do what you will"

dreams, interpretation of, 23, 27

drugs, experiments with, 263, 265

du Bellay, Jean and Guillaume, 6, 11

Dublin Blasters, 61

du Deffand, Marquise, 216–17

dueling, 62, 66, 171

Duellist, The (Churchill), 188

Duffield, Francis, 128–29, 130, 131, 134, 188

Dunstan, St., 27

earthquake at Lisbon (1755), 209–10

Eastbury, Blandford Forum, 95, 96, 97

Edgerley, Sophia, 143

eighteenth century, life in the early, 32–39

election of 1754, 155

Eleusinian Mysteries, 139, 187

Elizabeth I, Queen, 25–26

"Enochian" (occult language), 28

Epistles of Clio and Strephon (love letters), 43, 75

Erasmus, 5, 8l 19

Essay on Government (Lee), 195

Essay on Man (Pope), 37, 99, 134, 176, 178, 209

Essay on Woman (Potter), 134, 143, 175–81, 200, 204–5

eunuchs, 72

Everlastings, the, 65–66

"Evil, be thou my good" (Miltonic maxim), 44

executions, watching of, 134, 135, 210

exorcism, 62, 97, 115

Fanny Hill (Cleland), 81–93, 197

fiction, using living people as characters, 236, 237

Fielding, Henry, 82, 83, 92, 104, 114

"Fine Modern Gentleman, The" (Jenyns), 41

flagellation, 72, 85, 87–88, 217–18, 231, 252

flesh, diet of human, 240

flogging. *See* flagellation

Flogging block, The (Swinburne), 252

forgiveness of sins, significance of, 193

fortune-telling, 122

Fowke, Martha, 43–44, 75, 97

Fowke, Thomas (brother of Martha), 153

Fox, Charles James (son of Henry), 59, 211

Fox, Henry, 147, 167, 171

Franklin, Benjamin, 154, 188, 193, 201

Frederick, Prince of Wales (son of George II, known as Fred), 99–105, 122, 123, 125–26, 147, 148, 149

Freeman's Journal, 205

Freemasonry, 62, 63, 132, 241–42

Freud, Sigmund, 113

Fruit-Shop or *A Companion to St James's Street, The,* 44, 144, 204

funeral of Whitehead's heart, 192

gambling, 9, 99, 204, 205, 238

gaming houses, 42

Gandhi, Mahatma, xvii

gang life, 18th century, 38–40

Gardner, Gerald (witch expert), 187

Gargantua, 2, 7–20

George II, King, death of, 162
George III, King. *See also* George,
  Prince
  early years of the reign of, 162, 169
George, Prince (son of Frederick, later
  George III), 126, 147–48, 150–51,
  162–65, 171–72, 174, 201, 202
ghosts, 62, 63
  attend club meeting, 65–66
Glastonbury, mysteries of, 27
Gordon riots (1780), 202
Grand Tours, 41, 50, 63–64, 95,
  105–7, 113
Grenville, Richard (Lord Temple),
  155, 156, 174
guillotine, xvi–xvii, 219

Hakluyt, Richard, 27
Hall-Stevenson, John, 156, 188, 203–4
hanging
  decline in percentage of, 211
  lower limits meriting, 37
  watching, 134
"Harem, The" (Toast of Divan Club),
  111
heart, Whitehead leaves his, in will, 191
Hell-Fire, cult of, 34
*Hell-Fire Club Kept by a Society of
  Blasphemers, The*, 47
Hell-Fire clubs, 47–52, 56, 110, 121,
  266
  at George and Vulture Inn, 66, 99,
    108, 110, 131, 186
  at Medmenham, 121, 123
  at Oxford University, 64–65, 206
  in Ireland, 61–63, 140, 205
"Hell is the place for me" (said by
  Aucassin), xv
Hells Angels, 266
Henry VIII, King, 5, 25, 128, 136

heretics, torture of, xvi
high treason, 57
highwaymen, viewed with favor, 38
hippies, x, 114, 265
*Histories of Gargantua and Pantagruel,
  The* (Rabelais), 7–12, 19
History of England (1660–1715)
  (Ralph), 104
Hoadly, Bishop Benjamin, 48, 53
Hogarth, William, 67, 99, 109, 127,
  133, 134, 135, 159, 167, 172
Holy Ghost Pie (meat dish), 48, 110
homosexuals, 88, 170, 206, 230, 266
horoscopes, 25
"Hymn to Proserpine" (Swinburne),
  257
hypnosis as a means to seduce, 261

idolum tentiginis (cock-shaped hobby-
  horse), 141
illegitimate child, 79–80
immorality, a defense of, 60
immorality and profanity, Government
  order to suppress, 47
incest, 38, 204, 227, 232, 242
Indolence, Castle of (fictional), 116–20
Infidel, the. *See* Dashwood, Rachel
  Frances Antonina (daughter of
  Francis)
infidels, slaughter of, xvi

Jeremy Twitcher, 181. *See also*
  Sandwich, Earl of
Jesus Christ, 4, 198
Jezebel (Crowley), 261
John, Friar (later Abbot of Thélème),
  13–14, 17, 22
Johnson, Dr. Samuel, 132, 168, 170,
  201
Johnstone, Charles, 196–201

Jonathan Wild (Fielding), 92, 104, 222

Juliette (Sade), 221, 222–26, 229, 235–43, 248, 269

Justine (Sade), 219, 222, 228–35, 148
 has to turn a water wheel, 234
 her death, 240
 her thrashing described, 231–32

Kabbalah (Jewish cult), 24–25
Kama Sutra, 134, 196
Keller, Rose, 217
Kelley, Edward, 27–29, 259, 260
Kepler, Johannes, 26
Kidgell, Rev. John, 64, 175–79
kidnapping, 195
Kit-Cat Club, 42, 43, 44, 50
Koestler, Arthur, x
Koran, the, 111

Lady of Pain. *See Dolores*
Langley, Thomas, 143
Lascelles, Rev. Robert (nicknamed Panty), 204
LaVey, Anton, 266–67
lawsuits and trials, as a basis for erotic books, 69, 74
Leary, Timothy, 265
Lee, Mrs. *See* Dashwood, Rachel
le Fay, Morgan, 12
Leicester, Earl of, 26
Lens, Peter, 61
lesbianism, 84, 204, 227, 237, 243
Lewis, Matthew Gregory, 249
Liber Legis (Crowley), 262
Lilliburlero (song), 50, 51
Lisbon earthquake (1755), 209–10
Lloyd, Robert, 136, 160, 169, 180, 182, 191
Louis XIV, 32, 227

Louis XV, 36, 38, 91, 189,
 stabbing of, 210
Lovelace (fictitious libertine), 60
Luther, Martin, 5, 19
lynching by teams of horses, 210
Lyttelton, Lord, 115, 117, 122, 135, 181

Macclesfield, Baron, 47, 48, 49, 53
Machen, Arthur, 260
Madimi (child-spirit), 28–29
magic, 21–26, 63, 64, 75, 122, 259–60
Maldoror (Lautreamont), 250
Mallet, David, 43, 97, 114, 167, 168, 211
Manfred. *See Castle of Otranto*
Mansfield, Jayne, 266
Manson, Charles (multiple murderer), xvii–xviii, xx, 265, 267
man-traps, 206
Marx, Karl, xvi
Mary, Queen, threat to kill by black magic, 26
masks to hide identification of women, 142
Masons. *See* Freemasonry
Masque of Alfred (Thomson and Mallet), 114, 167
masturbation, 77, 243
Mathers, S. L. Macgregor, 260, 262
mediums, 28–29
Medmenham Abbey, 128–29, 130–45. *See also* Order of Friars
Melcombe, Lord. *See* Dodington, George
Melmoth the Wanderer (Maturin), 215, 249
Memoirs of a Woman of Pleasure. See Fanny Hill
Menken, Adah, 258
Merlin (magician), 10, 21–22

Middlesex, Wilkes's stand as MP in, 201
Milnes, Richard Monckton (later Lord Houghton), 253
Milton, John, 44. See also Paradise Lost
mock-monastery, 197–98
Mohocks, 39–41, 45, 61, 266
Monk, The (Lewis), 249
Mons, Angel of, 260
Montagu, Edward Wortley, 165
Montagu, Lady Mary Wortley, 43, 55, 95, 111, 142, 149
More, Thomas, 5
Morgan le Fay, 12
Morning Post, The (London), 200
Motteux, Peter, 19, 74
Murder Considered as One of the Fine Arts, On (de Quincey), 250
Murray, Fanny (Lord Sandwich's mistress), 143, 176, 180
Mysteries of Udolpho, The (Radcliffe), 214–15

naked host, visitors received by, 61
Nature and obedience, 46
"Nature's single precept is to enjoy oneself, at the expense of no matter whom" (Sade), 225–26
Nazi insignia, 266
necrophilia, 135, 242
Newcastle, Duke of, 152, 165, 166
New Justine (Sade), 229. See also Justine
New Learning, cult of, 3, 5, 18
Newton, Sir Isaac, 35
Night Thoughts (Young), 60, 94, 104
Nineteen Eighty-Four (Orwell), 225
North Briton (newspaper), 169–70, 172, 174, 180, 212
November 1st, significance of, 228

Nun in her Smock, The (Curll), 73, 75, 82
Nuns of Medmenham, 141–43,
nymphs and hogsheads, 140

Occult Philosophy (Agrippa), 194
Occult Philosophy (Paracelsus), 23
"Oeconomy of Love, The" (Armstrong), 76, 81, 91, 115, 204
onanism, 72
120 Days of Sodom (Sade), 218, 226–28
One More Effort (Sade), 244, 248
Order of Friars of St. Francis of Wycombe, The, xi, 121–22, 129, 130–36. See also Medmenham Abbey
Order of the Golden Dawn, 260, 262
orgasm, described poetically, 180
orgies, 47–48, 62, 63, 222, 227, 237
at Medmenham, 141
Otranto. See Castle of Otranto
outlawry, 182
Oz (magazine), xix

palmistry, 122
Pamela or Virtue Rewarded (Richardson), 82
Pantagruel (son of Gargantua), 11, 17
Panty (nickname of Rev. Robert Lascelles), 204
Paracelsus, 22, 23, 25, 64, 92
Paradise Lost (Milton), 44, 52, 86, 251
Paris, alleged origin of name, 8
parodies on religious tracts, 178
Parsons, Richard, 1st Earl of Rosse, 62
patriotism, 54, 99
Patriot King (Bolingbroke), xii, 125
Pego Borewell (fictional author with suggestive name), 177

Pererius, Benedict, 23
permissiveness, 81, 121, 244, 269
Perrault, Agnes, 143
perversion (Sade), 220
phallic statues, 158, 177
Philip, Duke of Wharton, 50–60
philogynists, sect of, 204
Philosopher's Stone, 27
Phoenix Club, Oxford, 206
phrenologist's report on Sade's skull,
    247
pillory, 73
Pitt, William, The Elder, 103, 153–54,
    155, 164–66, 171
pleasure, pursuit of (Sade), 220
"Plot upon Plot" (ballad), 40
Poems and Ballads (Swinburne), 252
politics in the 1750s, 146–55
Politics of Ecstasy (Leary), 265
Pope, Alexander, 37, 43, 55, 72,
    73–74, 78, 81
Potter, Thomas, 133–34, 135, 138, 143,
    155, 156–57, 175, 176, 177–80,
    181, 191
Powys, John Cowper, 2, 262,
pox, cures for, 69. See also venereal
    disease
prayer book, revision of, 193
prayer books with false bindings, 136
Priapus (phallic garden-god), 124
Prime Minister, the self-styled
    (Wharton), 58
prisoners, ill treatment of, 219
prostitution, 77, 79, 141, 218, 227, 28,
    255. See also Fanny Hill
psalms, smutty parodies of, 134
pyromania, 205

Quackery Unmask'd (Spinke), 70
quasi-religious names, use of, 131, 132

Rabelais, Francois, 2–20
Radcliffe, Ann, 214–15, 222
rakes, 41–46
Ralph, James, 104, 125, 154
rape, 73, 82, 228, 266
Rasputin, 29, 260
reform movement in politics (1770s),
    211
reign of the Boot and the Petticoat,
    168
religious habits used by mistresses, 141
Revett, Nicholas, 123, 135
Richardson, Samuel, 55, 60, 82–83,
    105
Richelieu, Duc de, 41, 56, 64, 91, 141,
    152–53, 216
ritual of the Order (bogus) of
    St. Francis, 138–39
Robespierre, Maximilien, xvi, 60, 224
Robinocracy, 34, 37, 96, 101, 103
Roland, Madame, xvi–xvii
Rosemary's Baby (film), 267
Rosicrucian Lamp, Everlasting,
    66–67, 186, 190
Rousseau, Jean Jacques, xviii
Rule of Thélème. See "Do what you
    will"

Sabbatai Zevi of Smyrna, 24
Sacred Magic of Abra-Melin the Mage
    (tr. Mathers), 262
sacrifices for virility, 64
Sade, Marquis Donatien Alphonse
    Francois de, 216–47, 248–51, 267
sadism, 252–53, 259. See also Sade
Sandwich, Earl of, 67, 110, 133, 134,
    143, 167, 174–77, 180, 181, 189,
    194, 198
Sarah, Baroness Le Despenser (wife of
    Francis Dashwood), 191

Sarah, Duchess of Marlborough, 101
Satan, Church of, 266–67. *See also* Devil
Scarlet Woman, magician's need for, 262
Schemers, the, 55, 56, 92
scourging, 73, 106. *See also* flagellation
scowerers, 38, 39, 40
scrying. *See* crystal-gazing
scrying stones, 128, 143
Secret History of Clubs (Ward), 45
secret service, 26
Secrets of the Convent, 174
see-through clothes, 150
Selwyn, George, 135, 197, 210–11, 259
Sepher Yetzirah (Book of Formation), 24
Seven Deadly Sins seen as virtues, 266
Seven Years War, 152, 197, 210, 216
sex, determination of, in case of Beaumont d'Éon, 189
sex and cruelty: do they go together? (Sade), 224
sex deviations (Sade's 600), 218
sex magic, 263
sex manual, 76
Shelley, Percy Bysshe, 251
"Sir Industry" (in Thomson's poem), 119
skull
    as candleholder, 52
    as drinking vessel, 140, 206
Smollett, Tobias, 168, 169
snobbery, 100
Sodality of the Friends of Crime (Sade), 237–38, 241, 247
sodomy, 38, 89, 218, 224, 227, 263
sorcery, 63–64, 133, 140. *See also* black magic; magic

South Sea Bubble, 34, 51
Spanish fly (aphrodisiac), 80, 218
Spectator, The, 35, 39, 40
spiritualism, 27–28
spit, roasting humans on, 67, 206
Spring (Thomson), 98
Stanhope, Sir William, 132, 134, 138
Sterne, Laurence, 202–3, 204
"St. Francis of Wycombe." *See* Dashwood, Sir Francis
St. Leger, Colonel Jack, 62
Strawberry Hill, 128, 211, 212, 213, 214
Stuart, John (later 3rd Earl of Bute), 148–51, 154, 162–74
Summer (Thomson), 97
Swinburne, Algernon Charles, 252–59
syphilis. *See* venereal disease
Syphilis (Fracastoro), 74

Talbot. *See* Kelley, Edward
Talbot, Lord, 153, 163, 171
"Taste the sweets of all things" (said by Dashwood), 106
Tate, Sharon, murder of, xvii, 267
telepathy, 23, 26
Temple, Lord, 155, 181
"Temple" at Wycombe, 124
Ten Commandments, proposed amendments to, 96
terror, novels of, 214–15
Thélème, Abbey of, 13–20, 205
Thélème, rule of. *See* "Do what you will"
Therese Philosophe (de Montigny), 91–92, 222
Thomas Aquinas, St., 5
Thompson, Dr. Thomas, 125, 132, 134, 139, 145, 191

Thompson, Edward, 138, 142, 157, 192

Thomson, James, 97–98, 113–22, 127

"Times, The" (poem on homosexuality), 159, 170, 204

Tom Jones (Fielding), 82, 104

transvestites, 45, 63, 135, 188–89,

Treatise of Flogging (Meibomius),

Treaty with France (1763), 171

Tristram Shandy (Sterne), 202–3, 204

Trithemius, Abbot, 26

"Trivia" (poem by Gay), 39–40

Trophonius's Cave, 158, 203

True Briton (newspaper), 53–56, 59, 60, 266

tub, rolling, 39

Tucker, John, 121, 131, 134, 183–84

Tumblers, 39

Turpin, Dick, hanged, 38

Urquhart, Sir Thomas, 19

Vansittart, Arthur, 134

Vansittart, Henry (brother of Arthur), 134, 140, 196

Vansittart, Robert (brother of Arthur), 134, 135, 140

venereal disease, 70, 77, 80. *See also* pox, cures for

Versailles, 38

Vicar of Wakefield (Goldsmith), 168

vices anglais, 44

Voltaire, 91, 96, 97, 98, 107, 153, 209, 210

wafers, blood-red triangular, 140

Walpole, Horace (son of Robert), 4th Earl of Orford, 107, 112, 128, 135, 136–37, 140, 142, 143, 153, 164, 166, 167, 169, 174, 182, 197, 211–15, 216, 217

Walpole, Sir Robert, 34, 35, 53, 56, 95–96, 98–103, 112, 113, 132, 133

Walsingham, Sir Francis, 26

Warburton, Bishop, 133, 177, 181

West Wycombe Hill, caves in. *See* caves, meetings in, at West Wycombe Hill

Whaley, Thomas "Buck," 205–6, 208

Wharton, 2nd Marquis of. *See* Philip, Duke of Wharton Whigs,

Whitehead, Paul, 132–33, 134, 135, 138, 139, 140–41, 142, 143, 153, 167, 174, 182–83, 191, 203

ghost walks, 194

White's Club, 45, 101

wife-swapping, 29

Wilkes, John, 131, 134, 136, 139, 155–61, 167–82, 185, 187, 189, 190–91, 192–93, 196, 197, 198–99, 200–3

Winter (Thomson), 97

witchcraft, 138–40

Wizard, the enchanting. *See* Indolence

women, admittance to clubs, 47, 63

Women's Lib (Sade and), 235

Wraxall, Nathaniel, 140

Yeats, William Butler, xviii, 115, 260

Young, Edward, 50–52, 60, 94, 95, 97, 104, 127

Zionists, xvii

Zohar (occult handbook), 24, 44

BOOKS OF RELATED INTEREST

Eden in the Altai

The Prehistoric Golden Age and the Mythic Origins of Humanity

by Geoffrey Ashe

John Dee and the Empire of Angels

Enochian Magick and the Occult Roots of the Modern World

by Jason Louv

Occult Paris

The Lost Magic of the Belle Époque

by Tobias Churton

Rosicrucian America

How a Secret Society Influenced the Destiny of a Nation

by Steven Sora

Secret Societies of America's Elite

From the Knights Templar to Skull and Bones

by Steven Sora

Infernal Geometry and the Left-Hand Path

The Magical System of the Nine Angles

by Toby Chappell

Foreword by Michael A. Aquino, Ph.D.

Afterword by Stephen E. Flowers, Ph.D.

The Fraternitas Saturni

History, Doctrine, and Rituals of the Magical Order
of the Brotherhood of Saturn

by Stephen E. Flowers, Ph.D.

The Miracle Club

How Thoughts Become Reality

by Mitch Horowitz

INNER TRADITIONS • BEAR & COMPANY

P.O. Box 388

Rochester, VT 05767

1-800-246-8648

www.InnerTraditions.com

Or contact your local bookseller